Library of
Davidson College

THE OTHER SCENE:
PSYCHOANALYTIC READINGS
IN MODERN SPANISH AND
LATIN-AMERICAN LITERATURE

PUBLICATIONS OF THE SOCIETY OF SPANISH AND SPANISH-AMERICAN STUDIES

Luis T. González-del-Valle, *Director*

STEPHEN M. HART

THE OTHER SCENE: PSYCHOANALYTIC READINGS IN MODERN SPANISH AND LATIN-AMERICAN LITERATURE

SOCIETY OF SPANISH AND SPANISH-AMERICAN STUDIES

©*Copyright, Society of Spanish and Spanish-American Studies, 1992.*

The Society of Spanish and Spanish-American Studies promotes bibliographical, critical and pedagogical research in Spanish and Spanish-American studies by publishing works of particular merit in these areas. On occasion, the Society also publishes creative works. SSSAS is a non-profit educational organization sponsored by the University of Colorado at Boulder. It is located in the Department of Spanish and Portuguese, University of Colorado, Campus Box 278, Boulder, Colorado, 80309-0278. U.S.A.

International Standard Book Number (ISBN): 0-89295-065-X

Library of Congress Catalog Card Number: 91-62080

Printed in the United States of America

Impreso en los Estados Unidos de América

This text was prepared by Sandy Adler, Foreign Language Word Processing Specialist for the College of Arts and Sciences, University of Colorado at Boulder.

CONTENTS

Introduction 1

I. Drama and the Staging of Desire 7

    The "Family Romance" of Spanish Romantic Drama 7
    Obstacle-Love 10
    Marriage 12
    Identity 16
    Lorca and the Art of Repression 18
    Bodas de sangre and the Prisonhouse of Gender 20
    La casa de Bernarda Alba: The Bear and the Dawn 23
    Carlos Fuentes and the Dream of Conquest 29

II. Novel, Nationhood and Oedipus 41

    Martín-Santos: Castration and Representation 41
    Pedro Páramo and the Dream of the Dead Father 51

III. *Écriture féminine* and the Political Unconscious 63

    The Political Unconscious: From Luisa Valenzuela to
      Rosario Castellanos 72

IV. Poetry, Culture, Neurosis 87

    Vallejo: Incest and the Matriarchal Utopia 87
    Pablo Neruda: Revolution, Culture and Paranoia 96
    Vicente Aleixandre and the "Other Scene" 107

    Conclusion 121

    Works Consulted 123

    Index 141

*For my father, Bryan,
and my mother, Barbara*

PREFACE

Earlier versions of three sections in this volume have been published elsewhere. Parts of Chapter I appeared as "The Bear and the Dawn: Some Versions of *La casa de Bernarda Alba*" (*Neophilologus* 73 [1989]: 62-68), and "The 'Family Romance' of Spanish Romantic Drama" (*Romance Studies* 16 [1990]: 59-71). Part of Chapter III appeared as "Rulfo's *Pedro Páramo* and the Dream of the Dead Father" (*Forum for Modern Language Studies* 26 [1990]: 62-74). I am grateful to these journals for their permission to reproduce some of the material in the present volume.

Some of the sections of this work were originally given as lectures; the essay on Rulfo at the Queen Mary and Westfield Modern Iberian and Latin-American Research Seminar; the section on Vallejo at the University of Pittsburgh; the essay on *écriture féminine* at the Kentucky Foreign Language Conference; the section on the Political Unconscious at a meeting of the Association of Hispanists of Great Britain and Ireland; and the piece on Clarice Lispector at the University of London's Department of Extra-Mural Studies. For the feedback on those occasions I remain very grateful. Special thanks are in order also to the staff and postgraduate students at the University of Kentucky, who encouraged my research, in ways perhaps unbeknown to them, during my stay as Visiting Associate Professor there in 1989. Last but not least, thanks to colleagues and students at the Department of Hispanic Studies of Queen Mary and Westfield College, without whose guidance none of these essays would have reached fruition. I am also deeply grateful to the comments and suggestions for improvement made by the readers of the Society for Spanish and Spanish-American Studies at Boulder, Colorado. I have given a list in the abstract of those who have helped me. This is not to suggest that they are responsible for the mistakes here, which I feel duty bound to claim as my own.

INTRODUCTION

At one point in *The Interpretation of Dreams* (1900), Freud alludes to an idea of one of his contemporaries, G.T. Fechner, who had proposed in his study *Elemente der Psychophysik* (1889) that "the scene of action of dreams is different from that of waking ideational life" ("der Schauplatz der Träume ein anderer ist als der des wachen Vorstellungslebens"). Freud comments: "it is not clear what Fechner had in mind in speaking of this change of location of mental activity; nor, so far as I know, has anyone else pursued the path indicated by his words" (*Complete Psychological Works* IV, 48). Freud then indeed takes the first step along the very route delineated by Fechner's words, putting to one side any "anatomical interpretation" and turning instead to propose that this phrase be understood as referring to "a *mental* apparatus built up of a number of agencies arranged in a series one behind the other" (IV, 49). Freud obviously found this a suggestive insight. In a letter to Fliess dated February 9, 1898, Freud commented that this particular passage from Fechner was the only sensible remark he had found on the literature of dreams (V, 563 n. 1). Freud returned to this idea later on in *The Interpretation of Dreams* and explored the path outlined by Fechner in another direction, this time emphasizing the theatrical and cinematographic overtones of the word *Schauplatz*: "we should picture the instrument which carries out our mental function as resembling a compound microscope or a photographic apparatus, or something of the kind. On that basis, psychical locality will correspond to a point inside the apparatus at which one of the preliminary stages of an image comes into being" (V, 536). Fechner's phrase has obviously triggered a set of associations for Freud which go beyond the rather anodine nature of Fechner's original statement. The cinematographic metaphor grew perhaps out of the word *Schauplatz*, especially in terms of its literal meaning of "show-place."[1]

A similar trigger response seems to have emerged in the later Freud-Lacan interface. Whereas Freud responded to the hidden visual metaphor lurking within the word *Schauplatz*, the concept which fired Lacan's imagination was the otherness of *der andere Schauplatz*. The "other" is a fluid concept within Lacan's work since, as one commentator has pointed out, it can mean "you for me, me for you, anybody for anybody else, and also the first who made you as you define yourself: with your first name, your given name, your identity" (Clément 24). The use of the term "Other" with a capital "O" is no less ambiguous. As Wilden suggests, it is not possible "to define the Other in any definite way, since for Lacan it has a functional value, representing both the 'significant other' to whom the neurotic's demands are addressed (the appeal to the Other), as well as the internalization of this Other (we desire what the Other desires) and the unconscious subject itself or himself (the unconscious is the discourse of—or from—the Other)" (*Speech*

263-64). Lacan makes a significant reference to the concept of *der andere Schauplatz* in his essay "La Direction de la cure" (1961):

> —si le désir est en effet dans le sujet de cette condition que lui est imposée par l'existence du discours de faire passer son besoin par les défilés du signifiant;

> —si d'autre part . . . en ouvrant la dialectique du transfert, il faut fonder la notion de l'Autre avec un grand A, comme étant le lieu de *Schauplatz*, dont parle Freud dans le *Traumdeutung*)

> —il faut poser que, fait d'un animal en proie au langage, le désir de l'homme est le désir de l'Autre. (*Écrits* 628)[2]

Once more we see that the use of the term *der andere Schauplatz* expands upon and exceeds the implications of the originator text. While Fechner had used the term to refer to the place where dreams are acted out, and Freud used it to describe the site of the Unconscious, Lacan goes one step further and turns *der andere Schauplatz* into "the locus of the deployment of the Word." This comes as no surprise from a psychoanalyst who saw the unconscious as "structured like a language."[3] What is intriguing, however, about this process of semantic remanipulation is that it throws into stark relief the elusiveness of the term, since each time it refuses to allow its present user to fix its meaning for eternity.

Lacan's subsequent musings on the relations between the Other and desire in the context of "the other scene" are evocative. As he suggests: "le désir de l'homme est le désir de l'Autre." Anthony Wilden interprets the second "de" as indicating a subjective genitive, explaining that "man desires insofar as he is Other." To substantiate his argument Wilden quotes from Lacan to the effect that man's desire is "less ignorance of what he demands, which can after all be defined or limited, than ignorance of whence he desires" (*Speech* 115). The slippery nature of terms such as "other/Other" in Lacan's work extends, one could legitimately argue, to other more unobtrusive aspects of his syntax, including prepositions such as "de." In the phrase quoted above "de" could modify an objective genitive as well as a subjective genitive. To Wilden's "man desires insofar as he is Other" might be added other possibilities such as "man's desire is the Other's desire," "man's desire is for the Other," or simply "man desires the Other."[4] If one explores for a moment the ramifications of this last possibility ("man desires the Other"), it offers at least the satisfaction to the translator that it is as ambiguous because as laconic as the original French. Its implication is that man is unable to desire anything other than the language of the Other and that ultimately desire is a linguistic phenomenon. It is within language that the desires of humankind have been lodged, and specifically in those memory banks of desire, literary texts. Literature is precisely the language of desire in that language can do nothing else than desire and since, as Lacan suggests in the above fragment, man is "an animal at the mercy of Language," his desires are not pre-linguistic but structured like a Language, and, one might add, structured like literature.

In the following psychoanalytic readings of Spanish and Latin-American literature, my choice of texts has been eclectic. I have not sought to offer a comprehensive study of literary trends or national literary traditions or even of specific literary texts. The texts I have chosen traverse genre boundaries (since they are drawn from drama, novel and poetry) as much as national boundaries (the texts are from Spain to Mexico to Argentina). But underlying each of my analyses of different types of literary text is this idea that the literary text is the space in which the "other scene" is played out. I have also chosen certain texts because of the various ways in which, as I hope to show, they duplicate, echo and even pre-empt some of the main insights of psychoanalytical theory ranging from Freud's "Family Romance" to Lacan's "Name-of-the-Father."

Chapter I focuses on drama and the ways in which it stages desire. It has three sections; the first analyzes Spanish Romantic drama performed during the period 1834-1844 in the light of Freud's concept of "Family Romance" and touches on the discussion of obstacle-love, marriage and identity. The second part of the chapter focuses on the role of repression in García Lorca's drama, focusing on two plays, *Bodas de sangre* (1933) and *La casa de Bernarda Alba* (1936). The third section analyzes the expression of the dialectic of Self and Other, Conscious and Unconscious in Carlos Fuentes's play *Todos los gatos son pardos* (1970), which recalls the story of the struggle in 1519 between Moctezuma and Cortés.

Chapter II concentrates on what might be called the "male novel," comparing and contrasting Luis Martín-Santos's *Tiempo de silencio* (1962) and Juan Rulfo's *Pedro Páramo* (1955) in the light of Lacanian and neo-Lacanian psychoanalytical theory. The analysis of Martín-Santos's novel centers on the interplay of castration and representation, and the section on Pedro Páramo employs Freudian and Lacanian theory in order to delineate the role of the father figure in Rulfo's novel. In the case of both novels the individual search for roots is related to the search for a national identity.

Chapter III focuses on the "female novel"; it takes as its point of departure the concept of *écriture féminine* in order to discuss a selection of twentieth-century novels written by women in the light of this concept. The novels are *La casa de los espíritus* (1982) by Isabel Allende, *El mismo mar de todos los veranos* (1978) by Esther Tusquets, *Perto do coração selvagem* (1944) by Clarice Lispector, *Cambio de armas* (1982) by Luisa Valenzuela, and a selection of works by Rosario Castellanos. In the work of especially the last two writers, the discussion centers on the notion of the "political unconscious."

Chapter IV concentrates on poetry and analyzes the role ascribed to "culture" and its links with paranoia in the work of three poets, César Vallejo, Pablo Neruda and Vicente Aleixandre. In Vallejo's poetry the portrayal of culture is intermeshed with an Oedipal fascination with the mother figure; the section on Neruda's work focuses on the value ascribed to culture in his pre-political and political poetry. The analysis of Aleixandre's work begins with a discussion of its Freudian and Surrealist roots and reviews the ways in which his poetry strives to capture a pre-Symbolic realm which ostracizes the notion of culture.

Psychoanalysis as a theoretical discipline has had a rather mixed reception in the Spanish-speaking world which contrasts markedly with its impact in the Anglo-Saxon world. In Spain during the Franco regime, for example, it was actively discouraged, and in Spanish America it has had a rather checkered history, only managing to achieve something approaching an autonomous tradition in Argentina.[5] The interplay of literary and the Hispanic canon likewise has taken the form of a sporadic and often muted dialogue. The corpus of psychoanalytical readings of Spanish and Latin-American literary texts, despite some recent studies, remains an area of investigation which is still caught at what, to use Lacan's term, might be called the "mirror stage," namely, passively reflecting rather than being a reflective agent.

When used as a means of informing the interpretation of literary texts, psychoanalysis (whether Freudian or otherwise) has occasionally met with active resistance, the test case being criticism on the work of García Lorca. It was in the pages of the British journal *Bulletin of Hispanic Studies* that an exchange of words about Lorca's work occurred which threw into sharp relief the contours of the two camps. In an article published in 1976, J.M. Aguirre took to task two critics, Carlos Feal Deibe and Rupert C. Allen, over their (Freudian) psychoanalytical readings of Lorca's work. After briefly quoting Deibe, Aguirre launches into his colorful attack:

> No hay duda de que tales interpretaciones hechas desde una realidad fundamentalmente no poética, pueden conducir, y de hecho conducen, a resultados no ya sólo sorprendentes, sino, con mucha frecuencia, estrambóticos, por lo menos desde el punto de vista de la crítica estrictamente "literaria." Tratar de "explicar" el simbolismo de la obra de García Lorca mediante criterios antropológicos y psicoanalíticos es lo mismo que pretender "explicar" el juego del croquet, citando a Jung. En otras palabras, esos autores están empleando un "instrumento desmesurado," algo así como una apisonadora para planchar un par de pantalones. Además, cuando tal instrumento es usado como poseedor de propiedades talismánicas para encontrar la "verdad" del símbolo, el resultado de tal uso conduce al establecimiento de "verdades" muy dudosas. (129)

The main distinction Aguirre seems to be drawing relates to the inappropriateness of using a certain critical apparatus in order to analyze the literary text, expressed in the apparent absurdity of ironing one's pants with a steamroller and the (at least to me) less apparent absurdity of using Jung to explain croquet. The metaphors Aguirre uses are intriguing. Jung, if one wishes, surely *could* be used to "interpret" the game of croquet; Aguirre is aware of this and provides a footnote reference to a relevant passage in Jung which, on the face of it, would seem to weaken his argument (131 n.6). Literature, after all, shares with croquet the quality of "game." Aguirre's second metaphor is more revealing. While it would clearly be absurd to iron one's pants with a steamroller, the use of a metaphor of this kind simultaneously reveals Aguirre's (subconscious) assumption that the aim of literary criticism is "to iron out the creases" of the literary text, making it more readable, culturalizing its untidiness. This is presumably what Aguirre means by "crítica estrictamente 'literaria.' " It is doubly ironic that the "pants" should, in Aguirre's metaphoric transposition, represent Lorca's work, especially if one considers that Lorca's homosexuality made him an ambiguous wearer of male garments. Many of Aguirre's points were countered in an article published the following year in *Bulletin of Hispanic Studies* by Carlos Feal Deibe, who argued that Aguirre consistently contradicts himself (311-14).

What ultimately emerges from this exchange is that the anti-psychoanalysis lobby will often accuse the pro-psychoanalysis critic of using Freudian knowledge as if it were a "superior" type of scientific knowledge which can unlock the "truth" of the text, in short, as if it possessed "propiedades talismánicas para encontrar la 'verdad' del símbolo" (Aguirre's words, see above). However, one of the crucial insights of modern psychoanalytical readings of literature is that the knowledge of psychoanalysis (particularly in its neo-Freudian or Lacanian forms) is neither "absolute" or "superior" to the knowledge encapsulated within literature. Aguirre is not alone in his dismissive approach to psychoanalysis and, for this reason, it should be stressed that psychoanalysis deconstructs some of the barriers erected arbitrarily between different fields of knowledge.[6] As Shoshana Felman suggests, "there is no longer a clear-cut opposition or a well-defined border between literature and psychoanalysis: psychoanalysis can be intraliterary just as much as literature is intrapsychoanalytic. The methodological stake is no longer that of the application of psychoanalysis to literature but, rather, of their interimplication in each other" (49). Following the path indicated by Felman's insight, the present study attempts to open up a more sustained dialogue between some major texts of the Hispanic canon and the revolutionary knowledge of psychoanalysis. If it is able to stimulate further investigation in the field of psychoanalytical readings of Hispanic texts its purpose will have been well served.

NOTES

1. Most dictionaries translate *Schauplatz* as "scene, stage, theater" (*New Schöffler-Weis* 321). Strachey's translation of this word as "scene of action" is a justified embellishment. The literal and etymological meaning of *Schauplatz*, however, derives from the verb "to show" and "place."

2. One of the principles which follows from these premises is that:

> —if desire is an effect in the subject of that condition which is imposed on him by the existence of discourse, to make his need pass through the defiles of the signifier;

—if on the other hand ..., by opening up the dialectic of transference, we must ground the notion of the Other with a big *O* as being the locus of the deployment of the Word (the other scene, *eine andere Schauplatz,* of which Freud speaks in the *Traumdeuiung*);

—it must be posited that, as a facet of an animal at the mercy of Language, man's desire is the desire of the Other. (*Speech* 114)

3. See Thom.
4. Lacan's own multiple translations of gnomic statements from Freud's text are a favored trope of his style. Typical is his multi-layered translation of Freud's phrase "Wo Es war, soll Ich werden" (see *Speech* 133-34 and Bowie 145-47).
5. While Freud's work was influential to a degree in Spain in the 1920s, mainly through the Spanish translation of his work published in 1922 and the promotion of his ideas by the Spanish Surrealists, during the Franco years after the Civil War psychoanalysis was overtly and covertly suppressed; see Castilla del Pino. Psychoanalysis had a greater impact in Latin America, largely as a result of the emigration of European psychoanalysts to the subcontinent prior to or during World War II; see Vezzetti. Marie Langer, for example, who had worked with Freud, left Vienna, settled in Buenos Aires and founded the influential Asociación Psicoanalítica Argentina in 1942; for more information about Langer's practice, see Langer. Melanie Klein's ideas spread to Latin America via Buenos Aires through the pioneering work of Arminda Aberastury; see Perrota. Argentina soon established itself as a major center for the transmission of new psychoanalytical trends, particularly in the 1970s, in the form of the Instituto de Estudios Psicoanalíticos, based in the University of Córdoba, which specialized in Lacanian theory. Despite this, no individual has emerged in Spain or Spanish America who could claim the title of "Hispanic Freud."
6. Trend, for example, breezily dismisses psychoanalysis, and indeed symbolism, as constructs imposed from without: "The word *verde* (green), for instance, has been taken for a psycho-analytical symbol. Actually, when Lorca said that a thing was green, we knew that it was green, and that was that; it did not occur to us that he was consciously or deliberately symbolizing anything" (6). Ramsden, in a similar vein, implies that psychoanalytical readings introduce extraneous material into their analysis: "The other form of structure that is occasionally imposed on Lorca's poems came entirely from outside his work. Attempted interpretations in the light of depth psychology offer the clearest example. Here nothing is safe. Anything that sticks up is liable to be seen as a breast or a phallic symbol. As literary criticism aimed at the fuller appreciation of individual poems I find this unhelpful and pernicious" (vii). Ramsden's implication that his own criticism, contrary to other types of reading which came from "without," comes from "within" Lorca's work is not a tested assumption.

I
DRAMA AND THE STAGING OF DESIRE

In this first chapter I will be focusing on drama, Spanish Romantic theater, García Lorca's rural tragedies and a play by Carlos Fuentes; my theoretical backdrop will be, as in subsequent chapters, (mainly) the works of Sigmund Freud and Jacques Lacan. Drama is a particularly apt *locus* from which to establish links with Freudian theory, since it was the Greek drama of *Oedipus Rex* that Freud used in order to expound his revolutionary theory of the evolution of human personality. It was in *The Interpretation of Dreams* that Freud argued that while Sophocles "as he unravels the past, brings to light the guilt of Oedipus, he is at the same time compelling us to recognize our own inner minds, in which those same impulses, though suppressed, are still to be found" (364-65). His interpretation of Sophocles's play, as well as his interpretation of Shakespeare's *Hamlet*, were the (admittedly rudimentary) blueprint of what has come to be known as Freudian literary criticism. It is not a matter of coincidence that Freud should have used drama as a metaphor of the evolution of human personality, rather than, say, the novel (as Engels did) or poetry, for it is in drama, more than in any other genre, that we encounter the unravelling of the text in which the texture of human identity is woven.[1] In the following discussion, a concept drawn from psychoanalytical knowledge will be employed to elucidate some of the tensions underlying the works in question, the "Family Romance" in Spanish Romantic Drama, repression in Lorca's theater and the Other in Fuentes's *Todos los gatos son pardos*. My aim here has not been to employ psychoanalytical theory as a means of unlocking an otherwise impenetrable text, but rather to suggest that these texts "stage" the mystery of human desire in a way very similar to Freud's.

The "Family Romance" of Spanish Romantic Drama

The following analysis of the interplay between one of Freud's primary concepts—the *Familienroman* or "Family Romance"—and selected Spanish plays which were first produced in Spain at the height of the Romantic period, given the space available, will inevitably not be in any sense exhaustive. Rather I intend to concentrate on specific scenes from five major Romantic plays which seem to me to embody the conflicts and tensions operating within what Freud called the "Family Romance." The concept, and indeed the phrase "Family Romance," is an apt one to use in the context of Romantic drama, since "romance" is an ambiguous term which conjures up three separate but related meanings: i) pertaining to the vernacular languages of certain countries in southern Europe which descended from Latin, including Spanish, ii) a love intrigue, and iii) a fictitious narrative with a predominant love interest. The first meaning is merely coincidental to the subject-matter of this essay, but the second and third meanings are germane to the topic treated here in that they are concerned with the interconnection between life and art, between love and the ways in which it is narrativized. This idea will become clearer when set in the context of Freud's own discussion of the "Family Romance."

Freud's essay "Der Familienroman der Neurotiker" was first published in 1909 in a collection of essays edited by Otto Rank.[2] As Freud began this essay: "The liberation of an individual, as he grows up, from the authority of his parents is one of the most necessary though one of the most painful results brought about by the course of his development" (*Complete Psychological Works* IX, 237).[3] He goes on to argue that whereas normal individuals are able to achieve this liberation, neurotics are not and remain emotionally tied to their parents. He then identifies two stages of the "Family Romance," the first of which is asexual and the second sexual. The first stage often takes the form of fantasies in which the child's parents are "substituted for other parents normally of higher social standing" (239). The second stage, which is likewise expressed in fantasies, most typically takes the form of imagining the mother involved in secret love affairs. Both types of daydream are ostensibly born of the desire for revenge when the child's parents do not live up to his expectations but, as Freud notes, they are more appropriately seen as "an expression of the child's longing for the happy, vanished days when his father seemed to him the noblest and strongest of men and his mother the dearest and loveliest of women" (241).

One point immediately springs to mind in Freud's exposition: his constant recourse to the metaphor of literature. Thus he describes the child's feelings as "imaginative stories" which remind him of "historical intrigues"; they are also defined, rather emblematically, as "works of fiction" (240). Freud thus sees a non-problematic link between the fantasies of his neurotic patients and fictions embodied in literary form. At one point in his argument he makes this connection explicitly, arguing that neurotics and "comparatively highly gifted people" have one thing in common: a "peculiarly marked imaginative activity" (237).[4] What makes this link seem self-evident is the central term itself ("Familienroman") on which Freud hangs his theory of the neurotic. "Roman" is the German equivalent of the English "novel, work of fiction, romance," which indicates that Freud is using the metaphor of literature as a transparent device to describe the psychological phenomenon of the evolution of the human personality (*Cassell's* 499). This was indeed a recurrent turn of Freud's thought, as we have already noted above. This particular tendency in Freud's writings has led Shoshana Felman to suggest that literature and psychoanalysis are so entwined that we can say that literature in effect *inhabits* psychoanalysis ("To Open" 5-10). In this essay I shall be arguing that Spanish Romantic drama is a particularly rich field of investigation for the interlacing of literature and psychoanalytical knowledge. In terms of the family romance, it reveals time and time again the same blueprint: conflict within the family and mainly through the father-daughter relationship. Furthermore, Romantic drama—and its name is not coincidental —also offers in an archetypal form the basic constituents of the kind of romance to which Freud readily refers.[5] The ties between Freudian theory and Spanish Romantic drama are intermeshed to such an extent that, to reverse the priority of terms in Felman's insight, one might even say that in these plays psychoanalysis seems to *inhabit* literature.

My argument is not that the texts analyzed here can be specifically related to childish fantasies, or to claim that if one were (hypothetically) able to psychoanalyze the authors of the texts concerned, one could somehow "discover" that they were projections of emotions rooted in infancy. This would be to pay lip service to what Elizabeth Wright has identified as "vulgar Freudianism" (37-55). Rather I attempt to argue that Spanish Romantic drama elucidates some of the unconscious conflicts which Freud identified within the family unit when he said that "the whole progress of society rests upon the opposition of successive generations" (*Complete Psychological Works* 273). The texts studied here return obsessively to this very configuration, one which itself often results in the death of one of the parties involved. I am therefore attempting to invert the paradigm used by Freud, according to which psychoanalysis is the science which uses literature to confirm its own theories. Such a one-sided view of the relation between psychoanalysis has been revealed as a misreading, as Shoshana Felman points out. Instead I argue that literature and psychoanalytical knowledge are two parallel discourses which complement and inhabit each other.

The Spain of the early nineteenth century was one in which two salient discourses strove for supremacy. On the one hand was that of the voice of liberalism which had enjoyed a brief political existence in the 1812 Rising at Cádiz and which issued in the 384 articles of the 1812 Constitution. On the other hand was the discourse of its powerful political oppressors, the monarchy, the Church, the aristocracy, the country's wealth.[6] The ferocity of its opposition to liberalism was epitomized in the Ominous Decade (1823-1833) of Ferdinand VII's reign, when free thought was silenced, liberals persecuted and universities closed down "lest they disseminate the disastrous mania for thinking" (Peers 23).[7] That the ideology of Ferdinand's reign was phallocratic was ceremoniously displayed when war broke out in 1834 over the issue of whether a woman was able to ascend to the throne.[8]

Most of the plays discussed in this section were first staged in Madrid against the backdrop of the first Carlist War (1834-1839). The dates of the five main Spanish Romantic plays coincide, with the exception of Zorrilla's, with those turbulent years: Francisco Martínez de la Rosa, *La conjuración de Venecia* (1834); Duque de Rivas, *Don Álvaro o la fuerza del sino* (1835); Antonio García Gutiérrez, *El Trovador* (1836); Eugenio Hartzenbusch, *Los amantes de Teruel* (1837); and José de Zorrilla, *Don Juan Tenorio* (1844). These plays can be seen on one level as the cathexis of liberalism after ten years of political oppression. Spanish Romantic drama sought to undo the phallogocentric (k)not of Ferdinand's regime, exposing its authority as no more than a narcissistic image. Their art questioned the foundations of phallocracy in three seminal areas: love, marriage, and identity. I propose to look at the relevance of these concepts separately.

Obstacle-Love

The theme of love for which Spanish Romantic drama is famous is invariably a sexual love between a man and a woman which is frustrated by some social or metaphysical obstacle and eventually leads to the death of each of the protagonists. Romantic drama is thus a blueprint of what Freud called "obstacle-love" and which he described as follows:

> It is easy to show that the value the mind sets on erotic needs instantly sinks as satisfaction becomes readily obtainable. Some obstacle is necessary to swell the tide of libido to its height; and at all periods of history, wherever natural barriers in the way of satisfaction have not sufficed, mankind has erected conventional ones in order to enjoy love. This is true both of individuals and nations. In times during which no obstacles to sexual satisfaction existed, such as may be, during the decline of the civilizations of antiquity, love became worthless, life became empty, and strong reaction formations were necessary before the indispensable emotional value of love could be recovered. (Tanner 88)

In another sense anticipating Freudian knowledge, the plots of the plays reveal sexual instinct and the death drive to be co-substantial. It is because of their love that Álvaro and Leonor die in *Don Álvaro*, Manrique and Leonor in *El trovador*, and Diego and Isabel in *Los amantes de Teruel*. The precise nature of the obstacle which leads to their death is often difficult to establish. In some of the plays class-difference is an obstacle. Álvaro cannot marry Leonor in *Don Álvaro* and Manrique cannot marry her namesake in *El Trovador* because they are not of the same social standing as the woman. Yet, it is difficult if not impossible to extricate the role of what the Romantics called "fate" from this obstacle. The full title of *Don Álvaro o la fuerza del sino* requires that any interpretation of the play place "fate" at the center stage. The Romantic hero and heroine typically see fate, rather than the society in which they live, for example, as the sole cause of their misfortune. Rugiero, for instance, says to Laura in Act II, Scene 3 of *La conjuración de Venecia* that they are "desgraciados." Laura repeats this notion in Act III, Scene 1: "Soy tan desventurada." Spanish Romantic dramatists, as we can see, very much echoed the notion common to other European Romantic writers concerning the ubiquity of misfortune. One of the most famous nineteenth-century exponents of this pessimistic world-picture was, of course, the German philosopher Schopenhauer, who argued that: "it is absurd to suppose that the endless affliction of which the world is everywhere full, and which arises out of the need and distress pertaining essentially to life, should be purposeless and purely accidental. Each individual misfortune, to be sure, seems an exceptional occurrence; but misfortune in general is the rule" (41).

The opening lines of Álvaro's monologue at the beginning of Act III, Scene 3 seem to express Schopenhauer's philosophical point in poetic terms:

> ¡Qué carga tan insufrible
> es el ambiente vital
> para el mezquino mortal
> que nace en sino terrible!
> ¡Qué eternidad tan horrible
> la breve vida! ¡Este mundo,
> qué calabozo profundo
> para el hombre desdichado
> a quien mira el cielo airado
> con su sueño furibundo! (139)

Leonor, this time from *El Trovador*, voices similar sentiments:

> yo para llorar nací;
> mi negra estrella enemiga,
> mi suerte lo quiere así.
> Despreciada, aborrecida
> del que amante idolatré,
> ¿qué es para mí ya la vida? (Act I, 52)

The characters of Romantic drama name the obstacle to happiness in their lives using generic terms such as "terrible fate" or "black star," that is, fetishizing the obstacle as a force external to their own will. The nature of the obstacle can perhaps best be described using Jacques Lacan's term *le nom-du-père* or the Name-of-the-Father. If we compare the plots of the Romantic plays, we find that in most cases it is the father who lays down the law and forbids his daughter to enjoy the fruits of love and marriage, as, for example, in *Don Álvaro* and *Don Juan Tenorio*. In order for the power of the father to be fully effectual, however, it must embody an absent signifier. As Lacan suggests, the "signifier of the Father as author of the Law" is linked to the "murder of the Father" (*Écrits. A Selection* 199). This is the knot of resistance which is worked out in the typical Romantic play; don Álvaro, for example, kills the Marquis of Calatrava, and don Juan Tenorio kills Gonzalo. In each case, a father figure is murdered, and while this seems to destroy the obstacle, it in effect completes the Law and its power. In *La conjuración de Venecia* the role of father figure is played by Laura's uncle, Pedro Morosini, and in *El Trovador* by Leonor's brother, Guillén. In this latter group of plays, although the father is physically absent, the power of the Law-of-the-Father is enforced and the lovers are put to death or commit suicide.

It is in *Don Álvaro* and *Don Juan Tenorio* that what Freud called the "Family Romance" is most nakedly expressed. In *Don Álvaro*, the Marquis dies cursing his daughter: "Yo te maldigo" (Act I, Scene 8, 101). In *Don Juan Tenorio*, don Juan is haunted by the man he killed, Gonzalo, who, like the father who is dead but does not know he is dead, is reminiscent of the well-known father dream analyzed by Freud (*Interpretation of Dreams* 559).

He returns in the form of a statue. Even at this stage, Juan once more attempts to murder the father, but this time he is unable to do so:

> JUAN Iré, si;
> más me quiero convencer
> de lo vago de tu ser
> antes que salgas de aquí.
> (*Coge una pistola.*)
>
> ESTATUA Tu necio orgullo delira
> don Juan: los hierros más gruesos
> y los muros más espesos
> se abren a mi paso: mira.
> (*Desaparece LA ESTATUA sumiéndose por la pared.*)
> (Part II, Act II, 212)

Duque de Rivas had shown the Marquis of Calatrava's power surfacing in the fulfillment of the curse ("Yo te maldigo") he uttered to his daughter just before he died. Leonor's subsequent experience of misfortune in love tends to suggest that the curse has come true, but the curse, like language, remains invisible. Zorrilla, however, seems to go one step further in *Don Juan Tenorio*, for he reveals the power of the Name-of-the-Father returning in the figure of the statue. Gonzalo's statue, as a fixed image of his name, is a displaced representation of his power over others even after death and embodies his right to punish by death the "son-in-law" who affronted his authority, Juan Tenorio.

Marriage

Crucial to an understanding of Romantic love in these plays is the lovers' attitude towards marriage. As Tony Tanner has argued, marriage is the central subject for the genre which, in Spain at least, followed the emergence of Romantic drama—the bourgeois novel. Tanner's views are relevant to a discussion of Romantic drama. In the nineteenth century, Tanner argues, middle class society viewed marriage as sacrosanct, the "all-subsuming, all-organizing, all-containing contract" (15). Romanticism, Josipovici suggests, involved liberation from "a hierarchical social system and from a universe conceived on the model of the exact sciences" (180)[9] and, consistent with this view, the Romantics devalued Logic, Reason and the Reality Principle, turning rather to Unreason, Dream and the Imaginary. Yet the protagonists of the Spanish plays under discussion do not reject marriage; indeed, the archetypal Romantic hero and heroine desire marriage. Because, in the typical Romantic play, the lovers fail to get the consent of the girl's father, their love becomes unlawful. They are therefore constrained to adopt rebellious stances to authority, whether it be social, legal or familial.

The laws governing marriage in Spain in the 1830s specified that both sons and daughters needed their father's consent before getting married. A marriage which did not have paternal consent entailed loss of property and disinheritance from the family fortune. It was some thirty years later that the law changed (20 June 1862), at which point that consent became necessary only for sons under 23 years of age and daughters under 20 years of age. But according to the laws of the society contemporaneous with the plays, consent from the father was necessary before marriage could even be considered (*Don Álvaro* 79). In the event of an unfair refusal, recourse could be had to the law courts to overturn the father's decision, although this is not presented as even a remote possibility in the Romantic plays under discussion. The father's refusal is taken as a binding and irrevocable decision comparable to the will of God. Marriage is thus not presented as a feasible possibility within the lawful contours of the Romantic play. "If marriage is at the center," as Tony Tanner pertinently asks, "and the center cannot hold, what then?" (61). Spanish Romantic plays precisely explore this epistemological absence at the center of bourgeois society and reveal an obsession with the love which breaks the law, annihilates the legal institution by which men live and finally destroys the ego as well. The sexual desire experienced by the Romantic hero and heroine, through the agency of the Name-of-the-Father, becomes unlawful and subversive.

It is a commonplace notion that the society of nineteenth-century Europe was characterized by sexual repression; in this context the Victorian age springs to mind. In his penetrating study *Histoire de la sexualité*, however, Michel Foucault argues against this idea, contending instead that the issue of sexuality came to occupy a central place at this historical juncture: "Ce qui est propre aux sociétés modernes, ce n'est pas qu'elles aient voué le sexe à rester dans l'ombre, c'est qu'elles se soient vouées à en parler toujours, en le faisant valoir comme *le* secret" (49). Far from repressing sexuality, modern industrial societies, as Foucault has gone on to argue, have encouraged a proliferation of discourses about its nature and function:

> Entre chacun de nous et notre sexe, l'Occident a tendu une incessante demande de vérité: à nous de lui arracher la sienne, puisqu'elle lui échappe; à lui de nous dire la nôtre, puisque c'est lui que la détient dans l'ombre. Caché, le sexe? Dérobé par de nouvelles pudeurs, maintenu sous le boisseau par les exigences mornes de la société bourgeoise? Incandescent au contraire. Il a été placé, voici plusieurs centaines d'années, au centre d'une formidable pétition de savoir. (102)

Sexuality subsequently became an enigmatic space in which knowledge is lodged. This epistemological shift was accompanied by what Foucault calls an intensification of the knowledge and power associated with the body. Sexuality has led to "une intensification du corps—à sa valorisation comme objet de savoir et comme élément dans les rapports de pouvoir" (141), which has profoundly altered the power and sexual structures operating in the basic unit of bourgeois life, namely, the family. Since the middle of the nineteenth century, "le dispositif de sexualité, qui s'était développé d'abord dans les marges des institutions familiales (dans la direction de conscience, dans la pédagogie), va se recentrer peu à peu sur la famille" (145). The family becomes the central space in which sexuality is embodied in discourse: "Une demande incessante naît alors de la famille: demande pour qu'on l'aide à résoudre ces jeux malheureux de la sexualité et de l'alliance" (146).

A similar preoccupation with the family as the unit wherein the tensions of sexual knowledge are played out underpins Spanish Romantic drama. The central pivot of the Romantic play, put simply, is the desire of two young people to marry (and therefore unite two families). Likewise, the separate members of the respective families are implicitly involved in their liaison, and this often has catastrophic consequences. In *Don Álvaro*, for example, the protagonist kills both of Leonor's brothers (Carlos and Alfonso) as well as her father, the Marquis of Calatrava. In the same play, Alfonso stabs Leonor to death, just before he himself dies (Act V). Family relationships often have unsuspectedly complicated ramifications.[10] In the last scene of *La conjuración de Venecia*, for instance, we find out that Pedro Morosini, who has been hounding Rugiero because he is in love with Pedro's niece, is in fact Rugiero's father. This makes the two lovers Laura and Rugiero cousins, unbeknown to themselves. The two rivals for Leonor's love in *El Trovador*, Nuño and Manrique, arch-enemies and apparently from very different social backgrounds (Nuño is the son of a nobleman, Manrique the son of a gypsy), turn out to be brothers, as revealed in the last scene of the play (although there is a hint of this in Act III). Family relationships thus are stretched to the breaking point by sexual passion. Illicit family relationships are the ghosts waiting in the wings of the Romantic play. The ties of the (k)not of the bourgeois family are tightened up and undone simultaneously. The "family romance" articulated in Spanish Romantic drama, far from being simply a sentimental tale of a love frowned upon by society, turns into a morbid reflection on the forbidden pleasures of incestuous desire.

One result of the epistemological shift in the modern era towards sexuality as a space of power and knowledge has been the demise of the power formerly attached to nobility and "blood." As Foucault argues: "Ce sont les nouvelles procédures de pouvoir élaborées pendant l'âge classique et mises en oeuvres au XIXe siècle qui ont fait passer nos sociétés d'une symbolique du sang à une analytique de la sexualité" (195). This social tension is apparent in Spanish Romantic drama in the conflict between honor ("blood") and sexual instinct. Almost as an act of obeisance to the Golden Age, the heroes of the Romantic plays are preoccupied, at times obsessed, by their own honor and its corollary, "limpieza de sangre."[11] In some ways, honor acts in these plays as a ghost of the past, a set of values from a previous era which continue to haunt the present. Don Juan's attitude is simply one of rebellion against the values of the past. As his *leitmotiv* goes: "Por donde quiera que fui, / la razón atropellé, / la virtud escarnecí, / a la justicia burlé, / y a las mujeres vendí" (101). The most intriguing example of this complex conflict of discourses occurs in *Don Álvaro*. Like the typical Romantic hero, Álvaro has mysterious origins. In Act I, Scene 2, three possibilities are put forward. Álvaro is i) a pirate, ii) the son of a Spanish grandee and a

Moorish queen, and iii) an Inca. In any of these possible scenarios, Álvaro embodies the discourse of the outsider, the outlaw, the Other:

TIO PACO	La otra tarde estuvieron aquí unos señores hablando de lo mismo, y uno de ellos dijo que el tal don Álvaro había hecho sus riquezas siendo pirata . . .
MAJO	¡Jesucristo!
TIO PACO	Y otro, que don Álvaro era hijo bastardo de un grande de España y de una reina mora . . .
OFICIAL	¡Qué disparate!
TIO PACO	Y luego dijeron que no, que era . . . no lo puedo declarar . . . finca . . . o brinca . . . una cosa así . . . así como . . . una cosa muy grande allá de la otra banda.
OFICIAL	¿Inca?
TIO PACO	Sí, señor, eso, Inca . . . Inca.
CANONIGO	Calle usted, tío Paco, no diga sandeces. (80)

Reaction to each of these guesses at Álvaro's origins is one of surprise, and even scorn: "Don't talk nonsense," the Canon says. For the phallocentric discourse of common sense, Álvaro does not make any sense; he is banished from the confines of the discourse of the Official, the Canon and Tío Paco. His Otherness with regard to the discourse of common sense surfaces enigmatically in the text when Tío Paco fails to articulate the word "Inca." Álvaro's foreignness is, indeed, something about which he is extremely touchy. When Alfonso insults him on account of the impurity of his blood, in Act V, Scene IX, Álvaro seems to lose his mind:

DON ALFONSO	Soy un hombre rencoroso que tomar venganza sabe. Y porque sea más completa, te digo que no te jactes de noble . . ., eres un mestizo, fruto de traiciones.
DON ÁLVARO	(*En el extremo de la desesperación*) Baste. ¡Muerte y exterminio! ¡Muerte para los dos! Yo matarme sabré, en teniendo el consuelo de beber tu inicua sangre. (*Toma la espada, combaten y cae herido DON ALFONSO*) (216)

The blood which Álvaro lacks (it will be his consolation, he says, to drink the "inicua sangre" of his enemy) is a symbol of the old world which his own sexuality is bound to destroy. Yet, ultimately, Álvaro is barred from marrying Leonor and giving her his name because of his blood.[12] His last act of rebellion is to commit suicide, a vogue which reached epidemic proportions in nineteenth-century European society, thereby attempting to defy the Law-of-the-Father, since suicide, as Foucault argues, represents "une manière d'usurper sur le droit de mort que le souverain, celui d'ici-bas ou celui de l'au-delà, avait seul le droit d'exercer" (182). Like Leonor in *El Trovador*, Álvaro commits suicide in order to usurp divine prerogative. But by attempting to escape the Law, Álvaro succumbs to its power for, as Foucault reminds us, "la loi ne peut pas ne pas être armée, et son arme, par excellence, c'est la mort" (189).

The rationale behind the Romantic hero's desire for death is related to the power ascribed to love. In the absence of the power/knowledge of love, the Romantic lover ceases to exist. As Manrique says to Leonor in *El Trovador*: "¿Me amas, es verdad? Lo creo, / porque creerte deseo / para amarte y existir, / porque la muerte me fuera / más grata que tu desdén" (Act I, 57). This reaches catastrophic proportions in *Los amantes de Teruel*, where simply to express hatred for the lover is enough to make him expire on the spot:

> Mi desgraciado amor, que fue su vida
> Su desgraciado amor es quien le mata;
> Delirante le dije: "Te aborrezco";
> El creyó la sacrílega palabra
> Y expiró de dolor. (95)[13]

Love is seen as the cornerstone of the Romantic identity. Without it, the sense of a coherent identity disappears. Echoing the Freudian paradigm, the cathexis of the id ends in sex or death.

Identity

Identity is invariably depicted as unknowable in Spanish Romantic drama. The Name-of-the-Father is unable fully to *name* the individual. There are various examples in the Romantic plays of individual identity being an unknown quantity, some of which have already been touched on. Álvaro's origins, for example, as we have seen, are obscure; Rugiero and Laura in *La conjuración de Venecia*, as we find out at the end of the play, are cousins. Nuño and Manrique are revealed to be brothers at the end of *El Trovador*. Related to the issue of indecipherability is the use of masks in these plays. Both *La conjuración de Venecia* and *Don Juan Tenorio* have frequent recourse to this dramatic technique. In *Don Juan Tenorio*, Act I, Scene 12, Juan and Luis take off their masks to reveal their previously unknown identities (97), and later on in the same scene Gonzalo does the same (98). It is by imitating Luis that Juan is able to seduce Luis's fiancée on the eve of her wedding. In *El Trovador* Manrique owes his very existence to a case of mistaken identity. Azucena, who at one point had stated that she avenged her mother's death by burning one of the Count don Lope de Artal's sons, reveals in Act III and confirms in Act V that in fact she burnt her own son by mistake and brought Manrique up as if he were her own son. The characters of Romantic drama spend much of their time in the dark about the identity of others, and also about their own. Identity is thus shown to be a fluid, perpetually changing state. Fixity of identity is revealed as an illusion.

This sense of the gliding nature of the signifier of identity is exemplified by characters adopting aliases in *Don Álvaro*. In Act II, after her father's death, Leonor runs away, intending to spend the rest of her life in a hermitage, and she does so dressed as a man. In Act III, Álvaro changes his name to Fadrique, and Carlos changes his name to Félix. This leads to the extraordinary situation in which Álvaro saves Carlos's life and then looks after him without realizing that he is Leonor's brother. In Act V, Álvaro changes his name once more to Padre Rafael. The fact that Álvaro has adopted a false identity leads to the even more extraordinary situation in which he happens to be in a retreat which is, by a coincidence verging on the fantastic, a stone's throw away from the cave where Leonor is living—dressed as a man—in anonymous solitude. The conflict of these different identities is epitomized by the scene when Álvaro is asked by Alfonso, whom he has just fatally wounded, to confess him (in his capacity as a priest):

DON ALFONSO	Ya lo conseguiste . . . ¡Dios mío! ¡Confesión! Soy cristiano . . . Perdonadme . . . salva mi alma . . .
DON ÁLVARO	(*Suelta la espada y queda como petrificado.*) ¡Cielos! . . . ¡Dios mío! ¡Santa madre de los Angeles! . . . ¡Mis manos tintas en sangre . . ., en sangre de Vargas! . . .
DON ALFONSO	!Confesión!, ¡confesión! . . . Conozco mi crimen y me arrepiento . . . Salvad mi alma, vos que sois ministro del Señor . . .
DON ÁLVARO	(*Aterrado*) ¡No, yo no soy más que un réprobo, presa infeliz del demonio! Mis palabras sacrílegas aumentarían vuestra condenación. Estoy manchado de sangre, soy irregular . . . Pedid a Dios misericordia . . . Y . . . esperad . . . cerca vive un santo penitente . . . podrá absolveros . . . Pero está prohibido acercarse a su mansión . . . ¿Qué importa? Yo que he roto todos los vínculos, que he hollado todas las obligaciones . . . (217)

The conflicting selves within Álvaro's personality begin to split apart. In the last few moments before his death, Álvaro achieves an awareness of his schizoid personality which drives him to madness. The blindness of the characters with regard to others as well as with regard to themselves is often presented as the cause of their downfall and death. Thus when Alfonso sees Leonor emerging from the nearby cave, he jumps to the wrong conclusion, believing that she has been cohabiting surreptitiously with don Álvaro all along, and dutifully stabs her to death. This event is indeed typical of Romantic drama in its emphasis on the tragic consequences devolving from ignorance of personal identity. Identity, as these Romantic plays, and particularly *Don Álvaro*, suggest, is no more than a name which is one link in a chain of self-substituting signifiers. Its fixity is the (elusive) fixity of language.

Related to this disruption of the Cartesian sense of a self-defining and self-sustaining ego are those points in the plays when individuals lose their minds and are absorbed into the world of madness. Álvaro goes mad at the end of the play in the minutes before he jumps off a cliff. In the last scene of *La conjuración de Venecia*, Laura likewise loses her mind. A similar snag in the tissue of the text occurs when characters faint, as does Pedro in the same scene of the same play, or Inés when she first sees Juan, and Centellas and Avellaneda when they see the ghost of Gonzalo (*Don Juan Tenorio*, Part I, Act III, Scene 4, 148; Part II, Act II, Scene 2, 211). In these cases the discourse of the Other is actualized; its power, whether it be a ghost or the beloved, is so unsettling as to produce a temporary loss of sanity or consciousness.

In their unravelling of the concepts of love, marriage and identity in nineteenth-century Spain, the Spanish Romantic plays reveal a world which is in the process of dissolution. As a result of their epistemological rebellion against the social institution of marriage as specifically encapsulated in the Law-of-the-Father, the Romantic hero and heroine experience a painful deconstruction of the Cartesian sense of the self. The Spanish Romantic play typically relives a sequence of events which can be related to what Freud has called the "Family Romance," the imaginative liberation of the individual from the authority of his parents. A fitting expression of the internecine conflict of the Carlist War which historically frames its reality, Spanish Romantic drama articulates a conflict between the ideology of the past and the discourse of the future. Blocked from social admission to the paradise of sexual love, the Romantic personality seeks refuge in suicide (death in life) or insanity (a living death).

Lorca and the Art of Repression

Federico García Lorca is the single most studied Spanish dramatist of the modern era.[14] Ever since his untimely death at the hands of Nationalist soldiers at the outbreak of the Spanish Civil War, Lorca has functioned for millions of Spaniards as a symbol, or rather a symptom, of the repression characterizing Franco's regime.[15] Yet perhaps more intriguing than the primary repression which Lorca suffered in the sense of being executed is what might be termed "secondary repression," the repression he experienced as a gay individual living in Spanish society in the first few decades of this century and the ways in which this repression formed his art.

Lorca's gayness has often functioned as a smokescreen which inhibits rather than unveils the specificity of his work. In those studies published soon after Lorca's death, critics tended to pass over his gayness in silence. In this way they were following the example set by some of Lorca's best friends who, as Christopher Maurer points out, "chose to know nothing about it" (xi). A good example of this was Ángel del Río's biography-*cum*-criticism study published in 1952. Ángel del Río's first premise is that "la infancia de Lorca, fue, a juzgar por todas las referencias, completamente normal" (12-13). Those aspects of Lorca's life that did not fit into his criterion of normality were referred to obliquely. Ángel del Río refers to Lorca's gay affair with a Spanish sculptor, Emilio Aladrén, as "algún episodio en su vida íntima, sentimental, al que él se refería después velada y doloridamente" (36). Other biographies create a similarly white-washed image of Lorca's personal life. J.B. Trend, in a gesture designed clearly to combat rumors, states: "The Lorca I knew was certainly not over-sexed. On the contrary" (6).[16]

On the other hand, there were those critics who used Lorca's gayness as a tool against him. Typical of what Ian Gibson calls "the traditionalist, Catholic mentality of the Spanish Right which was responsible for his death" was the snide reference to Lorca's "doubtful sexuality" which appeared in a Huelvan paper on 10 September 1936 (*Death of Lorca* 200). Great play was made by the Nationalist authorities of Jean-Louis Schoenberg's so-called "revelations" twenty years later that Lorca had been murdered as a result of a gay jealousy intrigue, since they saw it as a way of minimizing their own role in his death (149-55). In his study *Federico García Lorca: L'homme et l'oeuvre* (1956), Schoenberg had proposed the idea that Lorca had been killed off because of the "homosexual jealousy" of a certain Ramón Ruiz Alonso; Lorca had supposedly scorned the group of homosexuals, communists and pederasts based in Granada to which Ruiz Alonso belonged (106-22). Schoenberg's allegations have since been revealed to be pure fabrication, notably by Ian Gibson, but it is intriguing that one of the premises of Schoenberg's thesis, namely the "impure pederast" as contrasted with the "pure gay," should reoccur in a more recent balanced study of Lorca's gayness.[17] Paul Binding's book *Lorca: The Gay Imagination* (1985), in discussing Lorca's poem to Walt Whitman, for example, draws a distinction between the "classical" homosexual and the "pederasts" and "urban faggots" who form part of the "neurotic riff-raff" of the "gay scene" (139).[18]

Binding's "gay" approach to Lorca's work is a fruitful one which has opened out the debate about the presentation of sexuality in Lorca's work. There are a number of epistemological problems, however, involved in an approach of this kind. One of the premises of Binding's argument is that Lorca is more "true" to his inner feelings when he is able to express his gay emotions in an untrammelled way; he comes closest to this in his "Oda a Walt Whitman," his play *El público* and his recently divulged *Sonetos del amor oscuro*. A further consequence of this reasoning is that when Lorca portrays the sexual repression experienced by women in his rural tragedies or blacks in his New York poems, Lorca is expressing his own sexual fix via a displaced artistic image.[19] But this is to ignore the artistically formative nature of repression for, as Lorca's work—his plays as much as his poetry—clearly shows, repression is not external to but intrinsic to artistic representation. Rather than expressing a muted, gay desire, Lorca's theater deconstructs the very idea of sexual gender. As we shall see, in his use of the image of "blood" in *Bodas de sangre* (1933) and his portrayal of the mother-daughter relationship in *La casa de Bernarda Alba* (1936), Lorca unties the notion of sexual difference.

Bodas de sangre and the Prisonhouse of Gender

At one stage in *This Sex Which is Not One* Luce Irigaray refers to what might be called the "prisonhouse of gender":

> How can we speak so as to escape from their compartments, their schemas, their distinctions and oppositions: virginal/deflowered, pure/impure, innocent/experienced ... How can we shake off the chain of these terms, free ourselves from their categories, rid ourselves of their names? Disengage ourselves, alive, from their concepts? Without reserve, without the immaculate whiteness that shores up their systems. You know that we are never completed, but that we only embrace ourselves whole. That one after another, parts—of the body, of space, of time—interrupt the flow of our blood. (212)

Bodas de sangre expresses a similar sense of entrapment within the "compartments" of gender, along with a frustration that the "flow of our blood" is interrupted. As in Irigaray's quotation, these two insights are linked in Lorca's play, and I propose to discuss the role of both ideas, but, for reasons that will hopefully become clear, in reverse order.

No study of *Bodas de sangre* can avoid battling with the meaning ascribed to "blood" in the play. The references to blood early on in the play tend to portray it as an image of a fluid and unstoppable libido. In the lullaby which occurs at the beginning of Act I, Scene 2, the image of blood occurs juxtaposed with the image of water and male virility (the horse which alludes to Leonardo and to his "unstoppable" passion).

> Duérmete, rosal,
> que el caballo se pone a llorar.
> las patas heridas,
> las crines heladas,
> dentro de los ojos un puñal de plata.
> Bajaban al río.
> ¡Ay, cómo bajaban!
> la sangre corría
> más fuerte que el agua. (24-25)

Here Lorca is echoing Freudian knowledge on two counts. Firstly, in his portrayal of libido in terms of fluidity; one of Freud's favorite metaphors for the id was the "great reservoir of libido."[20] Secondly, Lorca, in the allusion to the horse, itself a phallocentric emblem, is echoing Freud's interpretation of libido as phallic.[21] Other early uses of the image of blood in the play tend to confirm this initial impression that Lorca is presenting libido as fluid and phallic. Thus the mother refers to her late husband's procreative abilities in terms of his blood: "Tu padre sí que me llevaba. Eso es buena casta. Sangre. Tu abuelo dejó a un hijo en cada esquina. Eso me gusta. Los hombres, hombres; el trigo, trigo" (14). This libido can also be expressed not only as *eros* but also as *thanatos*, as in the case of Leonardo's blood; again Lorca seems to be echoing Freudian knowledge: "¿Qué sangre va a tener? La de toda su familia. Mana de su bisabuelo, que empezó matando, y sigue en toda la mala ralea, manejadores de cuchillos y gente de falsa sonrisa" (72). The awesome destructiveness of libido is confirmed when the mother describes her son's death, the central image again being blood: "es tan terrible ver la sangre de una derramada por el suelo. Una fuente que corre un minuto y a nosotros nos ha costado años. Cuando yo llegué a ver a mi hijo, estaba tumbado en mitad de la calle. Me mojé las manos de sangre y me las lamí con la lengua. Porque era mía" (73). Images of capitalism and possession occur ("nos ha *costado* años . . . era mía") and allude to the crude economic forces underlying child-rearing. The mother's grotesque action—drinking the blood of a dying man—is an image of frustrated desire: the desire of desire, a structure whose rhetorical strategies will gradually overcome the play. Procreation, family lineage and the repression of blood which this social system institutionalizes finally explode in a cathexis of blood.

Judging by the images of blood we have seen so far, Lorca seems to be using "blood" as an emblem of a libido which is fluid and phallic. However, if we look at other instances of the use of this image in *Bodas de sangre*, we detect that it has opposite connotations. Later on in the play, especially in the opening scene of Act III, blood comes to take on feminine connotations; we are listening to the "mythical" conversation between three woodcutters:

LEÑADOR 1.º
Se estaban engañando uno a uno y al fin la sangre pudo más.

LEÑADOR 3.º
¡La sangre!

LEÑADOR 1.º
Hay que seguir el camino de la sangre.

LEÑADOR 2.º
Pero sangre que ve la luz se la bebe la tierra.

LEÑADOR 1.º
¿Y qué? Vale más ser muerto desangrado que vivo con ella podrida. (94)

On the face of it, this passage extends some of the associations attached to the image of blood that we have already noted. Thus the first woodcutter (who seems almost the mouthpiece of the id) states that the id will seek cathexis no matter what the cost: "Vale más ser muerto desangrado que vivo con ella podrida." On one level this image can be read as meaning that libido is an asocial (phallic) force which, when expressed (as semen), will lead to death. The image used here is, however, unsettling in that the axis of comparison is between retained, rotten blood (a life which is worse than death) and expressed blood (a death which is better than life). Blood functions in this particular image with specifically feminine connotations, since it can also be construed as female blood which is either menstrual blood ("sangre podrida") or blood expressed in the form of a foetus. As Gilbert and Gubar have pointed out, "one of the primary and resonant metaphors provided by the female body is blood" (296). Because it is not gender-specific, blood functions in Lorca's text as a rhetorical agent which unties the notion of sexual difference. This would explain why Lorca uses the image of the moon at this juncture in the play, given its primeval associations with the female lunar cycle. Lorca thereby uses the single image of blood to convey both masculine libido and feminine procreation. The image of blood in Lorca's work, far from lending a spurious coherence to the play, deconstructs the very notion of gender.

Pointing in a similar direction, when the first woodcutter describes what is superficially the moment of orgasm for the eloping couple, he does so in terms which hover ambiguously between masculine and feminine attributes:

LEÑADOR 1.º
Ahora la estará queriendo.

LEÑADOR 2.º
El cuerpo de ella era para él y el cuerpo de él para ella.

LEÑADOR 3.º
Los buscan y los matarán.

LEÑADOR 1.º
Pero ya habrán mezclado sus sangres y serán como dos cántaros vacíos, como dos arroyos secos. (95)

The last image, which describes the lovers' bodies as empty vessels—empty pitchers and empty streams—contradicts the popular understanding of sexual fulfillment as plenitude and suggests a closer parallel may be with menstruation. Lorca seems indeed to be clothing the reference to sexual fulfillment with the image of the loss of menstrual blood. We find a similar image structure in *Yerma*, where the protagonist relates women's blood specifically to the desire for procreation: "Cada mujer tiene sangre para cuatro o cinco hijos, y cuando no los tienen se les vuelve veneno, como me va a pasar a mí" (137). As María tells Yerma, confirming this insight, being pregnant is like having a bird "dentro de la sangre" (135). Both images point to the unstoppable nature of the procreative instinct, which drives blood out of the female body either as menstrual blood or in the form of a child.

By fusing together male and female biological functions on the one hand and uniting sexual fulfillment with procreation through the central image of blood on the other, Lorca gives voice to an androgynous form of sexuality/creativity. Since it cannot achieve adequate expression within the forms of sexual gender according to which one is either a man or a woman, it is not surprising that this androgyny contains within it the seeds of its own frustration. Because of its entrapment within the prisonhouse of gender, Lorca viewed the sexual impulse as intrinsically characterized by unfulfillment. Again Lorca's work seems to be unravelling the same knot of desires that Freud was. The Viennese psychoanalyst, in one of his more pessimistic statements, had argued that "we must reckon with the possibility that something in the nature of the sexual instinct itself is unfavorable to the realization of complete satisfaction," and he could offer no explanation why this might be so (Mitchell and Rose 32). Lorca's insight into the prisonhouse of gender itself detects perhaps the cause behind the effect described so masterfully by Freud.

La casa de Bernarda Alba: The Bear and the Dawn

One very striking feature of *La casa de Bernarda Alba* is that, unlike *Bodas de sangre*, there are literally no men in the play; Bernarda Alba has no sons, the play opens with the funeral of her late husband, and we never once witness the elusive Pepe Romano on the stage. *La casa de Bernarda Alba* is, thus, more than any other of Lorca's plays, a "drama de mujeres en los pueblos de España," as the sub-title runs. The play dramatizes the archetypal moment of conflict and repression that characterizes the mother/daughter relationship as Freud saw it:

> Occasions for conflict between a daughter and her mother arise when the daughter begins to grow up and long for sexual liberty, but finds herself under her mother's tutelage; while her mother, on the other hand, is warned by her daughter's growth that the time has come when she herself must abandon her claims to sexual satisfaction. (*Interpretation of Dreams* 358)

Yet Bernarda, unlike the rather homely mother visualized in Freud's quotation, is a tyrant who will not transfer sexual power to her daughters, consistently refusing to co-opt them into sexual womanhood. Her power, as in the truly totalizing power of the tyrant, will die with her, thereby denying sexual succession, as the end of the play suggests.

The mother-daughter relationship articulated in Lorca's play is a social paradigm of Freud's psychological system of repression. Just as, in Freud's view, the suppressed sexual wish is inhibited from cathexis by the second system of the super ego (which is itself admissible to consciousness), thereby producing "unpleasure," so Bernarda, through her tyrannical system of control, forces her daughters to experience "unpleasure," to which their names amply testify (e.g., Angustias, Magdalena, Martirio). Bernarda is not only the harbinger of the "dawn" of consciousness, as her surname literally implies; she is also the bear who gives the hug of death to Adela, as her first name suggests. As J. Rubia Barcia has pointed out, Bernarda "es nombre de origen teutónico, que quiere decir 'con fuerza o empuje de oso.' "

While the conflicts within the family unit are the phanopoeic indicators of Lorca's tragedy, its melopoeic roots run deeper.[22] The true mechanics of Lorca's play take place within rhythm. Lorca regarded rhythm as one of the most important constituents of the theater: "Hace falta mucho y muy cuidadoso ensayo para conseguir el ritmo que debe presidir la representación de una obra dramática. Para mí, esto es lo más importante" (*Obras completas* II, 970). The drama of Lorca's work, as this quotation suggests, is enacted not only on the "visible" level of dialogue. It springs from the latent rhythms of the play, which are assimilated to the biological rhythms of the human body. It is in the space inhabited by rhythm that what Derrida calls the "double scene" unfolds, with its supplemental ability to disrupt the security of settled referents by signifying in excess of the captivating power of referentiality.

Julia Kristeva, in her important work, *La Révolution du langage poétique* (1974), has drawn attention to the rhythmic pulses which underlie the literary text in a way which extends and complements Lorca's original insight. The literary text, according to Kristeva, is articulated by means of a dialectic between the Semiotic, namely the free play of motile desire characteristic of pre-verbal consciousness, and the Symbolic, which entails the thetic splitting ("coupure"), fixation and subsequent codification of the flux of the semiotic process (17-100). This shuttle between the Semiotic and the Symbolic is evident on a primary level in *La casa de Bernarda Alba* in the sexual drive/repression dialectic around which the play is thematically articulated. Yet it is also present in the oscillation between poetry and prose in the play. While in the earlier *Bodas de sangre* the over-riding mode had been the poetic (so much so that a reviewer of a performance of the play in New York accused the actors of "speaking as if they had just eaten whole libraries full of seed catalogs"[23]), in *La casa de Bernarda Alba* prose is the dominant mode. However, during those brief moments when poetry does appear in Lorca's later play, it obtains the full force of the semiotic. A good example is the singing of the reapers as they return to the fields in Act II, to which the sisters listen ecstatically:

> Ya salen los segadores
> en busca de las espigas;
> se llevan los corazones
> de las muchachas que miran.
> Abrid puertas y ventanas
> las que vivís en el pueblo;
> el segador pide rosas
> para adornar su sombrero. (48-49)

As a review of a recent performance of *The House of Bernarda Alba* suggested of this moment, the women "close their eyes, loll against walls and chairs and achieve what is almost a silent, collective orgasm as they dream of male freedom" (de Jongh).

In general, the semiotic occupies the space of the Erotic and the Imaginary in Lorca's play, which are often mutually dependent.[24] The ecstatic space of the Imaginary is sparked off by the elusive Pepe Romano, who only exists by virtue of his absence, perpetually differing and deferring the pursuit of unmediated presence, in which all the daughters are implicated. At least three of the daughters are known to love Pepe Romano; Angustias is his official legal future bride, Adela is his secret lover, and Martirio's love for him is demonstrated by her act of stealing the portrait from Angustias in order to place it under her pillow. This portrait is a doubly empty representation for, within the representational confines of the play, it betokens a presence never actualized. It is precisely in the space between the re-presentation of Pepe Romano and his hypostatized primary presentation that the tragedy of the repressive system is articulated. Just as body is disconnected from image, so word is separated from its referentiality, giving rise to the free play of the Sisyphus-like anguish of unrequited passion.

A similar type of empty *imago* is also articulated in the difference between Bernarda and Adela. In Bernarda's eyes, Adela represents the discourse of the Other, expressed disarmingly in Act II when the clashing color of her green dress invades the staid conformity of the stage. The greenness of Adela's dress, itself ostensibly an image of life versus the death imagery of white/black, however, is ambiguous, since green, in Lorca's private world of symbols, invariably contains the seed of its own death.[25] In Bernarda's eyes, Adela's discourse is a threat to her power structure, and the method she finally chooses of suppressing the divergent discourse is that of a wily trick which deceives Adela into thinking that Pepe Romano is dead, thereby causing her to take her own life.

Adela's suicide is the climactic actualization of the unnameable silence which had woven its way through the syntax of the play from its initiation. Throughout the play, Bernarda obliges those around her to be silent. She demands silence in Act I during her husband's funeral and again at the end of the play in order to conceal the fact that Adela was not a virgin when she died. Indeed, Bernarda's desire for silence is linked to her negation of sex, speech, time and even life.[26] By perpetually calling for silence, Bernarda articulates a desire to close the text of the play, or the play of the text, thus enacting a type of linguistic censorship from within the play itself.

It is intriguing, given the radical nature of the critique immanent in Lorca's play, that the dramatic structure should be conventional. Lorca's dramatic output evolved from an earlier, more experimental mode to the more conventional stage machinery of the trilogy of tragedies *Bodas de sangre*, *Yerma* and *La casa de Bernarda Alba*, universally acclaimed as his most important works. Within these three major plays, a movement towards prose and social issues is balanced by a progressive disinterest in poetry and metaphysical issues (*La casa de Bernarda Alba* xxix-xxxv). Rather like Gustave Flaubert, who forced himself to write *Madame Bovary* even though his aesthetic taste leaned more towards imaginary and exotic worlds (as in *Salammbô* and *La Tentation de Saint Antoine*), so Lorca decided to fasten down the hatches on the world of the Imaginary in his masterpiece *La casa de Bernarda Alba*.[27] In rigidly writing against his poetic grain, Lorca committed a type of creative suicide and produced a genuinely "strong" work of art. By castrating his drive toward and desire for the semiotic, Lorca fetishized the thetic threshold and produced a rigidly genre-bound play. Repression, or *Verdrängung*, to use Freud's term, of the Imaginary was articulated in terms not only of the ideational content of the daughters' suppressed dreams but also the form-giving intention itself.

Lorca's use of a conventional dramatic structure is also more effective as a means of conveying repression. Looked at in this way Adela has been "penned up" within a patriarchal text. As Gilbert and Gubar suggest:

> As a creation "penned" by man ... woman has been "penned up" or "penned in." As a sort of "sentence" man has spoken, she has herself been "sentenced": fated, jailed for he has both "indited" her and "indicted" her. As a thought he has "framed," she has been both "framed" (enclosed) in his texts, glyphs, graphics, and "framed-up" (found guilty, found wanting) in his cosmologies. (13)

It is therefore not surprising that the agent who "sentences" Adela, her mother, should be portrayed in the play as embodying the power of patriarchy. If one were to characterize the *dramatis personae* of *La casa de Bernarda Alba* according to sex (which, in a patriarchal society is, as Kate Millett has pointed out, "aggression, intelligence, force and efficacy in the male; passivity, ignorance, docility, 'virtue' and ineffectuality in the female" (28), then Bernarda seems masculine.[28] Bernarda herself postulates an unbridgeable chasm between the sexes: "Hilo y aguja para las mujeres. Látigo y mulo para el varón" (15). Her daughters are indeed involved in domestic activities, specifically "rabiando por la boda," as the grandmother points out (33). However, Adela is the spanner in the patriarchal works for, by standing up to the *mujer viril* which her mother is, she initiates a power dilemma which will lead to her or her mother's death, if the power and gender structure is to remain static. Unlike her more passive sisters, who sit around sewing and embroidering and waiting for a marriage that will never happen, thereby accepting the system of negation and endless postponement of presence, Adela seeks to grasp the center of her aspirations and, in a highly Romantic gesture, attempts to achieve the putative unmediated presence afforded by love. Though her action leads to her eventual death, in a deeper sense her gesture of defiance is a victory, since her death signals a transcendence of the system of eternal repetition. As so often in Lorca's work, the only space in which the unmediated presence of passion can be actualized is in death. *Eros* and *thanatos*, the Janus faces of the id, are shown to be one and the same.

The tragedy of *La casa de Bernarda Alba* lies in the inability of the patriarchal social system to change its social contract of exchange and sacrifice, for, as Irigaray has argued, patriarchal society, in terms of its rites and its laws of exchange, is a deeply sacrificial society ("Women" 6-18). The sacrificial victim immolated on the altar of society's conscience in Lorca's play is, quite clearly, Adela. The terrible irony is that the punishment she receives for breaking the phallocratic code is meted out by a woman, and her mother to boot. Bernarda, as this final act of cruelty shows, has fully internalized the phallocratic system of masculine dominance, using it for her own ends. Adela, once her process of self-discovery leads her to question the ontological postulates of the patriarchal system, exchanges this new-found, paranoiac (because anti-patriarchal) knowledge for her life.

Let us re-assess Adela's crime against society. Firstly, she flouted her mother's authority by flirting with the man who was to be Angustias's legal partner in marriage. There are some indications that Adela went further than simply teasing Pepe Romano by walking past the window in the nude when she knew he was outside. The fact that Bernarda is so adamant that "la hija menor de Bernarda Alba ha muerto virgen" (91) suggests very strongly that Adela was not a virgin when she died.[29] There is a further indication that Adela not only had pre-marital relations with Pepe, but that she was also carrying his child. This occurs when she takes fright, in an almost exaggerated way, at the story of the girl in the village who had given birth to an illegitimate child, which she had killed and hidden, whereupon her misdeed is discovered and she is killed by the villagers.

> MARTIRIO (*Mirando a Adela*)
> ¡Que pague lo que debe!
>
> BERNARDA (*Bajo el arco*)
> ¡Acabar con ella antes de que lleguen los guardias! ¡Carbón ardiendo en el sitio de su pecado!
>
> ADELA (*Cogiéndose el vientre*)
> ¡No! ¡No!
>
> BERNARDA
> ¡Matadla! ¡Matadla! (66)

The anecdote acts as a reminder of the harsh fate awaiting those who trespass beyond the bounds permitted by phallocratic society and acts as an indirect prophecy of Adela's fate.

The fact that Bernarda is prepared to kill her own child shows how much her own femininity has been perverted. For in Bernarda's eyes marriage and child-rearing are inescapably linked to capitalism; this is shown by the fact that she repeatedly refuses to allow her daughters to marry anyone below their social standing, notwithstanding her daughters' wishes. They thus undergo a double repression, "surplus-repression" as well as repression. Herbert Marcuse, in his study *Eros and Civilization*, has argued that, while Eros is the tendency towards a complete oneness with the world, the erogenous zones of the body have been gradually reduced to the genitals in order to leave the rest of the body free, as a tool, for the tasks of society. The scarcity which justified this surplus repression is no longer a historical necessity, but in present-day society corresponds to the laws of capitalist production, which demand that more and more be produced in order to maintain the money surplus. The daughters not only suffer this type of surplus repression; they also suffer the repression caused by their inability to be integrated in terms of labor within society. The role of the female within the paternalistic society of Spain at the turn of the century was limited to bringing up a family. The only means of work and income—child-bearing—available to their sex is, thus, also being denied to the daughters. Even here, it should be pointed out, while it offers social status, marriage in a patriarchal society is repressive to the extent that it presupposes "that the mother should nurture the child without payment, before and after the birth, and that she should continue to nurture both man and society—a totem before any designated, identified or represented totem".[30] It is this double-edged repression which makes the plight of the daughters so desperate.

The ultimate effect of these two specific types of repression is to create an incestuous household in which marriage and communication are not viable. As Lévi-Strauss has pointed out, "exogamy and language have fundamentally the same function—communication and integration with others" (493). By remaining unwilling to exchange her daughters, except at a deliberately inflated price, Bernarda is attempting to create after her own image a silent (*infans*), narcissistic society in which no exchanges are transacted.[31] Thus her repeated admonitions to silence throughout the play take on a more sinister significance as the expression of a desire for a *regressus ad uterum*, in which the house becomes the womb and the daughters remain unborn. Bernarda's gesture is uncannily similar to specific utopian myths in which, as Lévi-Strauss has pointed out, a vision of heaven where no women will be exchanged and in which one might "keep to oneself" finds expression (497). Again, this vision being evidently the dream-wish of a patriarchal society, Bernarda once more plays the role of the unwitting male master by upholding and validating the laws of a phallocratic culture. Since Adela attempts to elude the cultural law of marriage by giving away her sexual favors for nothing (as she exclaims in Act II, "¡Mi cuerpo será de quien yo quiera!"[42]), Bernarda has no option but to seek her destruction. Both Bernarda and Adela are trapped by the phallocratic society in which they live, whose laws supersede human compassion. In the final bear-hug Bernarda gives to Adela, she brings her the dawn of consciousness and its inevitable corollary, death.

It is at the point of death that Adela's role as a mediator between feminine sexuality and textuality becomes clear. Gilbert and Gubar have pointed to a link between the male act of imprisoning the female in his writing with the act of killing; he "stills" and "kills" her (14). Following Gilbert and Gubar's insight, Adela can thus be seen not only as an image of repressed female sexuality but as a textuality which is stunted and silenced before it achieves expression. We find a similar theme expressed in one of the poems of *Poeta en Nueva York*, "Vuelta de paseo":

Asesinado por el cielo.
Entre las formas que van hacia la sierpe
y las formas que buscan el cristal
dejaré crecer mis cabellos.

Con el árbol de muñones que no canta
y el niño con el blanco rostro de huevo.

Con los animalitos de cabeza rota
y el agua harapienta de los pies secos.

Con todo lo que tiene cansancio sordomudo
y mariposa ahogada en el tintero.
Tropezando con mi rostro distinto de cada día
¡Asesinado por el cielo! (*Poet in New York* 6)

The child "con el blanco rostro de huevo" can be compared to the foetus Adela is carrying, as yet not fully formed and having the "blank face of an egg." Images of stunted creativity such as the "amputated tree that doesn't sing" and the "butterfly drowned in the inkwell" are encapsulated by the central image of the poem, the "water, dressed in rags, but with dry feet." The liquidity of the libido has been stilled; its dry feet now prevent it from flowing forth. A disturbing level of the poem which, as we can see, echoes very much the type of insights we have seen at work in Lorca's rural tragedies, is the masochistic desire for repression, of being "cut down by the sky," which explains Lorca's fascination with Saint Sebastian, of all the saints the one who accepted his martyrdom without complaint.[32] Adela's death, as she is "cut down by the sky," on a primary level suggests what Gilbert and Gubar call the "penning-in" of the female body. But on a secondary level it suggests the necessary repression of desire before the mystery of gender can achieve full expression.

Carlos Fuentes and the Dream of Conquest

Theater has been described as the "Cinderella" of the Latin-American literary canon, which is reflected in the three problems which characterize its existence: firstly, a lack of adequate venues; secondly, the lack of a clearly identifiable national theatrical tradition; and thirdly, small audiences. This lack of a clearly identifiable theatrical tradition has tempted writers skilled in adjacent literary genres, such as César Vallejo, Rosario Castellanos, Vargas Llosa and Carlos Fuentes, to try their hand at drama, an exercise which has not always proved universally successful.[33] With the possible exception of Rodolfo Usigli, Latin America does not possess a dramatist of the stature of Spain's García Lorca. Yet, even if it is difficult to identify a coherent, native dramatic tradition in Latin America, individual dramatic works of great ingenuity are certainly not lacking, an example being Carlos Fuentes's *Todos los gatos son pardos*.

Carlos Fuentes's fame as a novelist has led to the marginalization of his theater. In the literary canon of contemporary Mexican theater, Fuentes's drama operates almost like a black hole, occasionally eliciting murmurs of attention but, in canonic terms, met by silence. David William Foster's comprehensive *Estudios sobre teatro mexicano contemporáneo* (1984) studies the work of José Agustín, Emilio Carballido, Celestino Gorostiza, Luisa Josefina Hernández, Jorge Ibargüengoitia, Vicente Leñero, Carlos Solórzano, Felipe Reyes Palacio and Rodolfo Usigli, but no mention is made of Fuentes's theater.[34] Merlin H. Forster's essay on Fuentes's drama lists only one article on Fuentes's *El tuerto es rey* and a handful of articles on *Todos los gatos son pardos* (191-92).

Todos los gatos son pardos, however, is a play which deserves more critical interest than the amount it has aroused to date. It explores the roots of power in the human psyche and offers suggestive parallels with the path beaten by Lacan in his own explorations of the Unconscious. Fuentes indeed refers to the French psychoanalyst in his introduction to the play:

> Hace algunos inviernos y muchas noches, Arthur Miller me decía en su granja de Connecticut que, desde niño, lo que le había fascinado en la historia de la conquista de México era el encuentro dramático de un hombre que lo tenía todo—Moctezuma—y de un hombre que nada tenía —Cortés. Más tarde, leyendo los escritos de psicoanálisis estructural de Jacques Lacan, encontré este pensamiento: el subconsciente es el discurso del otro. (*Obras completas* II, 1160-61)

This gives a clue about the way that Fuentes reads history. For, as this quotation makes quite clear, he does see history as a set of empiric realities waiting to be discovered, or even, perhaps, as an objective account of the narrative of the world. What clearly interests him is a structural, psychoanalytical reading of the past. The seed planted by Arthur Miller Fuentes later found flourishing in the arcane metaphors of Lacan's prose. In *Todos los gatos son pardos*, Fuentes psychoanalyzes Latin-American history, or rather two of its founding personalities, Cortés and Moctezuma, and reads their dilemma as a blueprint of the origins of the Latin-American individual. In this play, as James Stais suggests, Fuentes attempts to establish "de una vez para todas, la responsabilidad que tiene todo mexicano de identificarse con el verdadero origen de su ser" (468). In the process Fuentes has recourse to a myth of origin, but given the utopian, back-to-origins nostalgia expressed in his work, particularly his novels, this will not come as a surprise to many readers. As Fuentes suggested in an interview with Emir Rodríguez Monegal, the search for utopia implies a rejection of historiography: "Salir de la historiografía, de la reducción de la historia, para entrar en la dialéctica, que es hacer la historia y hacerla con los mitos que nos dan los hilos de Ariadne de todo ese pasado utópico y épico para convertirlo en *otra cosa*. A través del mito, re-actuamos el pasado, lo reducimos a proporción humana" ("Carlos Fuentes" 45).

What is also clearly evident from the quotation above is that the nodal point of Fuentes's drama is the meeting between Moctezuma and Cortés and his understanding that this historic meeting was also an encounter between Self and Other, the Conscious and the Unconscious. An immediate question which arises when we attempt to decipher history in terms of binary oppositions is *who* in this relationship stands for the Other and *who* for the Same. In his work *The Conquest of America: The Question of the Other* (1984), Tzvetan Todorov makes this parallel explicitly, showing how the indigenous population was perceived by the conquerors uniquely in terms of the Other. Spain had only finally banished the Other in the form of the Moors from Spanish soil in 1492, when the last Moors were finally expelled from Granada. As one commentator suggests: "Spain in 1500, vibrant with religious zeal and political unity after the expulsion of the last of its Moorish invaders, turned eagerly to the New World in quest of gold, souls, and land" (*National Geographic* 466A). The same metaphorical system employed by Spain to rid its own territories of infidels is used by Cortés to map out the new world of the Aztecs which he encountered in 1519. In his first letter to the Catholic Kings, for example, Cortés refers to how the Aztecs wear "unas mantas muy delgadas y pintadas a manera de alquizales *moriscos*" (my emphasis); their dwellings are "muy amoriscados," and their religious temples are described as "mezquitas" (30-31). This view of the conquest, namely from the point of view of the conquerors and colonizers, is the orthodox view handed down to us by the discourse of history.

Given that *Todos los gatos son pardos* is very much a Western view of the dilemma of history, given its language, plot structure, and its conception of character and myth, it is curious that Moctezuma should take on the role of Self, with Cortés playing the role of Other. This is suggested in an obvious way, in that the language spoken by Moctezuma—Castilian—is never perceived by him as Other. It is simply a transparent means of communication which we, as audience, accept to be the language of the Aztecs for the sake of dramatic convention, in the same way that we accept a dramatic soliloquy as "realistic."[35] The presentation of Cortés as Other is predicated on a number of additional structural devices. Firstly, in the opening scene of the play the prophetic dreams of the "soñadores," which prophesy the return of Quetazalcóatl (given the transparent reference to Freud's view of dreams as the "royal road to the Unconscious"), prepare the ground for Cortés's later entrance and give rise to an interpretation of his appearance as an embodiment of the Unconscious. The priest, Cihuacóatl, describes Moctezuma's frame of mind in ways which recall Freud's use of corporeal metaphors drawn from the field of architecture to describe the space inhabited by the Unconscious:

> En el infierno de tu imaginación, en el paraíso de tu deseo, en los subterráneos dorados de tu palacio o en la cima ensangrentada de tu pirámide, serás visitado por los fantasmas de tus ancestros. (Act I, 1177)

Yet Moctezuma is unwilling to countenance the revelation of the Unconscious and, in a classic act of primary repression, has the dreamers put to death in order to silence their knowledge. By killing the dreamers Moctezuma believes he can put their dreams to rest at the same time: "¡Mátenlos! ¡Asesinen a los sueños! ¡Asesinen a los soñadores!" (Act I, 1184). By murdering the dreamers Moctezuma rids his regime of the last vestiges of individual liberty for, as Tzompantecuhtli points out to Moctezuma, dreaming is the only freedom left for his citizens: "No nos has dejado otra libertad, señor" (Act I, 1182). As Moctezuma soon finds out, however—and here the play echoes Freudian knowledge—repression of the Unconscious leads inevitably to the "compulsion to repeat." When Cortés finally arrives he wreaks a vengeance which is worse than Moctezuma's wildest dreams, since the Spaniard single-handedly destroys a whole culture.

The unravelling of the Unconscious is also related to the unveiling of sexual desire. Thus it is not coincidental that when Moctezuma is being informed by Cihuacóatl about the roots of the power he enjoys as a monarch, he should be gradually undressing a young woman. As we read in the stage directions: "Moctezuma desnuda lentamente a la DONCELLA" (Act I, 1178). Likewise the first glimpse we have of Cortés is when he is making love with Marina:

> Oscuridad total y prolongada. Rumores de la noche tropical. A ellos se superpone el de un jadeo erótico. Iluminación baja. Sobre unas mantas, un hombre y una mujer desnudos hacen el amor. Son CORTES y MARINA. (Act I, 1186)

In the case of both men, the expression of the Unconscious is linked to a libido which is gendered and, in each case, phallic.

One other intrinsic characteristic of the Unconscious as portrayed in *Todos los gatos son pardos* is power. For the literary looking-glass which Fuentes chooses in order to unravel the meaning of the Conquest is the mystery of power (which is, by no means, the only vantage point he could have taken). In this, Fuentes no doubt drew inspiration from Lacan's work. The French psychoanalyst has described the revelation of the Unconscious in terms which are eminently applicable to Fuentes's play: "Such awe seizes man when he unveils the lineaments of this power that he turns away from it in the very action employed to lay its features bare" (*Language of the Self* 3). The play opens with a blinding light which is a metaphor for Moctezuma's power:

MERCADER.—Baja la vista, pastor . . .

PASTOR. -¡Qué luz tan intensa! No podría mirarla, aunque quisiera . . .

MERCADER.—Es la luz que irradia nuestro rey Moctezuma, encarnación del sol y dueño de toda la tierra conocida . . .

PASTOR.—Dicen que nadie tiene derecho a mirar a Moctezuma a la cara, salvo cuatro de sus parientes más allegados.

MERCADER.—Así debe ser. Mira fijamente el sol y te quedarás ciego. (Act I, 1168-69)

Moctezuma's power is described at the beginning of the play as Godlike, since, outside it, nothing exists. As Cihuacóatl suggests: "Fuera de tu poder, que es todo, solo hay nada" (Act I, 1176). Moctezuma embodies a power which cannot be unveiled or contemplated, since it is God-like.

This is no doubt the reason why the Conquest is represented in *Todos los gatos son pardos* as the point in history when the old images of God come tumbling down and a new "democratic" age is born. As Cortés says to one of his soldiers, Ordás, "lo que hemos hecho tú y yo es arrebatarle el privilegio de drama a la casta de los reyes y de los cortesanos. Actuamos este intenso misterio: nosotros, el pueblo de España, somos ahora los protagonistas . . ." (Act II, 1235), an idea which is implicit in the title: "*Todos* los gatos son pardos" (my emphasis). At this point in history, during the Conquest, as the argument follows, the power associated with the Godhead now comes down to earth. As Marina suggests forcefully to Moctezuma's head priest:

¡No creas más en los dioses, imbécil! ¡Obliga a los dioses a creer en ti! ¡Desenmascara a los dioses, imbécil, y detrás de cada máscara encontrarás el rostro de un opresor! ¡No le pidas más el cielo a los dioses; exígele la tierra a los opresores! (Act III, 1256)

As the plot unfolds it becomes clear that the play very much turns on this metaphor, that is, the sense in which the Gods are invisible and draw their power from their invisibility. The irony of the play is that it is in the act of unveiling its power that the Unconscious is destroyed. Thus once the "Gods" are unmasked and their true nature made evident, their power drains away.

The mirror is an ambivalent image in *Todos los gatos son pardos*. As Lanin A. Gyurko has pointed out, Fuentes had used this motif before; in his novel *La región más transparente*, for example, Fuentes describes at one point how the God Tezcatlipoca appears while Cortés and Marina are copulating, carrying in his hand a "phallus-mirror": "Violenta cópula de ambos. Aparece el AUGUR/CATLIPOCA, envuelto en trapos negros: baila y salta alrededor de la pareja; lleva en la mano el falo-espejo" (Gyurko 237). There is a hint that the mirror stands likewise for the power of the phallus in *Todos los gatos son pardos*, especially in one of the "conquest" scenes. At the beginning of Act II, for example, an Indian girl swaps her sexual favors for a mirror: "el SOLDADO corre hacia ella, la toma del talle, ella se zafa, él hace gestos de invitación; le ofrece el espejo, ella se acerca, se mira asombrada en el espejo, tiende la mano al SOLDADO, toma el espejo. El la besa. Salen" (Act II, 1207). The mirror also becomes a metaphor of the (divine) power possessed by Moctezuma. When he falls from favor in the eyes of his people, Moctezuma is described as "el espejo opaco de todos los poderes que oprimen a los hombres" (Act III, 1249), an image which echoes the earlier prophecy of one of the soothsayers: "has hecho que el poder se vea en el espejo del crimen" (Act I, 1187). Like Oedipus, Moctezuma sees his own crime in the prophecies made by the soothsayers, which reflect the truth at him as if their words were a mirror.

Fuentes's use of the mirror to depict the disastrous creation of a new world in Latin America has some suggestive parallels with the anthropological musings of Claude Lévi-Strauss (Clément 77). In his study *Anthropologie structurale*, Lévi-Strauss refers to an incident which he found paradigmatic of the links and the distances that are necessary for the proper cohesion of society. In the distant past, a tribe of Indians had joined the Mandans of North America and learned from them how to grow corn. Before long, however, the Mandans asked the other tribe to leave for the following reason:

> It would be better for you to cross the river and build your village there, because our customs are far too different from yours. Since our young people and yours are not familiar with each other's customs, there could be disputes and these might lead to war. Do not go too far, because peoples who live far apart are like strangers and war may erupt between them. Travel northward until you can no longer see the smoke from our houses, and there build your village. This way we will be close enough to be friends and yet not far enough apart to become enemies.

Cathérine Clément quotes this passage and refers to how this idea of "correct distance" occurs in myths "wherever chance encounters have led to catastrophe." She argues, for example, that it "figures in the story of Oedipus, who is reunited too closely with his mother." And she further points out: "Lévi-Strauss discovered the correct distance in the stark model of primitive society: Lacan discovered it in the child."[36] This concept of correct distance can be applied to the relationship between the Old World and the New, as portrayed in the meeting of Cortés and Moctezuma. Discovery led to the correct distance not being maintained which itself resulted in catastrophe, which was at once cultural and discursive. Latin America became the Other of European discourse which it struggled to master and eventually destroyed. In Fuentes's play the meeting of the Old World and the New leads to the destruction of both civilizations. Moctezuma is eventually destroyed, and the last image we have of Cortés is of a man plagued by poverty and madness:

> Yo, un hombre que nada tenía, aplasté a un imperio . . . y mi propio imperio me aplastó a mí, un hombre que nada tiene. Mírame, Marina: fui la víctima de dos poderes: el derrotado y el victorioso . . . Marina, Marina . . . perdí tu tierra . . . y no gané la mía. (Act III, 1261)

A crucial part in the Conquest, which is echoed in Fuentes's play, was played by Malinche, or Marina, as she was also known. Malinche, the concubine-*cum*-interpreter, was given to Cortés by the Tabasco tribe in 1519, and she proved to be a decisive influence during the Conquest. She told Cortés, for example, about the legend that the white-skinned God Quetzalcóatl would one day return to the Aztecs. Cortés used this myth in order to persuade the Indian populations that he was destined to rule the Aztec empire.[37] Through Marina, Cortés achieved access to the power of language. He used the knowledge of the culture he sought to dominate in order to obtain its power. In a gesture typical of colonialism, that knowledge was translated into power.[38]

Great attention is paid to Marina's role in Fuentes's play. On one level she is reduced to a two-fold existence consisting of two bodily organs, her tongue and her sex. As Marina acknowledges at one stage: "Yo sólo soy la lengua" (Act I, 1188), and, as Cortés repeats later on in the play: "Eres mi lengua" (Act II, 1209). Marina's sexual function appears most nakedly in her first appearance on the stage when she is seen making love with Cortés, in a scene which acts almost like the primal scene of Latin-American history. Perhaps more important are her words when she gives birth to Cortés's son. Her soliloquy is reminiscent of the archetypal and universalist thrust of Octavio Paz's vision of the union of Cortés and Marina as a paradigm of the racial make-up of modern-day Mexico. Mexicans, he had argued, are "hijos de la Chingada," the union between the Spaniard male who "raped" the Indian native woman (*Labyrinth* 73-81).[39]

> Oh, sal ya, hijo mío, sal, sal, sal entre mis piernas . . . Sal, hijo de la traición . . . sal, hijo de puta . . . sal, hijo de la chingada . . . adorado hijo mío, sal ya . . . cae sobre la tierra que ya no es mía ni de tu padre, sino tuya . . . sal, hijo de las dos sangres enemigas. (Act III, 1252)

As the juncture in the play, Malinche becomes the mouthpiece for the destiny of the Mexican people. As Gyurko suggests, Fuentes consecrates Malinche as "the creator of a new people—the synthesis of Aztec and Spanish —and the person who heralds the birth of a new nation." As Gyurko goes on to point out, "from the beginning to the end of *Todos los gatos son pardos*, Malinche plays a role that far exceeds her historical significance. She constantly appears as a guiding spiritual presence, a figure of high moral idealism who speaks in extensive and eloquent monologues" (234).

In Fuentes's text, Moctezuma and Cortés are shown as involved in a game of masks which reflects back at the theme of representation. As in Spanish Romantic drama (see discussion above), the use of masks, or doubles, becomes part of a process of investigation, in *Todos los gatos son pardos*, into human identity. The double is a motif central to Fuentes's concept of literary creativity. As he pointed out in an interview with Rodríguez Monegal: "Hablamos de dobles: el novelista quisiera ser el gemelo de Luzbel, el curioso, el tentador, el condenado" ("Carlos Fuentes" 48). In Fuentes's play, the mask is central to the power games Moctezuma and Cortés play with each other. Moctezuma believes, for example, that by sending a simulacrum of his power, a double. But this ploy does not fool Cortés:

> (*CORTES toma con la mano la barbilla del DOBLE.*) ¿Por qué temes mostrarme tu rostro, Moctezuma? ¿O acaso temes conocer el mío? (*Lo suelta, ríe.*) ¡No somos sino máscaras! . . . Esperabas a los dioses. Los dioses han llegado. Las máscaras han caído. (Act II, 1238)

Cortés associates the coming of the Gods with the stripping bare of the mask, as we can see. As far as Moctezuma is concerned Cortés represents the Other who returns and explodes the dualism of conscious and unconscious levels of the personality. This idea comes to the fore in a significant exchange that Moctezuma has with his chief priest:

> MOCTEZUMA Dime, sacerdote: ¿no represento al sol en la tierra?
>
> CIHUACOATL.-Así es.
>
> MOCTEZUMA.- ¿Es demasiado pedir un poco de soledad a cambio de esa representación? Que no me miren, que no me toquen, que no me hablen. ¿No es suficiente estar y representar? ¿Es necesario estar sufriendo y representar mucho?
>
> CIHUACOATL.- Quien rechaza el poder es rechazado por el poder. Estos extranjeros quieren lo que tú rechazas: no solo representar el poder, sino usarlo para cambiar el rostro de nuestra tierra. (Act II, 1224)

Moctezuma seems here to be expressing a nostalgia for an appearance-essence dualism which could shield him from the oppressive nature of a historical dilemma he is unable to solve. This is no doubt the paranoiac motive behind his decision to send a double of himself to Cortés rather than himself, thereby reinstating a dualism based on essence versus representation which is, even as he speaks, in the process of crumbling. The double which he sends is a representation of a representation, since Moctezuma is the representation of the Godhead on earth. The appearance of Cortés, however, short-circuits the vicious circle of representation. The arrival of the Other deconstructs the dualism of personality and, in the process, fundamentally questions the myth of origins.

It will be clear from the preceding discussion that the motif of representation and its visual accompaniment, the mirror, are the focal points of Fuentes's drama. Other structural images, however, are employed in a traditional and non-reflective manner. One example is the image of blood which, as we have seen, was explored innovatively in Romantic drama; in Lorca's drama it became a means of deconstructing the notion of sexual difference. In *Todos los gatos son pardos*, however, blood is simply used as a metonymic link between the Amerindian and the Christian civilizations, both of which are patriarchal and sacrificial, as suggested when the blood of the youth sacrificed during the Aztec rite is likened to the blood of Christ's crucifixion. As we read in the stage directions: "El SACERDOTE 2, con las manos manchadas de sangre, también se acerca, coloca una mano sobre el pecho del Cristo, añade una huella de sangre a las de la crucifixión" (Act II,

1233). The blood of the Aztec sacrifice is thus in effect transformed into the blood which informs the sacrifice of Christ. Rather than stressing the disparateness of the Amerindian and the Christian cultures, Fuentes's text elides difference and slips into a discourse of the Same. The image of blood here has none of the metaphorical fluidity it possesses in Lorca's plays. By fusing two different cultural value-systems together through a binding metaphor, Fuentes is in effect privileging the archetype at the expense of its accidental representation and, true to the name of his father, privileging source at the expense of the physical reality of the body.

The use of traditional images in this way points to the presence of a degree of structural weakness in Fuentes's play. One of the semiotic flaws of the *Todos los gatos son pardos* is that, while it tends to re-evaluate the concept of representation as understood in the context of state power and its relationship to the god-head, this does not lead to a concomitant questioning of the motif of representation in a dramatic sense. Similar in this to the theater of Albert Camus and Jean-Paul Sartre, Fuentes's drama is revolutionary in content but unrevolutionary in terms of form (Laraque 32-37).[40] In *Todos los gatos son pardos* the issue of representationality is presented rather than re-presented. In its paranoiac refusal to countenance its own metadiscursive potential, Fuentes's text exhibits a structural lack. Although Fuentes's play would appear, thus, to possess certain structural defects, its investigation into the historical discourse of the Spanish conquest of America and its unravelling of the role of the Other in that struggle is, nevertheless, one of the most psychologically perceptive in modern Spanish-American drama.

NOTES

1. The reader will recall that Engels spoke of Balzac's "complete history of French society from which, even in economic details (for instance, the rearrangement of real and personal property after the Revolution) I have learned more than from all the professed historians, economists, and statisticians of the period together" (Jameson 10-11).

2. *Der Mythus von der Geburt des Helden*; see Freud, *Complete Psychological Works* IX, 236.

3. The essay is now translated simply as "Family Romances" (*Complete Psychological Works* IX, 237-41).

4. Freud made a similar comparison between the neurotic and the artist when he defined the latter as "originally a man who turns from reality because he cannot come to terms with the demand for the renunciation of instinctual satisfaction as it is first made, and who then in fantasy-life allows full play to his erotic and ambitious wishes" ("Formulations on the two principles of mental functioning," *Complete Psychological Works* XII, 218-26 [224]).

5. For a clear discussion of the usage of the term *romántico* and related cognates in Spain in the nineteenth century, see Shaw, "Spain . . ."

6. For a discussion of the 1812 Constitution and its political affect, see Solís. As Gabriel H. Lovett argues, it was in Cádiz that the Cortes "forged the instruments which put an end to the *Ancien Régime* and laid the groundwork for modern Spain" (I, 414). This was not, however, an easy historical transition. After the signing of the

Constitution, as Lovett goes on to point out, "the liberals finally came into open collision with the most cohesive forces of Spanish traditionalism, the Catholic Church, specifically over the issue of the Inquisition" (II, 470). For further discussion of the political struggle between the liberals and the traditionalists, see Lovett's chapter "Spain is Split Asunder" (II, 415-90).

7. For a discussion of this historical period, see Carr, esp. 79-209.

8. The Salic Law, which provides that females can never succeed to the throne, had been given to Spain by Philip V in 1713. Ferdinand's third wife, Maria Amelia of Saxony, died in 1829. Ferdinand, still childless and anxious to have an heir, married Maria Cristina, daughter of King Francis I of Naples. He abrogated the Salic Law in May 1830. His daughter Isabel was born on 10 October 1830. On Ferdinand's death three years later, Isabel was declared Ferdinand's heir, but Ferdinand's brother don Carlos, invoking the Salic Law, declared himself from Portugal to be Ferdinand's successor. The first Carlist War was to drag on for six years. For more information see Carr.

9. This sense of liberation was at the root of the great acclaim with which *Don Álvaro* opened in Madrid; see Andioc 63-86.

10. The plot of many Romantic plays has been criticized for being over-complicated; see Larra's pertinent critique.

11. For a brief discussion of the development of the doctrine of "limpieza de sangre" in the sixteenth and seventeenth centuries in Spain, see Elliott 220-24. This was a very common topos in Golden Age theater. Peribáñez, for example, in Lope de Vega's play *Peribáñez y el comendador de Ocaña*, bases his claim to authenticity on his pure blood: "Yo soy un hombre, / aunque de villana casta, / limpio de sangre, y jamás / de hebrea o mora manchada" (Act III, 149).

12. The heated exchange between Alfonso and Álvaro clearly also has a political edge. When *Don Álvaro* was staged in Madrid in 1835, the Spanish-American colonies were in revolt, and some had already declared independence from the Spanish throne. By calling Álvaro a "mestizo," and given that he is suspected of being an "Inca," Alfonso reflects the bitterness and contempt experienced by the colonial power for its wayward "daughters."

13. In *Don Juan Tenorio*, love itself becomes a religion in conflict with Christianity; see Mazzeo and Abrams. For a discussion of the role of the related theme of parallelism in Zorrilla's play, see Mansour, Ter Horst, and Mandrell.

14. For some idea of Lorca's presence in scholarship on modern Spanish drama, one can simply consult the *Year's Work in Modern Language Studies*. In the most recent publication available, in the section entitled "Literature, 1898-1936," the lion's share of research falls to Lorca, with three pages devoted to his work, which is about sixteen percent of the available space.

15. For an example of this tendency to see Lorca as symptomatic of Franco's repression, see Gibson, *La represión nacionalista*. For a discussion of this elegaic approach to Lorca's work, see P. Smith 110-11.

16. Similarly, José Luis Cano's study makes no reference to Lorca's homosexuality, nor does Ramsden in his study of the *Romancero gitano*.

17. Ian Gibson's point-for-point refutation of Schoenberg's thesis occurs in *The Death of Lorca* 176-82.

18. See also Sahuquillo 91-105. Sahuquillo's work is also particularly effective in showing how critics have consistently swept Lorca's homosexuality under the carpet; see 16-21.

19. This leads Binding to argue, for example, that homosexual desire is always present in Lorca's work, even if in a displaced form. Thus in his discussion of *Bodas de sangre*, Binding quotes a passionate outburst by the Novia and comments: "*Mutatis*

mutandis this (like Leonardo's speech) could be the cry of a young man who, after courtship, engagement, a wedding, after all the business of orthodox sexuality and house-planning, surrenders to his deeper and stronger desires and realizes (in both senses of that word) what he has been evading and denying for so long" (172). Surely this appeal to a level of emotion "deeper" than the surface values of heterosexual love betrays an adherence to the type of logocentrism that Lorca's drama seeks to undo. To see Lorca's theater as a *disguised* representation of homosexual desire is to reverse the sexual terms within the prisonhouse of gender, rather than to deconstruct its very premises. Of *Yerma* Binding argues that it is "intolerable that good, naturally maternal Yerma cannot have the children she so longs for; it is intolerable that good naturally parental homosexuals also cannot" (177). Yerma's recognition that "cuando paso por lo oscuro del cobertizo mis pasos me suenan a pasos de hombre" (Act II, Scene 2, 178), however, surely destabilizes gender rather than hinting at a hidden gay agenda. In his analysis of *La casa de Bernarda Alba*, Binding grinds at the same axe: "In his rage at the malformation of life to which the women of his drama—maybe even the terrible Bernarda herself—are subjected, Lorca must have been thinking of the denial of natural impulses and feelings of homosexuals in the conservative Spanish countryside" (189). In a cogently argued chapter on Lorca, P. Smith has shown that Binding's gay analysis of Lorca's drama falls prey "to the mirage of liberation" (118).

20. For a detailed discussion of the use of this image, see "The Great Reservoir of Libido" 63-66, Appendix B.

21. In his essay "Femininity," Freud argues that, although there is "only one libido, which serves both the masculine and the feminine sexual functions," libido is at root phallic since, as he further suggests, "the juxtaposition 'feminine libido' is without any justification." As he concludes, "more constraint has been applied to the libido when it is pressed into the service of the feminine function" (131). Feminists have been quick to point to the phallocentrism underlying Freud's view of the libido. For an excellent discussion of Freud's blindness to femininity, see Bowlby 40-59. It is one of the ironies of fate that in the Romance languages, following the lead of Latin, "libido" is a feminine noun.

22. Ezra Pound has defined "phanopoeia" as the ability within language to throw "a visual image on the mind" (42).

23. Review in *The New York Evening Post* (9 February 1935), quoted by Fernández Cifuentes (86).

24. See Lyon, "Love, Imagination and Society."

25. See Havard, "The Symbolic Ambivalence of 'Green,' " and Harris, "Green Death."

26. See Newbury and Dolan.

27. As Flaubert wrote: "Je crois que ma *Bovary* va aller, mais je suis gêné par le sens métaphorique, qui décidément me domine trop; je suis dévoré de comparaisons comme on l'est de poux, et je ne passe mon temps qu'à les écraser, mes phrases en grouillent" (Thibaudet 210). Lorca is reputed to have remarked enthusiastically about *La casa de Bernarda Alba*: "Ni una gota de poesía . . . ¡Realidad! ¡Realismo puro!" (*La casa de Bernarda Alba* xxix).

28. For a discussion of Adela's struggle against hierarchy, see Busette 86-88 and Bull.

29. See Havard, "The Hidden Parts of *La casa de Bernarda Alba*" 102-08.

30. Irigaray, "Women" 13. See also her vision of a utopian matriarchal culture, separate from patriarchal society, in which women would exchange commodities and labor freely (*Ce Sexe qui n'en est pas un*, esp. 189-93).

31. Bernarda is unwilling to let her daughters marry the first man who comes along. As she says to Poncia in Act I: "No hay en cien leguas a la redonda quien se pueda

acercar a ellas. Los hombres aquí no son de su clase. ¿Es que quieres que las entregue a cualquier gañán?" (20).

32. Dalí, as well as Lorca, was fascinated by Saint Sebastian; see Sánchez Vidal 212-13.

33. I borrow the term "Cinderella" from Catherine Boyle's lecture "Directions for Research on Latin American Theatre" given at the Institute of Latin-American Studies on November 15, 1990. For further information on the emergence of theater in Chile, see her study *Thematic Development in Chilean Theatre since 1973*. Castellanos's *El eterno femenino*, a witty drama about womanhood, has been staged in Mexico, but normally the second act is excluded; it is therefore clearly a play "para leídas." I owe this information to Sr. Raúl Ortiz y Ortiz, to whom Castellanos entrusted the manuscript of her play in 1973, a year before her death. César Vallejo, for his part, was unable to get any of his dramas staged either in Spain or France; for more information, see my study "El compromiso en el teatro de César Vallejo." Vargas Llosa has had a degree of success with his plays in Europe and Latin America, especially with *La señorita de Tacna*; for more information, see my "Vargas Llosa. 1936."

34. For a detailed discussion of pre-1950 Mexican theater, see Nomland. For a study of the modern dramatists of Mexico, see Burgess. For a good recent survey, see Taylor.

35. For a lucid discussion of dramatic convention, see Williams 3-8.

36. It is intriguing that the Mexican poet Rosario Castellanos also uses the motif of the mirror in order to portray the disaster of Conquest. In the poem "Malinche," Malinche destroys her daughter as if she were a mirror: "me aborreció porque yo era su igual / en figura y en rango / y se contempló en mí y odió su imagen / y destrozó el espejo contra el suelo" (Crow 100).

37. In this way Cortés was imitating a successful ploy also used before him by Christopher Columbus. When the latter's men arrived in San Salvador, for example, the native population believed they were "people from heaven"(Bradford 120).

38. Edward Said has some perceptive words to say about the way in which the colonizing nation uses its knowledge of the occupied nation in order to dominate it (31-49).

39. For further discussion of the Fuentes-Paz interface on this point, see Bower.

40. For further discussion of this play, see Chrzanowski and Peñuela Cañizal.

II
NOVEL, NATIONHOOD AND OEDIPUS

In this chapter the focus will be centered on the twentieth-century novel, and specifically Luis Martín-Santos's *Tiempo de silencio* (1962) and Juan Rulfo's *Pedro Páramo* (1955). At first glance, two novels could not be more different. Martín-Santos's Joycean style, his delight in the pyrotechnics of word-play, his flirtation with myths and the literary canon—in short, his defiant intertextuality—would seem poles apart from the sober, measured and even brittle style of Rulfo's novel. While not wishing to play down the obvious differences between these two texts, I shall be arguing that both are underpinned by one main structure, namely, the protagonist's search for self, and specifically the search for the identity of the nation, Spain in the first case and Mexico in the second, which is projected and experienced by the individual as an ever-absent but powerful alter ego. Perhaps more significant is the fact that both protagonists, Pedro in *Tiempo de silencio* and Juan Preciado in *Pedro Páramo*, re-enact the Oedipal journey.

Martín-Santos: Castration and Representation

> The literature of disease is more interesting to me than all the healthy books.
> D.H. Lawrence (Meyers 1)

In a book on the interrelation between literature and psychoanalysis it is only right that the psychoanalytical theories of a writer such as Luis Martín-Santos (1924-1964) should be mentioned. Martín-Santos was for the greater part of his life a practicing psychologist, and this is clearly reflected in his fiction as well as his major essay *Libertad, temporalidad y transferencia en el psicoanálisis existencial* (1964). In this essay Martín-Santos makes some perceptive points about the role of repression within the art form which can be related directly to his own vision, in *Tiempo de silencio*, of Spanish society as an alter ego which forces the ego to submit to repression and ultimately castration. His approach to his subject in the main, as might be expected, is that of an ego-psychologist. Martín-Santos's novels, however, both *Tiempo de silencio* (1962) and *Tiempo de destrucción* (1964), venture into areas which go beyond the ambit of Freudian ego-psychology and contain insights which are nearer in spirit to Lacanian or neo-Lacanian analysis.

In *Libertad, temporalidad y transferencia*, Martín-Santos on the whole uses Freudian parameters to discuss the psychic roots of the art form. Thus he argues that mankind is distinguished from other animals because of the surplus of sexual energy which informs every aspect of his life:

> Precisamente porque el hombre tiene un plus sexual, a partir de una instintividad genital y pregenital que no puede agotarse totalmente en la realización del acto carnal (ni aun en los individuos que mayores facilidades tengan y menos obstáculos para su realización), es por lo que su vida en muchos aspectos y hasta en su totalidad queda teñida de sexualidad. (118)

This surplus, Martín-Santos goes on to argue, must be sublimated: "El plus de esta sexualidad nos plantea como constante humana (y no como paradójico fenómeno antibiológico) el hecho de la sublimación" (118). Following Freudian knowledge, Martín-Santos sees sublimation as a result of repression, but he stresses that we should not see sublimation, and one of its corollaries, art, as simply a substitute cathexis of pent-up sexual energy:

> Hacer depender la sublimación sólo de la represión es un enfoque erróneo, tanto desde el punto de vista existencial como desde el punto de vista psicodinámico. La sublimación existe incluso en casos de pleno desenfreno sexual. De hecho, muchos de los individuos con mayores realizaciones culturales no son reprimidos sexuales, y, recíprocamente, muchos graves reprimidos son absolutamente improductivos. (119)

Insights such as these are certainly not absent from his novels. The connection between repression and art, for example, surfaces at various stages in *Tiempo de silencio*. When going to visit the studio of the German artist, Pedro remarks: "El número de desnudos que pinta indica el nivel alcanzado por la represión de un pueblo" (72), suggesting that art is a sublimatory outlet for a nation's surplus libido. It is interesting that both Matías and Pedro resort to Latin when confronted with paintings of nude women:

> —Jubilatio in carne feminae—inició Matías.
>
> —Pulcritudo vastissima semper derramata—continuó Pedro. (72)

The transference from one language to another is itself a symptom of repression; veiling libidinal desires within the official linguistic fig leaf of a revered ancient tongue associated with the Church. The relationship between libido and art is, however, far from easy. Libido is always apt to rebel against a socially-imposed culture, striving to achieve "algún irrealizable fin para el que el cuerpo de la hembra ha sido fabricado y hacia el que incesantemente tiende, a despecho de cuantas trabas y oposiciones trenza en torno a ella el confuso edificio de la cultura cuantas veces agrietado, otras tantas consolidado y acrecido" (221). Struggling against the edifice of culture, and its pre-condition repression, is to involve the individual in a Sisyphus-like struggle. Here Martín-Santos's novel seems to echo directly his theoretical text.

It is clear from statements such as these, and from his assertion that the sublimation of sexual energy can produce "neurotic symptoms" as well as "valuable cultural products" (*Libertad* 119), that Martín-Santos sees art as deriving from a sublimation of libidinal impulses. The artist, however, has greater control than the neurotic over his "symptom," the art form (120-21). The distinction Martín-Santos is drawing here is perhaps made clearer when he compares his own view of the symbol with the Freudian model: "El símbolo no puede interpretarse sólo al modo freudiano, como traducción de un dinanismo psíquico subyacente, sino también como realización formal y expresiva del ser del hombre, junto con su proyecto" (50). Here we can see a hint of the way in which Martín-Santos, on occasions, will move beyond the Freudian model. Freud's "self-determination" becomes "self-creation" in Martín-Santos's hands.

There are, however, points in his creative writing in which Martín-Santos is engaged in a dialogue with the discourse of psychoanalysis which seems to go beyond the hermeneutic limitations of ego-psychology, and particularly the latter's notion of the ego as a fixed though adjustable mechanism. One particular area in which Martín-Santos's novels seem to overlap with Lacanian and neo-Lacanian psychoanalysis concerns the issue of castration. The investigation into castration, particularly in *Tiempo de silencio*, has some striking similarities with Michèle Montrelay's psychoanalytical work. In her important study *L'Ombre et le Nom* (1977), Montrelay argues three points taken from Lacan. They are: i) "The unconscious is a structure or combinatory of desires articulated as repression," ii) "These representations can be called representations of castration, in as much as their literal articulation effectively deprives the subject of part of *jouissance*," and iii) "The stake is this *jouissance*, whose loss is the price of representation" (231-32). Representation, in Montrelay's view, is thus closely linked with castration, being its prelude and to some extent its pre-condition.

Let us review the final "self-castration" monologue of *Tiempo de silencio* in the light of this idea:

> ¿Pero yo, por qué no estoy más desesperado? ¿Por qué me estoy dejando capar? El hombre fálico de la gorra roja terminada en punta de cilindro rojo con su fecundidad inagotable para la producción de movimientos rectilíneos, aquí se está paseando orgulloso de su gran prepucio rojo-cefálico, con su pito en la mano, con un palo enrollado, dotado de múltiples atributos que desencadenarán la marcha erecta del órgano gigante que se clavará en el vientre de las montañas mientras yo me estoy dejando capar. (237)

On one level we must read this passage as referring to the non-creativity of the narrator compared to the "phallic man," whose ability to procreate takes on mythic proportions, and who is probably to be understood as an ironic projection of God the Father and Francisco Franco, whose "enormous organ" is able to pierce the womb of mountains. Whereas in his study *Libertad, temporalidad y transferencia en el psicoanálisis existencial*, Martín-Santos refers to castration in the context of the "castrating-mother figure" (80, 108), in *Tiempo de silencio* this castration is inflicted on the narrator, in theory, by a phallic God-*cum*-Franco figure, and, in effect, by a society which forces him to forego pleasure (pursue medical research) and obey social conventions (work as a doctor in the provinces). On one level, therefore, castration is to be understood as a metaphor of the annihilation of the individual by the society (Spain) in which he lives. A reading of this kind is confirmed by a similar passage in his unfinished novel *Tiempo de destrucción*. In the latter novel it is circumcision, rather than castration, which is the dominant image; the former is described at one stage as a painful religious rite similar to the ritual surrounding the selection process whereby the individual becomes a "Juez de Entrada" (229).

What is intriguing, however, about the castration-passage in *Tiempo de silencio* is the attitude of the narrator towards his ordeal. Pedro, like an inversion of neurosis, despairs of not despairing: "Y yo, sin asomo de desesperación, porque estoy como vacío, porque me han pasado una gamuza y me han limpiado las vísceras . . . y hay hombres como yo, que se van acostumbrando poco a poco a tomar mojama con un vaso de vino y es mejor que el caviar y que el arenque y que el fuá ese de las landes" (236). Pedro has literally been cleaned out; he seems almost non-existent. Yet his feelings are a complete mystery. The text does not give a coherent answer to his question: "¿Por qué me estoy dejando capar?" which initiates the dialogue. In order to try to answer this question we need to look briefly at the larger role of mythemes within the text.

Throughout *Tiempo de silencio*, the characters' actions are described as if they were rewritings of the lives of mythical characters drawn from Greek classical literature. Pedro's quest, for example, at various points recalls that of Homer's protagonist in *The Odyssey*.[1] His visit to a brothel becomes suddenly transformed into Orpheus' journey to the underworld and Ulysses' descent into Hades (82).[2] Pedro speaking to the Madame of the brothel suddenly becomes a dialogue between Oedipus and Electra (90). Pedro also re-enacts events from the life of Oedipus later on in the novel (162). Often these mythic re-enactions take on *esperpentesque* connotations. Going to prison, for example, turns into not only a *regressus ad uterum* but also the physical absorption of the individual into a gigantic digestive system (172; Lyon 75-76).

At the close of the novel Pedro suffers castration in much the same way that Oedipus is punished by blindness. Yet the presence of a mythic sub-text throughout the novel draws our attention to the possibility that Pedro's "castration" is to be understood, like many of the other events in the novel, on a displaced, metaphorical level. After all, the castration Pedro feels is not as "real" as the castration suffered by the eunuchs in Turkish harems to which Pedro refers. Pedro's castration is a relinquishment of the self in the face of social pressures. Rather than researching into cancer, he will have a steady job; rather than going to brothels, he will marry Dorita. Unlike the Turkish eunuchs, he does not scream, because "estamos en el tiempo de la anastesia, estamos en el tiempo en que las cosas hacen poco ruido" (237). It is comfortable to accept social laws: "¿Y por qué no estoy desesperado? Es cómodo ser eunuco, es tranquilo, estar desprovisto de testículos, es agradable a pesar de estar castrado tomar el aire y el sol mientras uno se amojame en silencio" (238). Yet there is a paradox here, since, although Pedro seems to be resigned to the idea of accepting dictatorship and silence, nevertheless we are faced with the text of the novel *Tiempo de silencio*, which has followed Pedro's quest and which is anything but silent on the matter of dictatorship.

If we have a second look at the narrator's state of mind at the conclusion of the novel, we might re-interpret what he says in terms of what Roland Barthes has called "the death of the author." Pedro's statement that "es agradable a pesar de estar castrado tomar el aire y el sol" suggests at the very least a radical split in consciousness between mind and body, almost as if the mind were talking about a body it no longer possessed. In one sense it could be argued therefore that the author has died in order to produce the text. The title of the novel, "The Time of Silence," could therefore be interpreted on two levels: firstly, as a metaphor for social conformism, and secondly, as a sign of the repression necessary for artistic expression to take place. On a superficial level, therefore, the novel concludes on a pessimistic note as the narrator accepts social law and commits personality suicide. But on a deeper level, castration is seen as the pre-condition of representation itself and thus of artistic formulation. Castration takes place at the end of the novel, thereby allowing the psychical dilemma to be formulated. Castration (and here Martín-Santos's text echoes Michèle Montrelay's insight) is the price paid for representation.

If we put forward an historical reading of the novel, the source of the power which castrates Pedro (and which also sets the text in motion) can be ascribed to Francisco Franco, since, as most critics have pointed out, *Tiempo de silencio* is a critique of Spain's Franco years (although it is set in the year 1949 specifically).[3] However, the power which castrates Pedro is diffuse and almost unnameable. It cannot be located simply within the person of General Franco, for it springs as well from the myths that Franco used to bolster up his regime, such as the Catholic Monarchs, Spain's imperial past, and the great figures of the Catholic Church. Martín-Santos's text, therefore, reads Franco's power diachronically, tracing it back to the birth of the Spanish Empire, in the same way that a psychiatrist is apt to trace the analysand's symptom back to an "abnormal experience" in the past (*Libertad* 125-58). It is significant, for example, that Pedro feels oppressed by the events of Spanish history, especially Spain's economic decline from the seventeenth century until the present day, a process which he seems to experience as if it were a personal tragedy. What is crucial here is Pedro's view of the role of language, and literature, in this historic decline. Throughout *Tiempo de silencio*, for example, the literature of the past is mercilessly criticized.[4] Pedro, for example, equates the culture of the past with an emptiness at the center of things when he refers to "ese *vacío* con forma de poema o garcilaso que llaman literatura castellana" (66; my emphasis). Pedro rejects the Spanish cultural tradition because of the hollowness of its rhetoric. Language is seen not only as a symptom but also a cause of Spain's dis-ease. The parallel between Spain and phallocentrism in *Tiempo de silencio* is clear from the metaphor which is used to describe Franco's power, the "órgano gigante" which we have already discussed. To this a third term must now be added, which I have called "miscourse," to conjure up the idea that "discourse" is always "missed."[5] Much of Martín-Santos's writing indeed revolves around the eternal triangle of Spain, phallocentrism and "miscourse."

We find parallels being drawn between this terrible trio of elements not only in *Tiempo de silencio* but also in *Tiempo de destrucción*. A particularly revealing passage runs as follows:

> Pero Demetrios, productor de un hijo, engendrador de hombres, de entrecano hocico, genesíaco varón, vencedor de la caduca mortalidad que a todos no aflige, qué serenamente, qué supercastellanamente, qué onésimamente sobre el pueblo, desde la colina, meditar podía en su superior cultura, intelectualidad rebosante, conocimientos—apenas progredientes, pero no totalmente olvidados—de un latín que alumbrara sus años mozos, en la infinita caterva de afluentes de los ríos españoles, en la lista también íntegra de los reyes de la monarquía goda que un día gozaron cetro, hasta que, despedazados por oso o a traición tonsurados, vieron concluir su trono como otras cosas concluyen, en los problemas de aritmética superior que, a fuerza de ingenio, era capaz de resolver haciendo caso omiso de las reglas de la desconocida álgebra arábiga y traidora, en la belleza del intransitivo, en la sintaxis rectamente entendida y con brillante estilo manejado, en el correcto uso del futuro perfecto de subjuntivo—a *quien hubiere leído las páginas de este mi libro de familia, en que cuidadosamente anoto las efémerides, prendas físicas o virtudes morales de mi hijo*—o bien de la forma perifrástica—a *quien hubiere de leer las páginas*, etc. etc. (92-93)

Demetrios would seem to be an image of the colonialist spirit of proud Castile spreading its culture and its language around the Iberian peninsular down the course of the ages. This rambling and fluid text, which gets caught up in its own grammatical conundrums (the reference to rivers is not insignificant), is allied to Demetrios's procreative abilities; he is an "engendrador de hombres." Genealogy, and specifically the power which is passed from father to son, is linked to the power inhering in language. This passage makes clear that Martín-Santos's work can be read as a concerted desire to reveal the insidious links between the notions of Spain, phallocracy and "miscourse." All three are symptoms of the same paralyzing disease—Lack. It is the terror of this existential Lack which is elsewhere described by Martín-Santos as the deepest of all primitive fears (*Libertad* 188). For Lacan, as for Martín-Santos, it is Lack which is simultaneously feared but at the heart of language, the cause of mankind's entry into the world of language and the Symbolic Order.

The trinity of Spain, phallocracy and "miscourse" necessarily means that women are projected in Martín-Santos's fiction as embodiments of the Other and thereby transformed into perpetual victims. Unlike in his theoretical works, where the castrating mother figure gets as much if not more exposure than her masculine counterpart, the woman in his fiction is more often than not vulnerable and, echoing etymology, is often wounded and killed. By being wounded and killed by the phallus, the woman is thereby turned from subject into object, from what Sartre in *L'Être et le Néant* has called *"l'être-pour-soi"* into *"l'être-en-soi,"* concepts which Martín-Santos discusses in *Libertad, temporalidad y transferencia* (37-40).[6] Since in Sartre's view *"le pour-soi"* is associated with self-consciousness and liberty, and *"l'en-soi"* with inanimate objects, the aim of the power of the phallus, in killing women, is to destroy their liberty, a quality which Martín-Santos, like Sartre before him, saw as constitutive of human life.

The three generations of women who live in the boarding house where Pedro lodges each fall foul of the law of male sexual aggression and exploitation. The grandmother and the daughter have been loved and left by men. Dora seems, at first glance, to have escaped exploitation by accepting the promise of marriage made by Pedro. But, as we witness at the end of the novel, she is stabbed to death by Cartucho, Flora's boyfriend, in revenge for the (putative) role Pedro played in Flora's death.

Yet it is Flora who is the paradigm of the aggression perpetrated on womankind by Spain, phallocracy and "miscourse."[7] Firstly, there are hints that the child she is carrying is the result of incest between herself and her father. This is suggested by three factors, i) Flora used to sleep in her parents' bed, ii) her boyfriend, Cartucho, insisted that he was not the father of the child, (wrongly) assuming that it was Pedro who made Flora pregnant, and iii) Muecas's eagerness in carrying out the abortion himself. Flora is therefore not only abused by Muecas, her father, but also becomes a victim a second time when he performs the abortion which causes the fatal hemorrhage. Her womb is abused a third time when Pedro, although drunk and unqualified to carry out an operation of this kind, performs a "scrape": "Es preciso primero colocarla en la adecuada posición ginecológica, dilatar luego el cuello de la matriz agarrotado por la naturaleza previsora y finalmente limpiar con un instrumento de aspecto de cuchara el interior del recóndito nudo" (109). The violation of her body does not end with death. Even after her burial, she is victim of a further violation, this time by the Law, and specifically in the guise of an autopsy. We may recall in this context that Martín-Santos seems to have regarded the Law as a form of institutionalized sadism. The right to judge others, as the narrator of *Tiempo de destrucción* suggests, gives the Judge "una cierta gratificación sádica al infligir con plena legalidad sufrimiento al prójimo" (180). Law, as the narrator of *Tiempo de silencio* suggests, is "siempre inhumana" (46). It is significant that Flora's post-mortal violation is experienced through a female consciousness, and specifically her mother:

> "Hija mía," "Hija mía," repitió desconsoladamente, para añadir luego con rabia: "Que me la están matando."
>
> —Aquí, señora, no matamos a nadie—replicó el joven jovial.
>
> Y decía la verdad.

> Pero ella insistía: "Que me la están matando." "Ay, que me la están matando." Más tarde, su lenta imaginación pareció llegar a precisar lo que temía: "Que me la están rajando toda, la pobre, que me la están abriendo." Sufría más de esta profanación que de la misma muerte y de las que—en vida—había sufrido previamente. (194)

The surgeon who performs the autopsy and his assistant, both of whom embody masculine consciousness, are unmoved. The autopsy carried out by the hands of the Law is seen as a greater profanation than her death at the hands of her father. It is significant that in contrast to the mother's groans during the autopsy, we do not witness as readers Flora's screams during the abortive operation carried out by her father. As readers we simply experience silence. The blow by the phallus puts the victim to silence. Again, it is not coincidental that when Dora is killed, this time by the phallic substitute of the knife, silence is the dominant chord of the passage:

> Quién es usted, dijo luego Dorita y Cartucho le contestó calla, calla de una vez, al mismo tiempo que le clavaba en el costado su navaja abierta, en un golpe seco y decidido que había dado más de una vez y mientras Dorita caía al suelo llenándose de sangre poco a poco encima de un charco que de noche parecía negro y que crecía, él se iba hacia afuera sin esperar siquiera a ver la cara que pondría él cuando volviera con su gran paquete de churros y se encontraba con que la venganza había sido ejecutada, que no hay plazo que no se cumpla ni deuda que no se pague. (232)

It is characteristic that Dora's executioner should say "calla, calla de una vez." Like Flora, she has been put to silence. In a phallocentric society, it is the women (Flora and Dora) who pay for the sins of the menfolk, ever subservient to what Martín-Santos elsewhere calls the "glorioso dominio fálico" (127).

The crime on which the narrative of the whole novel rests is Muecas's incest with his daughter. In his study *The Elementary Structures of Kinship*, Lévi-Strauss has argued that one of the cardinal laws of civilization is the prohibition of incest. He compares the need for the exchange of women within society, or exogamy, to the exchange of signs, words, language between individuals (479-93). In *Tiempo de silencio*, this taboo, and the law on which it rests, crumbles. The violation of incest is referred to at one stage in the context of primitive societies: "Como si no fuera el tabú del incesto tan audazmente violado en estos primitivos tálamos como en las montañas de yerba de cualquier isla paradisíaca" (44). When this taboo is, however, violated, a symptom of this violation is the dislocation of language as a social means of communication. Social intercourse leads to misunderstanding, its truth effect is displaced, and silence is valorized. A good example of "miscourse" is the false testimony produced by the extraordinarily lucid policeman who frames Pedro:

> —Sí. En realidad, yo la maté—reconoció agachando la cabeza.

> —¡Acabáramos!—dijo el policía, y dirigiéndose al mudo y continuo testigo del diálogo—¡Escriba! *Preguntado si conocía a la fallecida, contesta que sí que la conocía así como a su familia y a la casa en que habitaban por intermedio de su ayudante de laboratorio llamado Amador.* Punto. *Preguntado si había tenido algún contacto íntimo con ella, contesta que efectivamente había comprobado que no se le habían producido unas tumoraciones en la ingle que él creía que podrían desarrollarse a causa de un contacto fortuito con los ratones de experiencia de que regularmente se proveía en aquella familia y que él utilizaba para sus investigaciones sobre el cáncer.* Punto. *Preguntado sobre el día de la muerte él había acudido a la chabola y utilizado sus instrumentos quirúrgicos, contesta que*... (199)

While this awesomely well-constructed text has all the weight of truth, it is later dispelled by the three simple words repeated by the mother "El no fue" (202-03). The most convincing linguistic explanation of the event is revealed later to be also the most untrue. It is because of the treachery of "miscourse" that Pedro admitted to being guilty of a crime he did not commit; the deceptive nature of language also led Amador to "confess" that it was Pedro who killed Flora (121). It is essentially because of this misunderstanding that Cartucho kills Dora. "Miscourse" has fatal consequences.

Perhaps the most deconstructive use of "miscourse" occurs in the context of the narrator's allusion to archetype and Greek myth. I have argued above that the use of Greek myths as a sub-text in *Tiempo de silencio* is to be seen primarily in *esperpentesque* terms; thus, the characters fail miserably to measure up to the mythical figures they are compared to. The presence of "miscourse" in the novel also has implications for the relationship between the narrative and the mythic sub-text. Since the narrative consciousness desires to fuse these two levels together, this in effect leads to the production of a "neurotic" text. In his theoretical work, Martín-Santos has made the following statement about the mind of the neurotic:

> El proceso de encarnación de la existencia neurótica se realiza a expensas de lo antiguo y gracias a un continuo rechazo de lo nuevo. El mecanismo de elaboración del aparato *yo-super-yo* tiende en el neurótico a la circularidad. Ninguna situación o nueva persona es captada por el neurótico en su singularidad individual. Por el contrario, la deforma y mutila adaptándola al molde de una vieja situación o un antiguo personaje parental. (*Libertad* 90)

This description seems eminently applicable to the narrative consciousness of *Tiempo de silencio*. Like the neurotic patient, Pedro, or the text through him, fails to perceive difference. Throughout the novel, Pedro is the originator of the narrative consciousness, even if he is also what Henry James would call a "limited reflector" of that consciousness.[8] Pedro consistently reads experience in terms of mythical archetypes, as we have already noted. Other examples of his mythic misreadings are: Amador's tour of the slums brings forth for Pedro a comparison with Moses: "como muchos siglos antes Moisés sobre un monte más alto" (42). The fish on his dinner plate reminds Pedro of *ourobouros*, the self-devouring serpent which was a symbol of divine knowledge for the Gnostics (60). Sexual desire in particular arouses a desire for archetype. The pink light in the brothel allows the elusive archetype to be actualized. Here, it seems, the narrator is colluding in the fusion of the empiric and the archetypal levels: "No sólo la luz rosa consigue hacer desaparecer los puntos negros de la nariz o las arruguillas de los ángulos del ojo. También a los contornos desnudos de los cuerpos alcanza con su borrosa indeterminación, por lo que convertidos en objetos más táctiles que visuales, pueden sobreponerse con menor esfuerzo sobre el interno arquetipo al que el espíritu incansable busca coincidencia" (165). Later on in the novel, there is a similar reference to "el arquetipo de lo que deseamos desde la cama solitaria de los trece años de verdad, las pantorrillas que hemos comenzado a advertir en la calle" (219).

Given the text's neurotic desire to imitate archetype, it is not surprising that it should be characterized by linguistic repetition, since, as Martín-Santos has pointed out, a symptom of neurosis is repetition (*Libertad* 89). Thus Pedro's thoughts at one point become closed within six successive spirals of thought, themselves set in train by the image of the fish eating its own tail (a metaphorical image of self-conscious knowledge). Knowledge, it seems, is condemned to express itself in vicious circles. Such is the idea underpinning the description of Pedro's mind in terms of a "vacío espiroideo" (68) and "paraboloides espiroidales" in the context of the multiple graves in which Flora's body is buried (145). At times, words or expressions seem to surface in the text almost of their own volition: "Había estado apostado en vericuetos con oficio de camino, por los que había visto pasar sombras que—*maldito él*—le parecía que se encaminaba hacia—*maldito él*—el sitio que ya sabía dónde—*maldito él*—presupone lo que estaba haciendo" (104; my emphasis). The repetition compulsion seems to underpin the very workings of the mind: "Repitiendo: Es interesante. Repitiendo: Todo tiene un sentido. Repitiendo: No estoy borracho. Pensando: Estoy solo. Pensando: Hace frío. Pensando: Soy un cobarde. Pensando: Mañana estaré peor. Sintiendo: Hace frío. Sintiendo: Estoy cansado. Sintiendo: Tengo seca la lengua" (92). Repetition of this kind, in an almost hopeless desire to make sense of reality, is one of the characteristic features of Martín-Santos's text. As Michael Ugarte points out, this search for order and knowledge is "empty," since "symmetry will always fall victim to its own negation: displacement" (250).

The desire to make sense of reality is at the center of Martín-Santos's novels, and especially *Tiempo de silencio*. Epistemological dilemmas are filtered through the text of psychoanalysis, sometimes with a view to creating new psychoanalytical knowledge and sometimes in order to deconstruct that knowledge. But even when viewed ironically, Martín-Santos's text reveals that it is the knowledge of psychoanalysis which slowly pulls back the veil covering the insidious links between Spain, phallocracy and "miscourse." It is because of her links with phallocracy and "miscourse" that Spain is experienced alter-egoistically not as a mother but a stepmother. Ironically, it is her repression, and its corollary, castration, that—far from becoming a barrier hindering a freer type of literary expression—is actually a *sine qua non* of creative endeavor; the art is to use its power creatively. The final irony of *Tiempo de silencio* is that Pedro is obliged to submit to the prerogative of the alter ego, castration, before its power can be effectively represented.

Pedro Páramo and the Dream of the Dead Father

Rulfo's novel *Pedro Páramo*, since it is based on a search for the father, has often been seen to possess mythical meaning. The existence of mythical echoes in Rulfo's text leads Fuentes, for example, to argue that Rulfo's novel has a universal dimension. In *Pedro Páramo*, Fuentes argues:

> La imaginación mítica renace en el suelo mexicano y cobra, por fortuna, un vuelo sin prestigio. Pero ese joven Telémaco que inicia la contraodisea en busca de su padre perdido, ese arriero que lleva a Juan Preciado a la otra orilla, la muerta, de un río de polvo, esa voz de la madre y amante, Jocasta-Eurídice, que conduce al hijo y amante, Edipo-Orfeo, por los caminos del infierno, esa pareja de hermanos edénicos y adánicos que duermen juntos en el lodo de la creación para iniciar otra vez la generación humana en el desierto de Comala, esas viejas virgilianas—Eduviges, Damiana, la Cuarraca -, fantasmas de fantasmas, esa Susana San Juan, Electra al revés, el propio Pedro Páramo, Ulises de piedra y barro . . . todo este trasfondo mítico permite a Juan Rulfo proyectar la ambigüedad humana de un cacique, sus mujeres, sus pistoleros y sus víctimas y, a través de ellas, incorporar la temática del campo y la revolución mexicana a un contexto universal. (*La nueva novela* 16)

Fuentes is not suggesting that Rulfo inserts some classical myths unchanged into his text, since he describes Rulfo's characters as inverse reflections of classical prototypes; Juan Preciado embarks on a "contra-odisea"; Susana San Juan is an "Electra al revés." Despite their parodic function, however, the presence of these mythical allusions raises Rulfo's narrative in Fuentes's eyes to a "universal context." A similar bias underlies the contention of Luis Harss and Barbara Dohmann, who argue that *Pedro Páramo* is "a variant of the Mexican myth of the illegitimate child, born of rape, eternally in quest of the unknown father" (265), an idea which itself echoes Octavio Paz's notion that Mexicans are "hijos de la Chingada" (*El laberinto* 55-74), their national identity founded on the rape of La Malinche by Cortés during the Spanish Conquest.[9] In this discussion of *Pedro Páramo* I wish neither to follow the essentialist drive underwriting affirmations of this kind nor to submit that Rulfo's text has a universalist meaning. I intend to survey Rulfo's text from a psychoanalytical perspective precisely because *Pedro Páramo* returns to the Oedipal story made famous by Freud.[10] There is one specific way in which my critical practice will collude with the strategies of *Pedro Páramo*, and this concerns the death of the father. Julia Kristeva has argued that interpretation "necessarily represents appropriation, and thus an act of desire and murder" ("Within the Microcosm" 33), and in this sense my interpretation of Rulfo's text will collude in Pedro Páramo's death. The desire of the critic and the desire of the text thereby overlap. My text becomes the dream of the dead father seen as either an objective or a subjective genitive, a story about Pedro Páramo's death or the dream itself.

I wish to turn now to an intertextual configuration between *Pedro Páramo* and Freud's *Moses and Monotheism* (1939). As we shall see, both texts can be seen as archaeological palimpsests articulating the genesis of human consciousness. But, first, a few words about Freud's study. In his pioneering work, Freud argued that Moses, the founder of Judaism, was not a Jew but an Egyptian who led the Jews out of slavery in Egypt and introduced them to ethical monotheism, but was eventually slain by them. Memory of this act of parricide was subsequently repressed in the Old Testament account and certain changes were made to the biblical text in order to combat the Jews' sense of anxiety at having killed their God. Freud furthermore compares this narrative to the development of the mental life of the individual. The gap between the point in time when Moses was killed and the point when he is acclaimed as the founder of the Jewish religion is compared to the latency period in an individual's life when he suffers some great trauma and then subsequently suppresses knowledge of it (59-80).[11]

Freud takes his process of analogy one step further, and it is this particular step which is directly relevant to *Pedro Páramo*. Freud projects this basic narrative derived from the story of Moses to the evolution of the human race. Freud argues that:

> In primeval times primitive man lived in small hordes, each under the dominion of a powerful male . . . The strong male was lord and father of the entire horde and unrestricted in his power, which he exercised with violence. All the females were his property—wives and daughters of his horde and some, perhaps, robbed from other hordes. The lot of his sons was a hard one: if they roused their father's jealousy they were killed or castrated or driven out. Their only resource was to collect together in small communities, to get themselves wives by robbery, and, when one or other of them could succeed in it, to raise themselves into a position similar to their father's in the primal horde.

If the sons did manage to overpower their father they, "as was the custom in those days, devoured him raw" (81). The absolute power enjoyed by the father in the primal horde has some similarities with the kind of authority enjoyed by Pedro Páramo in Rulfo's novel. Pedro Páramo's power is total; he owns all of the women and all the land in the village, and his authority consequently has the irrevocable nature of a divine decree. Thus when he decides to destroy Comala, he merely needs to cross his arms in order for his will to be done. What makes the narrative of the genesis of human culture as advanced by Freud even more relevant to Rulfo's novel is the former's discussion of the genesis of the text recounting that history. For just as the priests repressed the memory of the murder of Moses, so the individual represses the memory of traumatic experiences; these experiences, however, despite repression, continue to survive in the form of what Freud calls "memory-traces." As Freud goes on to explain:

> What is forgotten is not extinguished but only "repressed"; its memory-traces are present in all their freshness, but isolated by "anticathexes." They cannot enter into communication with other intellectual processes; they are unconscious—inaccessible to consciousness. It may be that certain portions of the repressed, having evaded the process (of repression), remain accessible to memory and occasionally emerge into consciousness; but even so they are isolated, like foreign bodies out of connection with the rest. (94)

Again, we may notice a striking similarity with the way in which Rulfo's own literary text is structured. Like Freud's text enacting the birth of human consciousness, *Pedro Páramo* is a narrative full (if this is the correct word) of gaps and consisting of memory-traces relating to past events which are, to all intents and purposes, unconnected to the narrative which encapsulates them.

The most striking intertextual link between Freudian knowledge and *Pedro Páramo* is the fusion of the life of the individual with that of the human race. Freud argues in the same essay for a close link between individual and group psychology, mainly on the strength of his concept of an "archaic heritage" which is passed on from generation to generation (99-102). Rulfo's text, like Freud's, projects the discourse of the individual (the narrator) and the discourse of the human race into identical spheres of reference. In Rulfo's and Freud's text the search for the primal father is subject to transference from the space of individual consciousness to that of the evolution of the human species. Rulfo, we may remember, was himself obsessed by his own family tree and used to spend hours researching the identity of his ancestors.[12]

There is one other striking feature of *Pedro Páramo* which irrevocably returns Freud to mind, and this is its dream-like qualities. For the characters of Rulfo's novel have the uncanny presence (or lack of it) that our dead relatives have in our dreams, as suggested by Freud. In his *The Interpretation of Dreams* (1900), Freud gives numerous accounts of his patients meeting deceased relatives in their dreams. As Freud points out, it "very commonly happens in dreams of this kind that the dead person is treated to begin with as though he were alive, that he then suddenly turns out to be dead and that in a subsequent part of the dream he is alive once more" (560). We find a very similar process in *Pedro Páramo*. At the beginning of the narrative Juan Preciado (whom we assume to be alive) is looking for his father (whom we have no reason to believe to be dead) and meets a carter called Abundio (whom we also assume to be alive). Abundio tells Juan Preciado in the course of their conversation that Pedro Páramo died a long time ago (11), although we later see Pedro Páramo described as if he were alive. A woman Juan Preciado subsequently meets, Eduviges Dyada, tells Juan Preciado that Abundio, the man he was recently talking to, is dead (20). We later learn that this same woman, Eduviges Dyada, had in fact committed suicide some time before (34). To unsettle us still further we witness a scene in which the narrator himself dies (61).[13]

What is the reader to make of events of this kind? Given the Mexican context, this type of device is in some part comprehensible since, as Joseph Summers has pointed out, Rulfo's novel is based on the Mexican folklore belief in "ánimas en pena," souls condemned and unabsolved who wander the earth bodiless and overcome the living (88). The fact that the characters call other people dead means that they assume themselves to be alive. Yet once more this notion is reminiscent of the kind of "dead relative" dream studied by Freud. The Viennese philosopher gives an example of this type of dream: "a man who had nursed his father during his last illness, and had been deeply grieved by his death, had the following senseless dream some time afterwards. *His father was alive once more and was talking to him, in his usual way, but* (the remarkable thing was that) *he had really died, only he did not know it*" (*Interpretation of Dreams* 559). The death of the father figure, Pedro Páramo, as we shall see, has far-reaching epistemological implications for the rest of the characters in the story. They, like Pedro Páramo, are dead but they do not know it.

Freud makes one further point about dreams of this kind which is relevant to the present discussion; "if there is no mention in the dream of the fact that the dead man is dead, the dreamer is equating himself with him: he is dreaming of his own death" (560). Although Freud's statement is not completely applicable to Rulfo's text in the sense that the characters *do* mention Pedro Páramo's death, his overall point *is*. For Pedro Páramo is not simply a dead father but something more disconcerting and haunting, for he is a fading father who is still precariously there, a father who is dead but does not know it, and Juan Preciado's own death is obscurely tied up with this fact. Juan Rulfo himself has in fact made the point that many of the characters are not individuals in their own right but projections of the terrified mind of the narrator Juan Preciado. In an interview with J.C. González Boixo, Rulfo referred to the incestuous couple who appear in his novel in the following terms:

> No existen, es una alucinación que (Juan Preciado) tiene dentro del terror mismo. Por ejemplo, se le convierte en un montón de barro, de lodo, la mujer esa. Todo eso es absurdo, ¿no? Son alucinaciones que él tiene, de que encontró a esta pareja y de que esta pareja lo quiso dar alojamiento, son alucinaciones que preceden a la muerte. (89)

We are left with the disturbing possibility that not only the incestuous couple but all of the characters are projections of Juan Preciado's terror-stricken mind.

Lacan has taken up Freud's discussion of the primal father and extended this idea in order to reveal the affinity between the concepts of father and death. Lacan argues firstly that "the attribution of procreation to the father can only be the effect of a pure signifier, of a recognition, not of a real father, but of what religion has taught us to refer to as the Name-of-the-Father." The link between the potency of the father and what Lacan calls a "pure signifier" is a necessary one since, as Lacan goes on to argue, "there is no need of a signifier to be a father, any more than to be dead, but without a signifier, no one would ever know anything about either state of being." Our (un)knowledge of concepts such as the signifier and the father is predicated on the deep affinity between them. As Lacan goes on to point out, Freud could not have failed to be (un)aware of the knot binding these two terms together:

> How, indeed, could Freud fail to recognize such an affinity, when the necessity of his reflexion led him to link the appearance of the signifier of the Father, as author of the Law, with death, even to the murder of the Father—thus showing that if this murder is the fruitful moment of debt through which the subject binds himself for life to the Law, the symbolic Father is, in so far as he signifies this Law, the dead Father. (*Écrits. A Selection* 199)

The various father figures who appear in *Pedro Páramo*, since they are all already dead, claim their authority from their Name. Thus when Abundio asks Juan Preciado what his father is like, the latter replies that he knows him only as a Name:

> —¿Y qué trazas tiene su padre, si se puede saber?
>
> —No lo conozco—le dije -. Sólo sé que se llama Pedro Páramo. (9)

It is precisely as a result of his death that Pedro Páramo is endowed with the power to control the inhabitants of Comala. The central point of physical resistance within Rulfo's text, its (k)not of ambiguity, revolves around the space in the narrative when Pedro Páramo and the various other father figures in the novel fulfill the authoritarian and tyrannical role allotted to them in a phallogocentric society. When Comala refuses to mourn the death of his wife, for example, Pedro Páramo decides to curse the town:

> Enterraron a Susana San Juan y pocos en Comala se enteraron. Allá había feria. Se jugaba a los gallos, se oía la música; los gritos de los borrachos y de las loterías. Hasta acá llegaba la luz del pueblo, que parecía una aureola sobre el cielo gris. Porque fueron días grises, tristes para la Media Luna. Don Pedro no hablaba. No salía de su cuarto. Juró vengarse de Comala:
>
> —Me cruzaré los brazos y Comala se morirá de hambre.
>
> Y así lo hizo. (121)

Other father figures, such as Padre Rentería and the Bishop, likewise assert their own authority uncompromisingly. The priest refuses to bless his flock or to absolve Miguel Páramo, the man who raped his niece:

> "Hay aire y sol, hay nubes. Allá arriba un cielo azul y detrás de él tal vez haya canciones; tal vez mejores voces . . . Hay esperanza, en suma. Hay esperanza para nosotros, contra nuestro pesar.
>
> "Pero no para ti, Miguel Páramo, que has muerto sin perdón y no alcanzarás ninguna gracia."
>
> El padre Rentería dio vuelta al cuerpo y entregó la misa al pasado. Se dio prisa por terminar pronto y salió sin dar la bendición final a aquella gente que llenaba la iglesia.
>
> —¡Padre, queremos que nos lo bendiga!
>
> —¡No!—dijo moviendo negativamente la cabeza -. No lo haré. Fue un mal hombre y no entrará al Reino de los Cielos. Dios me tomará a mal que interceda por él. (29)

A similar authoritarian gesture is made by the bishop when he hears about the brother and sister who live together as man and wife:

> Yo me le puse enfrente y le confesé todo:
>
> —Eso no se perdona—me dijo.
>
> —Estoy avergonzada.
>
> —No es el remedio.
>
> —¡Cásenos usted!
>
> —¡Apártense! (56)

The point of resistance within the text, to which it incessantly returns, thereby enacting what Freud called *Wiederholungszwang* (the compulsion to repeat), is the textual space where the various father figures condemn the inhabitants of Comala, where what Lacan calls the *Non-du-Père* is articulated (*Moses* 75-77).[14]

The authority of the Father in *Pedro Páramo* is predicated on his death, as I have already argued. Yet it is precisely because the Father is by definition absent that the hegemony of what Lacan calls *Le-Nom(n)-du-Père* is unsettled. This epistemological disruption leads to a collapse of the dividing line between things normally thought of as separate. Through the crisis of phallocentric authority, Rulfo's world becomes one in which the difference between concepts, towns and people is elided; Rulfo's text dissolves into a dizzying discourse of Sameness. The catastrophic deconstruction of the phallogocentric system of knowledge leads to a disruption of the paradigm, producing what Barthes has defined as the "terrified metonym":

> Cet effrondrement catastrophique prend toujours la même forme: celle d'une métonymie effrénée. Cette métonymie, en abolissant les barres paradigmatiques, abolit le pouvoir de *substituter légalement*, qui fonde le sens: il n'est plus possible alors d'opposer régulièrement un contraire à un contraire, un sexe à un autre, un bien à un autre; il n'est plus possible de sauvegarder un ordre de la juste équivalence, en un mot il n'est plus possible de représenter, de donner aux choses des *représentants* individués, séparés, distribués. (221-22)

What Barthes calls the abolition of the paradigm is articulated on an explicit level in Rulfo's novel in the characters' inability to differentiate between life and death, as we have seen. A commensurate effect of the disruption of the Name-of-the-Father is the elision of the difference between past, present and future. As Rulfo himself pointed out when describing the creation of Pedro Páramo:

> I imagined the character. I saw him. Then, wondering how to handle him, I logically thought of a ghost town. And, of course, the dead live outside space and time. That gave me freedom to do what I wanted with the characters. I could have them come in, and then simply fade out. (Harss and Dohmann 270)

Yet the elision of any difference between concepts (such as life and death or past and future) is revealed most dramatically in the text's disruption of the ties within the family unit. Lacan describes graphically the effect of the lack of the Name-of-the-Father:

> It is the lack of the Name-of-the-Father in that place which, by the hole that it opens up in the signified, sets off the cascade of reshapings of the signifier from which the increasing disaster of the imaginary proceeds, to the point at which the level is reached at which signifier and signified are stabilized in the delusional metaphor. (*Écrits. A Selection* 217)

I shall return later on to what Lacan here refers to as the "delusional metaphor," but for the moment let us note that what Lacan calls the "cascade of reshapings of the signifier" is echoed in *Pedro Páramo* by the elision of the difference between individuals. The carter whom Juan Preciado meets at the beginning of the story, for example—though a complete stranger—turns out to be his brother:

> Fui tras él tratando de emparejarme a su paso, hasta que pareció darse cuenta de lo que seguía y disminuyó la prisa de su carrera. Después los dos íbamos tan pegados que casi nos tocábamos los hombros.
>
> —Yo también soy hijo de Pedro Páramo—me dijo.

> Una bandada de cuervos pasó cruzando el cielo vacío, haciendo "cuar, cuar, cuar." (9)

Differences are subsumed into identity. Another stranger whom Juan Preciado meets, Eduviges Dyada, then becomes as a mother to him:

> Perdóname que te hablo de tú; lo hago porque le considero mi hijo. Sí, muchas veces dije: "El hijo de Dolores debió haber sido mío." Después te diré por qué. (15)

Later on, the link between them changes slightly; Eduviges Dyada says to Juan Preciado: "yo estuve a punto de ser tu madre" (19), as if it were only because of a last-minute decision that she were not. This process whereby the differences between individuals within the family unit are elided continues when Juan Preciado meets a woman, Donis's sister, and becomes to her as a husband:

> Ella me dijo:
>
> —Donis no volverá. Se le notó en los ojos. Estaba esperando que alguien viniera para irse. Ahora tú te encargarás de cuidarme. ¿O qué, no quieres cuidarme? Vente a dormir aquí conmigo.
>
> —Aquí estoy bien.
>
> —Es mejor que te subas a la cama. Allí te comerán las turicatas.
>
> Entonces fui y me acosté con ella. (60-61)

Juan Preciado therefore acts as brother, son and husband in rapid succession with respect to people he has never met before. In the same way that any rigid definition underlying Juan Preciado's identity is subverted, so the relationship between other characters in the novel is rendered ambivalent. Donis and his sister, before Juan Preciado's arrival, had been living together as man and wife. As Donis' sister/wife tells Juan Preciado: "No es mi marido. Es mi hermano; aunque él no quiere que se sepa" (54). It is significant that Donis's sister/wife is the only unnamed woman in the text, as Donald Shaw has pointed out (*Nueva narrativa* 134). She occupies the nameless space which the Name-of-the-Father is powerless to control. The authority of the phallocratic system is debunked precisely through her namelessness. She stands outside categorization, outside language, occupying a limbo region between sister and wife.

A similar confusion surrounds the relationship between Bartolomé and Susana. Their father-daughter relationship is subverted by innuendoes to the effect that they live together as man and wife. An incestuous relationship is never mentioned explicitly in the text; the implication is only elicited in a displaced form. The first example of innuendo of this kind is the episode when Susana refers to her impression that Justina's cat had slept with her the night before:

> Anoche no echaste fuera al gato y no me dejó dormir.
>
> —Durmió conmigo, entre mis piernas. Estaba ensopado y por lástima lo dejé quedarse en mi cama; pero no hizo ruido.
>
> —No, ruido no hizo. Sólo se la pasó haciendo circo, brincando de mis pies a mi cabeza, y maullando quedito como si tuviera hambre.
>
> —Le di bien de comer y no se despegó de mí en toda la noche. Estás otra vez soñando mentiras, Susana.
>
> -Te digo que pasó la noche asustándome con sus broncos. Y aunque sea muy cariñoso tu gato, no lo quiero cuando estoy dormida. (92)

The reference to the cat "brincando de mis pies a mi cabeza" articulates in a displaced image the sexual act. The association between the cat and her father is confirmed when Susana subsequently hears that her father died that night: "—Entonces era él—y sonrió—. Viniste a despedirte de mí—dijo, y sonrió" (94). In the light of the latent sexual connotations of this scene, the flashback episode which immediately follows—the lowering of Susana down into the mine by her father—likewise functions as a displaced image of incest:

> —Más abajo, Susana. Más abajo. Dime si ves algo.
>
> Y cuando encontró el apoyo allí permaneció, callada, porque se enmudeció de miedo. La lámpara circulaba y la luz pasaba de largo junto a ella. Y el grito allá arriba la estremecía:
>
> —¡Dame lo que está allí, Susana!
>
> Y ella agarró la calavera entre sus manos y cuando la luz le dio de lleno la soltó.
>
> —Es una calavera de muerto—dijo.
>
> —Debes encontrar algo más junto a ella. Dame todo lo que encuentres.
>
> El cadáver se deshizo en canillas; la quijada se desprendió como si fuera de azúcar. Le fue dando pedazo a pedazo hasta que llegó a los dedos de los pies y le entregó coyuntura tras coyuntura. Y la calavera primero; aquella bola redonda que se deshizo entre sus manos.
>
> —Busca algo más, Susana. Dinero. Ruedas redondas de oro. Búscalas, Susana. (94-95)

The whole scene could be read as a symbolically veiled encounter with death through the agency of the father figure while searching for gold (sex). Sex, in fact, is associated closely with death throughout the novel, a *topos* epitomized in the scene when Juan Preciado sleeps with Donis's wife/sister and dies immediately afterwards. Furthermore, the latent metonymic link between sex and gold mining is catalyzed when we call to mind an earlier scene in which Pedro Páramo refuses Bartolomé's gold mine, since he is more interested in Susana's body. She is his best product, as Pedro Páramo goes on to say: "No me interesa su mina, Bartolomé San Juan. Lo único que quiero de usted es a su hija. Ese ha sido su mejor trabajo" (87). What is interesting about the ambiguity of the relationship between Bartolomé and his daughter is that their mode of mutual address thereby becomes fraught with epistemological uncertainty. In the discussion between Bartolomé and his daughter about her marriage with Pedro Páramo, the former says: "No me digas Bartolomé. ¡Soy tu padre!" (88), almost as if to suggest that, now he is to give her away in marriage, he can no longer be anything other than her father.

The crisis of phallocracy thus produces an elision of the hard-and-fast boundaries we associate with the concept of individual identity. The relationships between characters in *Pedro Páramo* are in a state of flux, which inevitably leads to the characters themselves being epistemologically unfixed. At times there is even slippage between male and female terms. When Juan Preciado is speaking with the person who is lying in the same grave as him the following exchange takes place:

—Tienes razón, Doroteo. ¿Dices que te llamas Doroteo?

—Da lo mismo. Aunque mi nombre sea Dorotea. Pero da lo mismo. (62)

It is significant that in the various cases of the elision of difference between individuals it is within the world of language that this (un)power is articulated. The disruption of the authority of the Name-of-the-Father leads to a disruption of the cut-and-dried lines separating one individual from the next and one word from the next. Social and linguistic authority are shown to be commensurate.

Pedro Páramo, as we can see, consistently dismantles the various oppositions which we (or common sense on our behalf) take for granted. The text articulates a "terrified metonym" (Barthes), thrusting the characters into the alienating presence of the "delusional metaphor" (Lacan). Put in another way, the characters experience what Roman Jakobson has called in a different context the "similarity disorder," meaning that the speaker suffers an aphasic disturbance whereby she can operate quite well in the metonymic dimension but experiences a breakdown in the metaphoric dimension (248). Rulfo's characters are unable to produce a metaphorical reading of their own lives; they simply replace a sister with a wife, or a stranger with a son, or a daughter with a wife, producing a metonymic reading which operates horizontally. A vertical metaphorical reading of their lives is repressed; all that they have left are gaps, silences and murmurs.

This breakdown in the metaphoric dimension has implications for the role that myth plays within the novel. Myth is often a verbal expression of a religious rite and thus seeks to channel mankind's violence while enforcing and promoting hierarchy within society.[15] In its emphasis upon duty, obligation and/or sacrifice, myth has often gone hand in hand with the representation of the self as separate, bounded and autonomous.[16] Rulfo's text, however, seeks to deconstruct myth. When Pedro Páramo dies, for example, nobody takes his place. As Alfred J. MacAdam has pointed out, it is "precisely the ironic aspect of Rulfo's manipulation of a mythic order that makes his text a satire and not a romance. Where one might expect a liberator or renewer of society, a new king, one finds only death" (89). Myth is grounded in logocentrism, and indeed phallocracy, in the sense that the hierarchy which it upholds is predicated on the assumption that certain individuals will lay down the Law over and above others. Myth, like other logocentric discourses within Rulfo's text, is subject, however, to verbal attrition; it is reduced to echoes, murmurs, silence, for *Pedro Páramo* is a text, as Sharon Magnarelli points out, "that is obsessed with voices, rumors, with second-hand discourse" (*The Lost Rib* 82). The various mythical narratives which underwrite *Pedro Páramo* are subverted. All that is left of their logocentric presence is a few rumors, a few echoes. The text becomes an echo chamber of mythical discourses, whether they be the story of Ulysses or the story of Orpheus, which are heard in part only, never in whole. Myth is expressed as a synecdoche, a metonym which lacks the larger part, rather like the scream of Toribio Aldrete which is trapped in one of Eduviges Dyada's rooms (37).

Juan Preciado, like Ulysses, goes in search of his homeland and all he finds is a pile of stones. As we read of Pedro Páramo at the closure of the novel: "Después de unos cuantos pasos cayó, suplicando por dentro; pero sin decir una sola palabra. Dio un golpe seco contra la tierra y se fue desmoronando como si fuera un montón de piedras" (129). It is characteristic that Pedro Páramo should die without saying a word, returning to the silence from whence he came. Again like another mythical archetype, this time Orpheus, Juan Preciado goes in search of Eurydice, but all he finds is a nameless woman who has been having incestuous relations with her brother. After sleeping with her, the narrator dies; her body is described as "derritiéndose en un charco de lodo," returning to the earth from whence it came. Finally, like Oedipus, Juan Preciado is destined to sleep with his mother, but he sleeps with a nameless woman; he is also destined to kill his father but he finds he is already dead. The lives of all the characters in Rulfo's novel (including Juan Preciado) are doomed to echo the destiny of the documents which Pedro Páramo intends to burn (but perhaps never does): "Déjalos aquí. Los quemaré. Con papeles o sin ellos, ¿quién me puede discutir la propiedad de lo que tengo?" (106). Since they are owned by Pedro Páramo, the characters, like the documents, can be discarded at will. And yet Pedro Páramo himself is eternally absent, existing in Name only, a dream conjured up by a self-destructive text. Juan Preciado becomes the crucial *missing link* in the history of the text, linked genetically to his father but always missing because his father is dead. Compelled to repeat the mytheme of the journey home, Juan Preciado returns to his origin only to come across absence, an absence which is as much found as invented, the dream of the dead father.

NOTES

1. See Palley 239-54.
7. See Cavilgia 453.
3. For more information on historical background to the novel, see Rey 236-38.
4. For further discussion of the role of the Generation of 1898, see Labanyi, *Ironía e historia* 15-40; see also Jerez-Farrán 119-32.
5. I have used the neologism "miscourse" to suggest how the discourse associated with Spain and phallocracy is always "missed" discourse, discourse which has missed its course. The reason I have used this neologism is to suggest that the very production of discourse is tainted in its origins. There is no true, original "discourse," there is only "miscourse."
6. For Sartre's discussion of these terms, see 30-34 and 115-49. Sartre was one of Martín-Santos's favorite writers, as he stated in an interview, "por su mayor proximidad a mi problemática moral" (Díaz 237).
7. For a discussion of the executioner-victim relationship in the novel, see Searle 45-52. For further discussion of the role of woman in Martín-Santos's novel, see Fiddian and Evans 30-46, Anderson 287-95, and Holdsworth 41-48.
8. Henry James argued that Frédéric Moreau in Flaubert's *L'Education sentimentale* and the heroine of *Madame Bovary* are "limited reflectors" of the consciousness of their creator (263).
9. See also Paz's discussion of *Pedro Páramo* in *Corriente alterna* and present study, p. 35.
10. This is of course not to deny that other critical perspectives are not valid systems of interpretations.
11. Of bioliterary interest is the description Harss and Dohmann give of their interview with Rulfo, which portrays the Mexican writer as an anxious, harassed person, reminiscent of an individual suffering from trauma. As they say of him rather mysteriously at one point: "There are blanks in his past"(248).
12. See Harss and Dohmann 249-51.
13. It is at the point in the narrative when Juan Preciado dies that, as Brotherston has pointed out, "his grammatical first person vanishes from the narrative and joins the collective unconscious" (74).
14. In order to stress the ambivalent role of the Father, Lacan uses the pun *nom(n)-du-Père*, which suggests how the Father simultaneously represents the Super-Ego (i.e., says *No*) and is the bearer of the *Name* denoting patriarchical authority.
15. See Girard.
16. See Benjamin 78-101.

III
ÉCRITURE FÉMININE AND THE POLITICAL UNCONSCIOUS

The epistemological dilemma faced by the twentieth-century female writer is epitomized in Rosario Castellanos's arresting poem "Meditación en el umbral":

> No, no es la solución
> tirarse bajo el tren como la Ana de Tolstoi
> ni apurar el arsénico de Madame Bovary
> ni aguardar en los páramos de Avila la visita
> del ángel con venablo
> antes de liarse el manto a la cabeza
> y comenzar a actuar.
>
> Ni concluir las leyes geométricas, contando
> las vigas de la celda de castigo
> como lo hizo Sor Juana. No es la solución
> escribir, mientras llegan las visitas,
> en la sala de estar de la familia Austen
> ni encerrarse en el ático
> de alguna residencia de la Nueva Inglaterra
> y soñar, con la Biblia de los Dickinson,
> debajo de una almohada de soltera.
>
> Debe haber otro modo que no se llame Safo
> ni Mesalina ni María Egipciaca
> ni Magdalena ni Clemencia Isaura.
>
> Otro modo de ser humano y libre.
>
> Otro modo de ser. (*Meditation on the Threshold* 48)

It is striking how many of the examples of female experience adduced in Castellanos's poem in her search for "another way of being" are drawn from the world of literature: Flaubert's Emma Bovary, Tolstoy's Anna Karenina. The threshold Castellanos is describing clearly has as much to do with our conception of women in literature, or literary women, as with women in everyday life. Indeed, it is only relatively recently that women's writing has ventured across the threshold of the literary canon. In the not too distant past women writers, with a few exceptions, were dismissed by their male contemporaries. Indicative of this approach is the comment made by the North American novelist Nathaniel Hawthorne in a letter he wrote to his publisher in 1855: "America is now wholly given over to a damned mob of scribbling women, and I should have no chance of success while the public taste is occupied with their trash—and should be ashamed of myself if I did succeed" (Showalter 101). Little has changed, the cynic might say, in 135 years. Even nowadays the work of women writers seems to be less worthy of academic scrutiny than the work of male writers. During the period 1986-1988, for example, only 9.9% of published scholarship on modern Spanish literature was concerned with women's writing. For modern Spanish American literature and modern Brazilian literature respectively the comparable figures were 5.5% and 13.3%.[1] Feminine writing within the literary canon, as these figures clearly indicate, is characterized by "lack."

Woman has, indeed, always been seen in terms of lack, deficiency, incompleteness. As Aristotle once stated with a phrase which feminists will never allow to slip into oblivion, "woman is, as it were, an impotent male, for it is through a certain incapacity that the female is female" (Mitchell, *Women* 115), a view which was echoed by one of the intellectual architects of the Western Renaissance, Thomas Aquinas (d. 1274), who viewed women as "mutilated males" (Flanagan 10). The parallels drawn between women and lack even permeate the discourse of twentieth-century ego-psychology. As Charlotte Wolff, a feminist psychiatrist, argues: "The effect produced by a group of women alone is different from that of a group of men. Women by themselves appear to be incomplete, as if a limb were missing. They do not come into their proper place and function without the male" (Auerbach 7). Yet, this sense of Lack, "as if a limb were missing," to quote Woolf's words, can also be a source of strength. It need not necessarily be seen solely in negative terms, for it could be argued that the discourse of womankind has now begun to speak *through* its absence, *through* its silence, *through* its lack. Since discourse itself can only emerge through the death of the signifier, through its own absence, the discourse of womankind can be seen as embodying the very lack of discourse. It stands nearer the absence, silence and death of words.

Virginia Woolf, in her paradigmatic work *A Room of One's Own*, makes some observations which are relevant to our discussion of lack, especially in the context of Charlotte Wolff's metaphor of a "missing limb." Virginia Woolf is describing her thoughts while having lunch at a Cambridge college:

> If by good luck there had been an ash-tray handy, if one had not knocked the ash out of the window in default, if things had been a little different from what they were, one would not have seen, presumably, a cat without a tail. The sight of that abrupt and truncated animal padding softly across the quadrangle changed by some fluke of the subconscious intelligence the emotional light for me. It was as if someone had let fall a shade . . . Certainly, as I watched the manx cat pause in the middle of the lawn as if it too questioned the universe, something seemed lacking, something seemed different. But what was lacking, what was different, I asked myself, listening to the talk? (18)

Woolf seems coyly unaware of the implications of her text, or at least that is the impression she wishes to give. But given the parallels between the manx cat shut outside while the sumptuous dinner takes place within and the earlier scene in which Woolf herself had been debarred from entry into a Cambridge College library, the manx cat stands—or better, sits—as a symbol of the female ostracized from the discourse of phallocratic society. Woolf's use of the cat as a symbol of femininity is perversely apt. She alludes to the symbolism which has linked cats almost in an archetypal manner to women. As Beryl Rowland has pointed out: "Aristotle stated that the female cat was peculiarly lecherous and wheedled the man on to sexual commerce. Misogynist clerics in the Middle Ages frequently repeated this evaluation, seeing man as the mouse and woman as the sleek, enticing, and predatory cat" (52).[2] Pointing in a similar direction, the persistent question in Woolf's text, "what was lacking," is clearly a reference—via the absent tail—to the phallus, the term Lacan used to signify the power adhering to the male within patriarchal society. But there is a deep irony in the historical fact that manx cats come from the Isle of Man and that one of their species should appear surreptitiously in Woolf's text to embody an ostracized female consciousness. There is a further irony, however, and this is the appropriateness of the fact that the manx cat has no tail and that the female writers whose work best illustrates the specificity of *écriture féminine* likewise have no tail/tale to tell. It was due to the type of ostracization epitomized by Virginia Woolf's experience that the need was felt by women writers to search for, in Castellanos's words, "another way of being," by writing a new literary canon into existence. What better way of doing this than by writing in a new language, one which was specifically feminine?

The concept of *écriture féminine* grew, rather surprisingly, out of the union of psychoanalysis and feminism. Freudian theory is, of course, anathema to the traditional discourse of feminism, which sees Freud's obsession with the phallus, penis-envy, female lack and hysteria as an apt illustration of his sexual credentials.[3] But gradually the discourse of what came to be known as psychoanalytic feminism emerged. Nancy J. Chodorow has identified three strands within this new discourse, which are object-relations and interpersonal psychoanalytical feminism, and Lacanian psychoanalytic feminism (184-98). The present essay will be specifically concerned with the third type of discourse as identified by Chodorow. An early example of Lacanian psychoanalytic feminism was the pioneering work carried out by Juliet Mitchell, who employed psychoanalysis to uncover the hidden (in the sense of unconscious) agenda of patriarchy in our society.[4]

In the years immediately before his death, Freud was intensely preoccupied with a question which he suspected was unanswerable. The question was superficially a simple one: "What does a woman want?" (Lacan, "L'inconscient" 29). Jacques Lacan felt inspired to carry on where his master left off, and in his seminar "God and the *jouissance* of The Woman," the French psychoanalyst attempted to address this issue. Lacan's answer, if it could be called an answer, was, predictably enough, controversial: "*The* woman can only be written with *The* crossed through. There is no such thing as *The* woman since of her essence—having already risked the term, why not think twice about it?—of her essence, she is not all" (144). In the course of that seminar Lacan also drew attention to his own belief in the undeniably phallic nature of the Symbolic order and the words which are rooted in that order, since woman is "excluded by the nature of things which is the nature of words" (144). Other of Lacan's insights likewise betray phallocentrism. In his account of the growth of human personality, for example, Lacan invariably invokes a paternal metaphor; thus the break in the relation between mother and child is presided over by the phallus. Lacan's concept of the *nom-du-père* as a site within which paternal authority as well as the language system is centered likewise suggests that the Symbolic order itself is androcentric (Mitchell and Rose 38). It is not surprising, therefore, that Lacan should speak of women as "excluded by the nature of things which is the nature of words."

These were the fruits of Lacanian knowledge that the body of psychoanalytic feminism could not digest whole. Luce Irigaray, for example, in her study *This Sex Which Is Not One*, argued that Lacan's androcentric discourse "like all the others—more than all the others?—that he reproduces in applying their logic to the sexual relation, perpetuates the subjection of woman" (104). What has been specifically excluded from the discourse of psychoanalysis, Irigaray argues, is the female body. A similar critique of Lacan's standpoint was voiced by the Argentine novelist Luisa Valenzuela, who promoted "un lenguaje femenino en absoluto emparentado con aquellas azucaradas palabras con las que hemos sido recubiertas a lo largo de siglos" (88). The Lacanian notion of the gliding of the signifier did not exclude, she went on to argue, the possibility of a feminine language: "El célebre deslizamiento del significado por debajo del significante—hoy tan vital como lo fue en su momento el encuentro fortuito del paraguas con la máquina de coser—no es necesariamente el mismo para cada individuo, y con mayor razón para individuos de distinto sexo" (89). By identifying with women—and especially witches—who in the past have suffered under the dictatorship of men, Valenzuela sought to create a "lenguaje hémbrico" (91), which itself echoes Irigaray's notion of women-speak (*parler femme*). When this central issue of the relationship between woman and language subsequently emerged in the pioneering work of Hélène Cixous, the role of the body had become a central metaphor. Cixous turned the knowledge of psychoanalysis on its head, starting from the basic supposition that a "feminine language" of necessity exists.

But what is meant by the phrase "feminine language"? The science of sociolinguistics has established that, in many societies, the speech of men and women differs; the more striking cases for which there is evidence pertain to non-European cultures. In Zulu, for example, a wife is not allowed to mention the name of her father-in-law, or his brothers, and she might be put to death if she broke this taboo. Likewise in some Amerindian languages the word a woman will use to denote her brother will be different from that used by a man. One of the more striking examples of different sexes speaking different languages came, rather appropriately, given the subject of our discussion here, from the New World. When Europeans first arrived in the Lesser Antilles and made contact with the Caribs who lived there they discovered that the men and women spoke different languages. As a contemporary report from the seventeenth century suggests:

> The men have a great many expressions peculiar to them, which the women understand but never pronounce themselves. On the other hand the women have words and phrases which the men never use, or they would be laughed to scorn. Thus in their conversations it often seems as if the women had another language than the men. (Trudgill 79-80)[5]

The surprise of the European observer is not fortuitous, given the fact that the language spoken by men and women in Standard Average European, from the point of view of lexicon, syntax and grammar, is identical. It is intriguing, therefore, that Cixous should be exploring the concept of a "feminine language" in the context of a European language that does not readily admit to any such distinction. Cixous's purpose in adopting a term of this kind, however, is not merely syncretistic. One important difference between her concept of *écriture féminine* and the idiolect spoken by women in non-European cultures concerns Cixous's emphasis on the written nature of her language.

In *La jeune née* Cixous argues that women must "write their own selves into writing" and in the process divest their writing of its phallocentric stamp by escaping the "language of the father." Playing on the double meaning of *voler* in French, Cixous imagines feminine writing to "fly" and "steal" simultaneously:

> It is not pure chance then that woman has something of the bird and the thief, as the thief has something of woman and bird: they pass, fall, enjoy the scrambling of orderly space, of disorientation, changing the place of furniture, things, values, breaking in, out, voiding structures, turning own and ownership upside down . . . A feminine text cannot be anything but subversive: if writing itself, it does so by the volcanic raising of ancient, established, encrusted surfaces.

These "established, encrusted surfaces" are the purview of phallocentrism, which must be subverted since, as Cixous goes on to argue, "if we enter society to become men, we have lost everything." This new type of discourse devolves from the female body, which has been suppressed from view under the historic weight of masculine discourse, becoming no more than a "disquieting stranger" (179). Bringing this *écriture féminine* into play involves integration with female libido which, according to Cixous, is "cosmic" (162), transcending the androcentric view of libido.[6] Cixous extends this idea: "The ideal harmony, reached by few, would be genital, assembling everything and being capable of generosity, of spending. That is what I mean when I speak of *écriture féminine*, that is what I talk about."

The impact of this notion of "feminine writing" was felt in Spanish literary circles in the early 1980s. In 1982, for example, Francisco Umbral suggested that "la nueva novela femenina . . . está floreciendo en España," identifying its characteristics as "realismo, intimismo, historias familiares, marginaciones sociales."[7] Women writers, however, were split over the issue as to whether their writing was generically different from male writing. Lourdes Ortiz and Adelaida García Morales were unconvinced; Ortiz suggested that "no existe un lenguaje específicamente femenino."[8] García Morales argued: "no creo que haya algo característico de las escritoras muy diferentes a los escritores." Some writers were more forceful about the differences. Martín Gaite's view was that "las mujeres siempre se han volcado en lo concreto, en los interiores . . . viendo sin ser vistos, y, por tanto, al escribir tienen la fuerza del testigo no apreciado", and Marta Traba argued that "si hay un texto o literatura femenina diferente," this was due to its "insistencia en el emisor" (Valls 13). Rosa Montero took a mid-way position. Thus, although "en cuanto arte, la literatura carece de sexo," nevertheless, Montero argues, "las mujeres viven el mundo de forma muy diferente a los hombres y se ven obligados a contarlo de forma a menudo radicalmente distinta" (Valls 13). Some women writers go even further. When questioned on this issue in a open discussion on the modern Spanish novel held at the MLA conference in Washington in December 1989, Marina Mayoral and Carme Riera both said categorically that not only is feminine language different, but language itself is feminine and men have been trying to conceal this truth since time immemorial. During a Feria del Libro Feminista held in Barcelona in June 1990, the Uruguayan writer Cristina Peri Rossi argued: "Las mujeres tenemos demasiados derechos prohibidos. Y yo quería subirme a los árboles, usar pantalones, fumar, e imaginar historias. . . ." (Piñol). As Elizabeth Ordóñez has suggested, this group of writers "desire nothing less than to escape being spoken of and to become the subjects of their own discourse" (53). As Carme Riera proposes pithily: "dejando de ser habladas comencemos a hablar" (Ordóñez 48).

It is clear that Cixous's theory of feminine writing cannot be applied indiscriminately to all writing composed by women. The work of the Chilean novelist Isabel Allende, for example, in its emphasis on plot and the delineation of character, falls outside the purview of *écriture féminine*. Perhaps more importantly, Allende's fiction presents feminism as an ideology which is restricted to the female sex and therefore simply an extension of femaleness rather than a revolutionary world-vision. In *La casa de los espíritus* (1982), for example, in a highly essentialist gesture, Allende presents the knowledge of feminism as locked into gender. Esteben Trueba's violent assertion of his dominance is part and parcel of his sex, just as feminism is the natural growth of Clara and her mother before her. By consistently translating political conflict into universalist sexual archetypes in *La casa de los espíritus*, Allende turns a potential political allegory into a naturalist symbol. Allende's metaphors, therefore, deconstruct the overt level of political commitment to feminism which lies like a patina on the surface of the text. The text's metaphors refer back to a biologically sexualized universe which sterilizes any putative politically revolutionary message.

One strategy used to differentiate women's from men's fiction is to compare and contrast the mythical sub-texts present in each of the two genres. Whereas novels written by men tend to allude—albeit ironically—to Greek myths and folklore (one thinks of the Ulysses narrative underpinning Martín-Santos's *Tiempo de silencio* and Juan Rulfo's *Pedro Páramo* [see Chapter II], and the Orestes narrative in Cela's *La familia de Pascual Duarte*), women's fiction tends to allude more readily to fairy tales. Fairy tales —especially the Cinderella story—are a recurrent motif, for example, in female development novels written by women in post-civil-war Spain.[9]

If one were to choose the work of one writer as an example of *écriture féminine*, it would necessarily be Clarice Lispector (1925-1977). Cixous has indeed proposed the work of the Brazilian authoress as the epitome of *écriture féminine* and has freely admitted the extent to which Lispector influenced her own writing after she first read Lispector in 1977. Critics have pointed to various similarities in the work of both writers: their joint espousal of fluid, open texts, their rejection of the phallocentric prison of binary oppositions, and their expression of a singularly feminine libidinal desire. Both writers are intent on "writing the body"; Cixous's contention, when describing her own work, that "Je suis là où ça parle" (translated by Fitz as "I am where it/id/the female consciousness speaks") might serve as an epigraph to Lispector's work.[10]

Lispector's first novel, *Perto do coração selvagem* (1944), published when she was just nineteen years old, treats themes which would remain the hallmark of her work for years to come: the preoccupation with specifically feminine experience, the sexual repression of women, the concern with capturing the fluidity of existence, and philosophical anguish. The protagonist of the novel is, in Giovanni Pontiero's words, "a conventional suburban wife with unconventional thoughts" (*Near to the Wild Heart* 189). Her dilemma seems simple enough: "How was she to tie herself to a man without permitting him to imprison her? And was there some means of acquiring things without those things possessing her?" (29). In order to break free from the bonds of phallocentrism, Joana strives to break down the binary logic which separates mind from body. She uses bodily metaphors to describe thought: "She was pervaded by long, integral muscles. Any thought descended through those smooth tendons only to tremble there in her ankles whose flesh was as tender as that of young fowl" (97).[11] In particular, Joana's interior monologues focus on a specifically feminine knowledge which is born from the body:

> How curious that I'm unable to say who I am. That is to say, I know perfectly well, but I cannot bring myself to say it. Most of all, I'm afraid of saying it, because the moment I try to speak, not only do I fail to express what I feel, but what I feel slowly transforms itself into what I am saying. Or at least, what makes me act is not what I feel but what I say. I feel who I am and the impression is lodged in the upper part of my

brain, on my lips—especially on my tongue—on the surface of my arms and is also coursing inside me, deep down inside my body, but where, precisely where, I cannot say. (19)

Joana's sense of identity is lodged, as she suggests, "especially on my tongue." This is typical of the novel as a whole. Beneath the linear movement of the plot the text expresses a desire to body forth that sense of linguistic identity which is specifically feminine and which cannot be defined, since it has "a quality of primary matter, something that might define itself but never came to be realized," or, as Joana puts it, "the mystery in itself" (131). It is characteristic that this new knowledge is associated not only with the feminine, but also with the world of words. For Joana's quest involves a radical re-thinking of the (man-made) laws of language: "Is 'never' man or woman? Why is 'never' neither son nor daughter? And what about 'yes'?" (15). Joana's search for a new language is implicit (and complict) in her search for femaleness. Joana is often *talking* with a mysterious *mulher da voz* (literally, "woman of the voice"), whose ideas, as Earl E. Fitz points out, "have a powerful if uncertain effect on Joana" (71). As she asks herself at one point: "Where was the woman with the voice? Where were the women who were merely female?" (*Near to the Wild Heart* 21).

Generally, the voice of womankind is characterized by its absence. What the narrator desires "still has no name" (64) and is expressed as "strange gibberish coming from her lips" (75). At certain Joycean moments of "epiphany," however, this deeper awareness of the body emerges in a new language, equivalent to what Cixous has called "avant-langage":

> Then she invented what she must say. Her eyes closed, submissive, she uttered in a whisper words born at that moment, hitherto unheard, still tender from creation—new and fragile buds. They were less than words, merely disconnected syllables, meaningless, lukewarm, that flowed and criss-crossed, fertilized, were reborn in a single being only to separate immediately, breathing, breathing . . . (127)

To emphasize its separateness from man-made language, this new linguistic world is inscribed within a neologism, "Lalande," which encapsulates an Amazonic world from which men are excluded. Otávio's husband is desperate to find out what he is missing:

> —Tell me again what Lalande means—he implored Joana. It's like angel's tears. Do you know what angel's tears are? A kind of daffodil, the slightest breeze bends it backwards. Lalande also means the sea at dawn, before anyone has set eyes on the shore, before the sun has risen. Each time I say: Lalande, you should hear the fresh and salty sea-breeze, you should walk the length of the beach still covered in darkness, slowly, stark naked. In a word, you will feel Lalande . . . (157)

This amazonic world is a pre-conscious world which conflates the divine ("angel's tears") and the physical ("daffodil"), a landless sea which the daylight of phallocentric civilization has not yet lit up. In attempting to body forth this "brave new world," Lispector, true to the spirit of *écriture féminine*, brings about "the volcanic raising of ancient, established, encrusted surfaces."[12]

Many other female writers, both in Latin America and Spain, have addressed some of the issues raised by Cixous, particularly in relation to the issues of gender and identity. But one other writer deserves special mention in this context: the Spanish novelist Esther Tusquets (b. 1936). While it cannot be said that Tusquets's work embodies *écriture féminine* to quite the same degree that Lispector's does, the notion of a feminine writing is invoked at certain key junctures in Tusquets's novels. Her first novel, *El mismo mar de todos los veranos*, published only a few years after the demise of the Franco regime in 1978, created a literary scandal, mainly because of its frank treatment of female sexuality and lesbianism. At one point in the novel, one of the characters begins speaking to her female lover in a new language which has some of the characteristics of Cixous's concept of *écriture féminine*:

> en los breves momentos en que mis labios se separan un poco de sus labios, la arrullo con palabras increíbles, tan extrañas, palabras que no he dicho a ningún hombre, que no dije ni siquiera nunca a Jorge, ni siquiera a Guiomar cuando era chiquita y no había adquirido todavía estos ojos duros de mujer que sabe, palabras que ignoraba yo misma que estuvieran en mí, en algún oscuro rincón de mi conciencia, agazapadas, quietas y al espera de ser un día pronunciadas, ni siquiera pronunciadas, sino salmodiadas, cantadas, vertidas espesas y dulcísimas en una voz que tampoco reconozco aunque debe ser forzosamente la mía, tantos años ocultas esta voz y estas palabras en un centro intimísimo y secreto, para brotar al fin en esta oscuridad grana, en este cubil con aroma a mar y a cachorro. (138)[13]

Similar to Cixous's conception of *écriture féminine* quoted above, this new voice transcends binary categories, such as between self and other; it is perceived as emerging simultaneously from a secret space *within* the self (*centro intimísimo y secreto*), and also from without (*una voz que tampoco reconozco*). Tusquets's text, however, gives a further twist to Cixous's notion of *écriture féminine*, since she uses its metaphors to express lesbian sexual desire, echoing Monique Wittig's theory of writing.[14] A description of this female voice which appears later on in the novel also emphasizes its alterity:

> empiezo a musitar también yo palabras muy extrañas, palabras que tampoco tienen sentido y que tienen sentido y que pertenecen a un idioma no aprendido, y recuerdo que ya me pasó otra vez con Clara algo semejante, pero esta vez yo no quiero detenerme, porque las palabras surgen en una embriaguez sin fin, y sé que han caído todas las barreras y se han bajado todas las defensas. (157)

A particularly significant feature of this passage is the suggestion that the language Elia has just begun to speak is *no aprendido*, which we must interpret as not learned from the phallocentric language men use. In this novel, indeed, the men do not speak.[15] As this particular passage continues it becomes clear that the new language spoken by women is associated with the body rather than the mind:

> este lenguaje no nace en el pensamiento y pasa desde allí hasta la voz hecha sonido: nace hecha ya voz de las entrañas y la mente lo escucha ajena y sorprendida, ni siquiera ya asustada o avergonzada, porque estamos repentinamente al otro lado—mucho más allá—del miedo y la vergüenza, y es evidente y claro que en cualquier instante yo tendré que morir, porque la ternura me ha traspasado como cien alfileres de diamante, la ternura me ha pisoteado y arrollado a su paso como el más terrible de los ejércitos en marcha, y me voy deshaciendo, disolviendo, desangrando en palabras, tan dulcemente muerta. (158)

Composed of pain and tenderness, this "avant-langage" spoken by the body is a feminine voice on the other side of words. The mind cannot understand its import: "la mente lo escucha ajena y sorprendida." As we can see, Tusquets borrows her metaphors from Cixous's notion of feminine writing, expanding it to encompass the full spectrum of sexual desire.

In their different ways, both Clarice Lispector and Esther Tusquets embody many of the crucial concerns underlying feminine writing. What is intriguing, however, is the fundamentally silent or absent nature of *écriture féminine* as figured in their work. At no point in their respective works does the female language speak out. It is constantly alluded to, it makes sporadic and tantalizing appearances, but is never brought fully out of the closet. The presence of female language is reported, but not spelled out, and reported speech by definition implies an absent speaker. Tusquets, for her part, describes the new language that her love bids her to speak without spelling out its words, while Lispector leaves us with a neologism, "Lalande," which hints at a new language and a new world of difference which is enclosed—silent and absent—within the master text, another way of being as yet unsaid.

The Political Unconscious: From Luisa Valenzuela to Rosario Castellanos

By Freud's own admission, the "unconscious" was his single most momentous discovery. As he wrote in the preface to the third English edition of *The Interpretation of Dreams*, "insight such as this falls to one's lot but once in a lifetime" (E. Jones I, 384). His "discovery" of the unconscious at the threshold of the twentieth century, however, was at first greeted in terms of a universalist hermeneutical strategy. It was therefore seen as true or untrue, and those who saw it as the latter, in a typically human gesture, laughed. G.K. Chesterton, for example, remarked scornfully that psychoanalysis was "some ridiculous mythology about every man having inside him a sort of aged and microcephalous monkey. Wistful and melancholy poems are written about how trying it is to have a monkey inside him, and ethical essays earnestly debate whether the man should own the monkey or the monkey the man" (Hoffman 70-71). Because of this new "lingo about the libido," as Susan Glaspell was to recall, "you could not buy a bun without hearing of someone's complex" (Hoffman 70-71).[16]

To avoid the self-defeating hermeneutics of arguments of this kind, we should perhaps readjust our notion of what is meant by the term "discovery" in the context of Freudian knowledge. In his quest for knowlege Freud often likened himself to an archaeologist or a *conquistador* (Bowie 14-44). Given the obsessively Greek turn of Freud's thought, we might do worse than interpret Freud's term in the light of Aristotle's use of the concept of *agnorisis*. As Aristotle suggests in chapter 11 of his *On the Art of Poetry*: "As the word itself indicates, a discovery ("agnorisis") is a change from ignorance to knowledge, and it leads either to love or to hatred between persons destined for good or ill fortune. The most effective form of discovery is that which is accompanied by reversals, like the one in *Oedipus*" (46). This description of discovery as leading "either to love or to hatred" and accompanied by a "reversal" is an idea that has great relevance to our later discussion of the work of Valenzuela, as we shall see. Perhaps more importantly, however, Aristotle's text proposes the Oedipus narrative as the most "effective form of discovery," and so it would prove to be in *The Interpretation of Dreams*. Given the rhetorical nature of the issues with which Aristotle is grappling here, a fundamental revision of the nature of Freud's discovery is surely called for. It is no longer appropiate to evaluate Freud's "discovery" in strict terms of truth or untruth for, as Fredric Jameson has convincingly argued, it is enmeshed, like any other, with the history which produced it. This idea leads Jameson to propose the unconscious in a new form as historicized and "political," an idea I wish now to analyze.

In his essay on T.W. Adorno contained within his book *Marxism and Form*, Fredric Jameson takes his starting point from the former's *Philosophie der neuen Musik* to elucidate the interplay between art (and particularly music) and society. The emergence of dissonance in nineteenth-century Western music is comparable, Adorno argues, to "the role which the concept of the unconscious plays throughout the history of middle-class *ratio*" (Jameson 21). The transgression of the consonant therefore functions "from the very outset as the disguised representation of everything that has to be sacrificed to the taboo of order. It substitutes for the censored instinctual drive, and includes, as tension, a libidinal movement as well, in its lament over enforced renunciation." The first atonal works are, Adorno argues, "transcripts in the sense of the dream transcripts of psychoanalysis" (Jameson 27). This leads Jameson to argue for a more historical awareness of Freud's own discoveries: "What if," Jameson asks, "the Freudian raw material . . . were itself but a sign or symptom of some vaster historical transformation?" (27). As he goes on to argue, the Freudian topology of the mental functions

> may be seen as the return of a new type of allegorical vision and as the disintegration of the autonomous subject, of the cogito or self-governing consciousness in Western middle-class society. Now such characteristically Freudian phenomena are no longer seen as permanent mental func-

tions awaiting throughout human history their discovery and revelations by Freud, but rather as new events of which Freud was at once contemporary and theorist. (27)

Jameson's historicization and politicization of Freud's concept of the unconscious is, of course, perfectly self-consistent, but his use of the concept remains impervious to paradigm shifts of consciousness other than Marxism. By solidifying the unconscious into a hierarchical historicity, Jameson suppresses the elusively self-deconstructive nature of Freud's text. As Leo Bersani has suggested:

> Freud provides us with both an interpretive discourse on these eroding forces, and an exemplification, within that very discourse, of the process of erosion. To read his work is to witness the coming-into-literature of a discourse which could, thanks to a scientifically validated theory, presume to dominate literature. But it is precisely at, so to speak, that metamorphic moment that the Freudian text also becomes a psychoanalytic text—that is, at the moment it dismantles its own discourse and makes immensely problematic the identity of the thinker "in" or "behind" the discourse. (12)

In the present discussion I intend to use Jameson's term "political unconscious," but without losing sight of Bersani's insight that the Freudian text from which it is drawn, far from being a bedrock of scientific truth, is itself subject to dismantlement from within. As we shall see, both Luisa Valenzuela and Rosario Castellanos focus on the role of political oppression in phallocentric society, identifying woman as the nodal point around which the mechanisms of repression cluster. While both authors depict women as inhabiting the space occupied by the political unconscious, they do so from different perspectives. In Valenzuela's work, political discourse operates within the text as an unconscious reality which exists in "the other scene" (*der andere Schauplatz*, to use Freud's term) beneath (or behind, or within) the explicit scenes of sexual passion. The life of political subversives in Argentina in the 1970s, during the "guerra sucia," is written like the unconscious mind, unmentionable, unknowable, but all-pervading precisely because of its absence. Castellanos, by contrast, captures political oppression within a wider ethnic and sexual frame which relates the Spanish conquest of America to the ostracization of women in modern-day Mexico.

In *Cambio de armas* (1982), Valenzuela explores the unconscious dividing line between sexual and political violence. Each of the *novellas* which compose *Cambio de armas* centers on the sexual relationship between a man and a woman, and this sexual relationship becomes in turn a synecdoche of political relations, with the political subtext standing in a relation of part to whole to the overt narrative space of the sexual relationship. In *Cambio de armas*, in a sense, Valenzuela is reversing the paradigm of the political thriller in which the protagonists would be involved in political machinations but their "true," inner selves would be revealed in their sex lives. In the political potboiler, politics is the discourse of the seen, sex the politics of the unseen.

Valenzuela reverses this paradigm in *Cambio de armas*, in which political repression becomes the unconscious discourse of the novel. The narrative seems thus to be colluding ostensibly with the government policy of abduction of subversives, on one level therefore echoing the subversiveness of Freud's text, which "dismantles its own discourse and makes immensely problematic the identity of the thinker 'in' or 'behind' the discourse" (Bersani's words quoted above). In "La palabra asesino," for example, the political discourse is reduced to the unseen level operating within the discourse of sexuality. This *novella* focuses on the masochistic/sadistic enjoyment of a woman who is at once sexually fascinated and morally repelled by her lover, whom she knows to be a political henchman: "Y se pregunta cómo y por qué llegar hasta la cama con el asesino, a sangre fría el asesino" (73).[17] Their love-making conjures up images of death (76), and politics becomes a murky underworld of which the narrator obtains knowledge only via her sexual relationship with her partner. The discourse of the political subversive is made to disappear, forced to operate like the Unconscious.

We meet with a parallel rhetorical gesture in "Cuarta versión." As the opening lines run: "Hay cantidad de páginas escritas, una historia que nunca puede ser narrada por demasiado real, asfixiante. Agobiadora" (3). When the political discourse emerges it is invariably in the context of what must be forgotten:

> Hola, se dijeron alegrándose de verse. Volver a verse era un alivio, en esas circunstancias, y también se dijeron, la situación está peor que nunca, aparecieron otros 15 cadáveres flotando en el río, redoblaron las persecuciones. Y alguien le sopló al oído: Navoni pasó a la clandestinidad. Olvidate de su nombre, borralo de tu libreta de direcciones. (8)

Forgetting names, dates, people, events becomes a way of life. It is not coincidental, for example, that forgetfulness should become the main narrative device structuring the narrative of "Cuarta versión." The protagonist, Laura, whose name recalls the unspoken name of the beloved in Petrarch's *Rime*, opens the narrative suffering from total amnesia: "No le asombra para nada el hecho de estar sin memoria, de sentirse totalmente desnuda de recuerdos" (113). Valenzuela's text, indeed, very skillfully expresses the sense of repression within Laura's own mind. Certain details tend to suggest that Laura's past has been relegated to the non-remembered realm of the Unconscious. One of these is the ominous and mysterious scar across her back: "esa larga, inexplicable cicatriz que le cruza la espalda" (119). In the section entitled "El pozo," there is a reference to the burning of Laura's feet: "Las paredes del pozo a veces resuenan y no importa lo que intentan decirle aunque de vez en cuando ella parece recibir un mensaje—un latigazo—y siente como se le estuvieran quemando la planta de los pies y de golpe recupera la superficie de sí misma" (130). As happens so often in Valenzula's text, the reference is synecdochal, as if uttered by a mind not totally aware of what is happening. This explains the image of the well into which the self of the victim frequently retreats. Another detail which seems to be more eloquent than its purely physical presence would tend to conjure up is the horsewhip. Merely seeing the whip is enough to make Laura break down and scream hysterically: "Y ella que no sabe de esas cosas, que ha olvidado los caballos—si es que alguna vez los conoció de cerca—ella se pone a gritar desesperada, a aullar como si fuera a destriparla o a violarla con ese mismo cabo del talero" (131). And yet the text has no reference to this form of torture carried out on Laura which might explain her otherwise unjustified psychotic fear. Laura's fear, in its Pavlovian nakedness, intimates that she has been violated at some time in the past by a horsewhip, but that the memory of this incident has been repressed from her conscious mind. The whip, therefore, becomes a physical symbol of a scene of torture which has been suppressed from view, relegated to the "other scene" of the Unconscious. It is almost as if the text itself, like Laura's mind, has been disconnected from its referential origins and moves amorphously in a no-man's-land, cut off from its own unconscious secret.

Throughout *Cambio de armas*, thus, there is a constant interplay between the levels of the conscious and the unconscious mind. This is particularly so in terms of the interchange between sexual and political discourse, which surfaces most effectively in the scene entitled "Los espejos." Though ostensibly a scene depicting sexual intimacy between a man and a woman, Roque's orders to the effect that Laura should watch what he is doing in the ceiling mirror turns the scene into a thinly veiled allegory of torture. The mirror, as in the work of Lacan, provides in Valenzuela's novel an alienated image of the self:

—Abrí los ojos y mirá bien lo que te voy a hacer porque es algo que merece ser visto. Y con la lengua empieza a trepársele por la pierna izquierda, la va dibujando y ella allá arriba se va reconociendo, va sabiendo que esa pierna es suya porque la siente viva bajo la lengua y de golpe esa rodilla que está observando en el espejo también es suya, y más que nada la comba de la rodilla—tan sensible—, y el muslo, y sería muy suya la entrepierna si no fuera porque él hace un rodeo y se aloja en el ombligo.—

¡Seguí mirando! (122-23)

In Valenzuela's text the body becomes alienated from consciousness, her leg and knee becoming almost separate from her body. The language of love turns gradually into the discourse of torture. Though under duress, Laura refuses to confess the identity of her colleagues, and her refusal is depicted in typically Lacanian terms as destroying the artificial sense of the self as projected by the mirror: "un no que parece hacer estallar el espejo del techo, que multiplica y mutila y destroza la imagen de él, casi como un balazo aunque él no lo perciba y tanto su imagen como el espejo siguen allí, intactos, imperturbables" (124). The split between self and reflected self as seen in the mirror is echoed in the split between victim and torturer. This ambiguity is centered around the ambivalent genitive form "la imagen de él," which could refer as much to the reflection of Roque as perceived in the mirror by Laura as to the image of himself which Roque possesses. The second meaning of the term would account for the way that Roque is unaware of the emotional and linguistic implosion experienced by Laura. True to the rhetoric of phallocentrism, which refuses to see anything other than a fixed image of itself, Roque retains the specious and specular solidity of the self as projected in the mirror. Laura, on the other hand, rejects this image, and by extension the knowledge, provided by the mirror: "ahora les sonríe a los múltiples espejos que le devuelven algo así como un conocimiento que ella rechaza de plano" (130). This "conocimiento" provided by the mirror is what Lacan would call a "méconnaissance," since it reflects a speciously fixed image of the self.[18]

Laura thus refuses to be integrated into the Symbolic Order of the world which Roque inhabits, an oppressive world based on repression, fear and torture. Laura's new identity, as conferred upon her by her captors, is centered on her new name which, as in the Lacanian concept of the mirror stage, is the point at which the subject is integrated into the Symbolic Order: "En cuanto a ella, le han dicho que se llama Laura pero eso también forma parte de la nebulosa en la que transcurre su vida" (113).

The section entitled "Mirilla" is an extension of the scene in which Roque forces Laura to watch him making love to her. This time, however, the mirror is replaced by two mysterious, unnamed peeping toms who look through the "mirilla" at Laura and Roque: "El le ha brindado más de una vez la posibilidad de verse en los espejos y ahora le está por dar la nueva posibilidad bastante aterradora de verse en los ojos de los otros" (134). Once more, the backdrop of torture during love-making is implicit rather than explicit. Roque uses his penis as if it were a weapon to break down Laura's defenses:

> El apareamiento se empieza a volver cruel, elaborado, y se estira en el tiempo. El parece querer partirla en dos a golpes de anca y en medio de un estertor se frena, se retira, para volver a penetrarla con saña, trabándole todo movimiento o hincándole los dientes. (135)

He forces her to howl like a dog and possesses her clinically, without pleasure: "él la sigue poseyendo con furia y sin placer" (136).

Through the interlacing of sexual and political levels, the sexual relationship between Laura and the Colonel echoes synecdochely the political struggle between terrorism and the military regime in Argentina in the 1970s. Through the central (k)not of power, the political is transformed into the unconscious missing term residing beneath the conscious, visible level of sexuality. The act of repression is enacted within Laura's mind (since she seems at the beginning of the story to be unaware of her past) and within the discourse of the text (which is itself subject to repression, gaps and forgetfulness).

At the point when she remembers her identity, however, Laura kills the man she has been living with. As the story concludes:

> Ella ve esa espalda que se aleja y es como si por dentro se le disipara un poco la niebla. Empieza a entender algunas cosas, entiende sobre todo la función de este instrumento negro que él llama revólver. Entonces lo levanta y apunta. (145-46)

The military colonel had attempted to convert the discourse of political hatred into sexual love, thereby anaesthetizing its danger. As he had told Laura only minutes before: "tenías órdenes de matarme y me odiabas aunque no me conocías ¿me odiabas? mejor, ya le iba a obligar yo a quereme, a depender de mí como una recién nacida" (144). But this reversal is itself reversed. The change from ignorance to knowledge, according to the Aristotelian formula, "leads either to love or to hatred." In Laura's case, it led back to the same story: hatred. The plan to translate the discourse of political opposition into the Unconscious backfires, and the terrorist fires into the Colonel's back.

Rather than simply repression, the work of the Mexican novelist Rosario Castellanos (1925-1974) focuses on oppression, which is often expressed in Castellanos's work by means of a social metaphor. A recurring motif in this context is the discovery of America by the Spaniards and the subsequent forfeiture by the Amerindian populations of their religion, their power and their language. In Castellanos's work the political unconscious emerges fragmentarily in the discourse of the Indians of present-day Mexico, who stand trapped within the prisonhouse of a language which they do not speak but in which they operate unconsciously. This idea forms the basis of one of her most famous poems, "Malinche," in which Castellanos projects herself as the "daughter" of the Indian race La Malinche turned her back on when she became Hernán Cortés's concubine-*cum*-interpreter.[19] A similar theme emerges in Castellanos's prose fiction. The opening lines of her novel *Oficio de tinieblas* (1962) delineate the meeting of the two races in stark terms:

> Y estos hombres vinieron como de otro mundo. Llevaban el sol en la cara y hablaban lengua latina, lengua que sobrecoge el corazón de quien escucha. Idioma, no como el tzotzil que se dice también en sueños, sino férreo instrumento de señorío, arma de conquista, punta de látigo de la ley. Porque ¿cómo, sino en castilla, se pronuncia la orden y se declara la sentencia? ¿Y cómo amonestar y cómo premiar sino en castilla? (9)

"Tzotzil" is a language banished to the world of the Unconscious and dreams (*que se dice también en sueños*), unlike Castilian which is identified as the language of authority and power. One of the unwritten assumptions of the *conquistadors* who brought the Spanish tongue to the New World at the end of the fifteenth and the beginning of the sixteenth centuries was that in exchange for bringing knowledge to the native population they would receive material tribute. As Cortés suggested in his first letter to the Catholic Kings,

> trataremos aquí desde el principio que fue descubierta esta tierra hasta el estado en que al presente está, por que vuestras majestades sepan la

tierra que es, la gente que la posee y la manera de su vivir, y el rito y ceremonias, seta o ley que tienen, y el fruto que en ellas vuestras reales altezas podrían hacer y della podrán recebir. (13)

This exploitative relationship is presented in Castellanos's fiction as the blueprint for the fabric of everyday life in modern-day Mexico. For even when Castellanos is describing a typical set of events in a Mexican village, the ideology of the Conquest is shown to flesh out the backdrop of the story. Such is the case, for example, with the short story "La suerte de Teodoro Méndez Acubal," which describes how an Indian finds a gold coin and is eventually charged with having committed theft, since it is deemed impossible that he could have acquired the coin by anything but illegal means. The owner of the jewellery store who denounces Teodoro Méndez Acubal to the police is "don Agustín Velasco, uno de los descendientes de los conquistadores" (*Ciudad real* 54).[20]

In this monochrome society language becomes a tool not for enlightenment but for oppression. When, in chapter VI of *Oficio de tinieblas*, for example, Remigio outlines the job requirements to his work force, he uses Spanish, a language they barely understand. Pedro, thus, "tuvo que conformarse a ciegas" (53). The Indians themselves accept their exploitation as something given: "Fue tu suerte de nacer indio" (53), they argue. Many of the *caciques*, therefore, are unwilling to teach their workers to read and write: "Indio alzado es indio perdido, decían. Cuando estos tales por cuales sepan leer y hablar castilla no va a haber diablo que los aguante" (56). The landowners are wise to the complementarity of knowledge and power: "Cuando los indios sepan lo que sabemos nosotros nos arrebatarán lo nuestro" (57).

The Indians are also shown as being kept in the dark about God since He is the source of power in a Christian society. In the short stories, for example, a parallel is consistently drawn between the ability to speak with God and the ability to speak Spanish. The feelings of Daniel Castellanos Lampoy described in *Aceite guapo* epitomize the awkwardness experienced by the Indian when using the tongue of the conqueror:

> Había ido olvidando lo que significaban las palabras, y ya no atinaba con el nombre de muchos objetos. Para hilvanar una frase buscaba arduamente las concordancias y no lograba expresarse con claridad ni con fluidez. Al sentir fija en él la atención de sus interlocutores un golpe repentino de sangre le sobrevenía a la garganta y se precipitaba a terminar en un tartamudeo penoso. (39)

Words get stuck in his throat; instead of a rush of words, Daniel feels a rush of blood. Rather than the transparency of a declared desire, Daniel is left with his brute physicality. Rather than language, body. Likewise, he is told that he has been wasting his time talking to the saints in the chapel, since they only understand Castilian. As Xaw points out to him: "Fíjate en la cara de santa Margarita. Es blanca, es ladina, lo mismo que san Juan, que santo

Tomás, que todos ellos. Ella habla castilla. ¿Cómo vas a querer que entienda el *tzotzil*?" (46).

Castellanos's promotion of Amerindia, implicit in the above quotations, raises epistemological problems, for though appearing to speak on behalf of those whom history declared to be the losers, Castellanos is nevertheless speaking the language of the conquerors. This irony is indeed inscribed in Castellanos's name; though expressing the lost voice of Amerindia she does so, true to the name-of-her-father, in the voice of the conqueror. Jean Franco has made some pertinent observations on this issue. The ideology embodied in Castellanos's novels is often, she argues, that of the conqueror; of *Oficio de tinieblas*, for example, she suggests that

> what mars the novel is, perhaps, not so much the shaky source of the story of the transposition from the nineteenth century to modern times but the fact that in making the child's crucifixion central to the novel, Castellanos tacitly acquiesces in the view of the literal-mindedness of the indigenous population propagated by positivism. (141)

The contradiction is especially apparent with regard to the depiction of the female protagonist of the novel. As she points out, "Castellanos's attempt to be true to history means that she dooms her protagonist" (146). Even so, it might be argued that Castellanos is not unaware of the epistemological roots of this historical dilemma. Rather than ignoring the linguistic issue she tackles it head-on and forces language to, in Bersani's words, "dismantle its own discourse" from within. The deconstruction of language is indeed the blueprint for Castellanos's parallel deconstructions of history, society and phallocracy. This point will be clearer if we examine more closely the subject of one of these deconstructive crusades—phallocracy—which is, in any case, a central preoccupation in Castellanos's work.

In Castellanos's eyes, those who suffer the greatest oppression in Mexican society, functioning as an underclass within an underclass, are women. In her essay "Woman and Her Image," Castellanos uses Simone de Beauvoir's study *Le Deuxième sexe* to analyze the ways in which women have been mythified and therefore rendered helpless (either through beauty or angelicness) concluding that "woman is stripped of her spontaneity of action, forbidden the initiative of decision, taught to obey the commandments of an ethic that is completely alien to her and has no more justification or basis than that of serving the interests, goals, and end of others" (*Reader* 240). In her essays Castellanos lists the means by which women are incarcerated within the phallocentric code (her most significant test case is the male requirement of virginity in his marriage partner), and then points to images of liberated women who range from real life, such as Sor Juana Inés de la Cruz, to the fictional such as Ana Ozores and Anna Karenina: "Each one in her way and in her own circumstances denies the conventional, making the foundations of the establishment tremble, turning hierarchies upside down, and achieving authenticity" (*Reader* 244). Strangely, however, none of the female characters in Castellanos's fiction ever manages to embody these feminist values. A typical example is Matilde Casanova, a character who appears in *Album de familia*. Despite being the recipient of the Nobel Prize for literature, Matilde suffers from an ability to balance the demands of work and motherhood:

> —No, yo era una fugitiva; yo estaba ocultando un crimen, expiando un remordimiento.
>
> —Pero remordimiento de qué, por Dios?
>
> —De mi estirilidad.
>
> —No eras estéril. Creabas. Tus más hermosos poemas datan de entonces.
>
> —Bajo ellos sepulté mi vientre, sepulté a mi hijo. Pesan más que toda la tierra, pero él vuelve a resucitar, otra vez, otra vez. (82)

Matilde cannot reconcile her own desire for artistic creativity with phallocratic society's desire that she have children; the strain becomes too much and she commits suicide.

The repression of women by men in the guise of society's needs is a recurrent theme in Castellanos's fiction, a typical example of which is her short story *El viudo Román*. Castellanos's story concerns the desire of a certain don Carlos to wreak revenge for his wounded honour against a family by singling out for ignominy the most vulnerable member of the family, Romelia the daughter, marrying her and then claiming that she was not a virgin. Romelia, similar in this to Estela before her who was likewise tricked on her wedding day, has, like Iphigenia, been "sacrificed on the patriarchal altars" (*Reader* 240). Despite the complacent words of Romelia's father, the archetypal "nobodaddy," it is clearly the women who pay the price for men's misdeeds. As Castellanos suggested: "In Mexico, when we utter the word *woman*, we refer to a creature who is dependent upon male authority: be it her father's, her brother's, her husband's, or her priest's" (261).

"Lección de cocina" is the master text of Castellanos's feminist deconstructive crusade. This short story opens with the narrator's unquestioning acceptance of her place within society (she is significantly unnamed), behind the proverbial kitchen sink: "Mi lugar está aquí. Desde el principio de los tiempos ha estado aquí. En el proverbio alemán la mujer es sinónimo de *Küche, Kinder, Kirche*" (*Album de familia* 7). The reference to a proverb immediately introduces a theme that is central to the story as a whole, since language, here epitomized by the proverb, is an instrument of oppression in that it maps out the boundaries of women's existence, as we shall see. The central metaphor of the tale springs from the domestic situation of women, epitomized by the beef which is being cooked for the duration of the story. This metaphor, and the ironic use it is subjected to, strongly recalls the same theme in the work of Sor Juana, whom Castellanos, as already noted, regarded as a symbol of a liberated woman within a man's world (*Reader* 222-25).

In a passage from her famous "Respuesta de la poetisa a la muy ilustre Sor Filotea de la Cruz," Sor Juana refers ironically to the Church authorities' argument that her intellectual energies might be better served if she were to take up cooking. Sor Juana turned this idea around, poking fun at the church dignitaries, by showing how her mind frequently became involved in the solving of intellectual problems during the preparation of food:

> Pues ¿qué os pudiera contar, Señora, de los secretos naturales que he descubierto estando guisando? Veo que un huevo se une y fríe en la manteca o aceite y, por contrario, se despedaza en el almíbar; ver que para que el azúcar se conserve fluida basta echarle una muy mínima parte de agua en que haya estado membrillo u otra fruta agria; ver que la yema y clara de un mismo huevo son tan contrarias, que en los unos, que sirven para el azúcar, sirve cada una de por sí y juntos no. Por no cansaros con tales frialdades, que sólo refiero por daros entera noticia de mi natural y creo que os causará risa; pero, señora, ¿qué podemos saber las mujeres sino filosofías de cocina? Bien dijo Lupercio Leonardo, que bien se puede filosofar y aderezar la cena. Y yo suelo decir viendo estas cosillas: Si Aristóteles hubiera guisado, mucho más hubiera escrito.
> (*Obras completas* IV, 459-60)

A similar line of argument emerges during Castellanos's narrative. The gradually cooking steak gives rise to various trains of thought, which gradually deconstruct the premises upon which phallocentrism is based. Firstly, the redness of the meat brings to mind the couple's recent visit to Acapulco and their sunburnt backs; its subsequent greyness, when she adds spice, reminds her of her ageing husband. Gradually self-awareness emerges. Marriage, she comes to see, has deprived her of her past and her identity: "Llevo una marca de propiedad" ("Lección de cocina" 14). The sexual act brings about a loss of life and a loss of language: "Cuando dejas caer tu cuerpo sobre el mío siento que me cubre una lápida, llena de inscripciones, de nombres ajenos, de fechas memorables. Gimes inarticuladamente y quisiera susurrarte al oído mi nombre para que recuerdes quién es a la que posees" (14).

Toward the end of the narrative, it becomes clear that the cooking process is a metaphor for the transformation of the human personality within time:

> Recapitulemos. Aparece, primero el trozo de carne con un color, una forma, un tamaño. Luego cambia y se pone más bonita y se siente una contenta. Luego vuelve a cambiar y ya no está tan bonita. Y sigue cambiando y cambiando y cambiando y lo que uno no atina es cuando pararle el alto. Porque si yo dejo este trozo de carne indefinidamente expuesto al fuego, se consume hasta que no queden ni rastros de él. Y el trozo de carne que daba la impresión de ser algo tan sólido, tan real, ya no existe.
>
> ¿Entonces? Mi marido también da la impresión de solidez y de realidad cuando estamos juntos, cuando lo toco, cuando lo veo. Seguramente

> cambia, y cambio yo también, aunque de manera tan lenta, tan morosa
> que ninguno de los dos lo advierte. (20)

The final insight of the piece is liberating. It is through the instrument of her oppression—here the metaphor of the meat reasserts its centrality—that the female consciousness has become cognizant of its chains and finally broken free. Rather like the Marxian paradox which asserts that it is only through and as a result of capitalism that the proletariat will break its chains and achieve true freedom, so Castellanos suggests that it is only through the agent of her own oppression—the domestic prision epitomized by the kitchen—that womankind will finally assert her freedom from phallocentric bonds.

In this chapter we have seen how certain concepts drawn from the body of psychoanalytical knowledge have informed the focus of feminine fiction written in Spain and Latin America. We have seen how the fiction of Clarice Lispector in Brazil and Esther Tusquets in Spain demonstrates striking parallels with Cixous's notion of *écriture féminine*, which itself is an offshoot of Freudian knowledge. The "feminine voice" which emerges in the novels of Lispector and Tusquets operates like the Unconscious since, unable to speak its truth, it remains silent. Luisa Valenzuela and Rosario Castellanos give a political edge to the silenced "feminine voice." Valenzuela unveils the insidious laws of patriarchal politics played out in a sexual relationship, while Castellanos explores the link between the social oppression of the subaltern and the repression of womankind. Each in their different ways, these four writers explore a notion of the Unconscious as "sexed" and "feminized" in order to demonstrate how the woman in contemporary society is debarred from entry into the master text of the patriarchal world.

NOTES

1. To give a rough indication of the critical prominence of women's writing the lines devoted to that subject were divided by the total number of lines of a given section in the *Year's Work in Modern Language Studies* and then expressed as a percentage. The percentages annually for the "1936 until the Present Day" section for Spanish literature, for example, were as follows: 1986 (5.9%), 1987 (10.5%), 1988 (13.3%); for twentieth-century Spanish-American literature, the corresponding figures were: 1986 (5.%), 1987 (5.3%), 1988 (5.8%); for modern Brazil: 1986 (18.6%), 1987-88 (8.1%); see the respective sections in vols. 48-50 of *Year's Work in Modern Language Studies*. The very high precentage for the modern Brazilian literature section corresponding to the year 1986 was mainly due to the large number of works published on Clarice Lispector that year. These figures can only be approximative, since the coverage on which the contributions are based is necessarily selective.

2. Virginia Woolf was not the first to make an association specifically between the woman and the manx cat. In 1881 Carlyle made the connection in a roundabout way using the middle term "Manx penny" in the expression: "[He] hadn't the heart to . . . watch a woman making a Manx penny of herself," as cited in the *Oxford English Dictionary*, which furthermore defines a "Manx penny" as "a coin stamped with the device of three legs arranged in a form suggestive of a Catherine wheel." Other

examples of metaphorical uses of the term manx likewise carry associations of oddness (VI, 146).

3. An example of this more traditional feminist approach can be found in Millet, esp. 176-203.

4. See Mitchell's essay "On Freud and the Destruction Between the Sexes" (1974) (*Women* 221-32), as well as her later study *Psychoanalysis and Feminism*, which attempts to integrate the knowledge of Lacanian psychoanalysis with the discipline of feminism. In this work she argues on behalf of Freud against the adoption of the psychoanalytical theories of Wilhelm Reich and R.D. Laing, arguing that a "rejection of psychoanalysis and of Freud's work is fatal for feminism" (xv). In the process she challenges Simone de Beauvoir and Kate Millett, among others, on their rejection of Freudianism (305-18 and 351-55).

5. Trudgill furthermore mentions that the anomaly between the speech of the men and the women in the case of the Lesser Antilles tribe cited may have been caused by the invasion of a foreign tribe (the Caribs) and their subsequent extermination of the male population of the Arawak people. I do not intend in the above discussion to give the impression that there are no distinctions in the speech of men and women in Standard Average European languages. Differences clearly do exist, although they are more subtle; see Wattman Frank.

6. In an interview with Andermatt Conley, Cixous elaborated on this point, taking Freud's model of the oral, anal and genital phases as a springboard in order to argue that feminine writing is built on genitality (138). In his earlier writings on infantile sexuality Freud isolated two pregenital sexual organizations, the oral-cannibalistic and the sadistic-anal. In 1925 his research led him to add a third stage which he called the phallic stage (*Basic Writings* 597-98).

7. *El País* (9 January 1982), quoted in Valls.

8. *El País* (17 June 1982), and *ABC* (11 May 1986), quoted in Valls.

9. Bergmann studies this motif in Laforet's *Nada*, Matute's *Primera memoria*, Moix's *Julia*, Martín Gaite's *El cuarto de atrás*, and Rodoreda's *La plaça del Diamant*.

10. Fitz succinctly summarizes the main similarities between Cixous and Lispector in his article "Hélène Cixous's Debt to Clarice Lispector: The Case of *Vivre L'Orange* and 'l'écriture féminine' "; see also Fisher. For a good discussion of the "writing the body" theme, see A. Jones. On the role of this concept in modern Spanish fiction see Ordóñez 47. For a discussion of the motif of writing the body in the work of Rosa Montero, see Gascón Vera.

11. At times Joana's body seems to have a will of its own. After the passage in which Joana hears that her aunt intends to send her away to boarding school, we read: "Joana's hands fidgeted, independent of her will. She observed them with mild curiosity and forgot them almost immediately. The ceiling was white, the ceiling was white. Even her shoulders, which she had always thought of as being so remote from herself, throbbed with life and began to tremble. Who was she?" (47).

12. For further discussion of Lispector's work see Fitz's general study *Clarice Lispector*; *Revista Iberoamericana* 126-27 (1984) is a special number devoted in part to Lispector's work. Other important studies are Pontiero, "Testament of Experience," Patai, and Lastinger. See also the bibliographies in Fitz, *Clarice Lispector* 140-55, and in Pontiero, "Clarice Lispector: An Intuitive Approach to Fiction" 79-85.

13. As far as I am aware there has been, to date, no book-length study of Tusquets's works. Important contributions are Vásquez, "Tusquets, Fitzgerald and the Redemptive Power of Love" (see also her article "Image and Linear Progression Toward Defeat in Esther Tusquets's *El mismo mar de todos los veranos*"); d'Ambrosio Servididio, "Perverse Pairings and Corrupted Codes: *El amor es un juego solitario*"

(see also her article "A Case of Pre-Oedipal and Narrative Fixation: *El mismo mar de todos los veranos*"); Gold 343; Bellver; Menteiga; Navajas; and Cleary Nichols.

14. For a discussion of the difference between the theories of Cixous and Wittig, see Griffin Crowder.

15. *El mismo mar de todos los veranos* is indeed notable for its absence of men; there are a few negative references to Elia's husband Julio, a few scenes recalling Elia's father (and notably the scene when he bought his wife a basket of roses [173-76]), but these pale into insignificance when compared with the preponderance of references to Elia's daughter, mother, grandmother and lover. The world of Tusquets's fiction is not only dominated in a physical sense by women, but the language of men is by the same token banished from that world.

16. In the eyes of his enemies the founder of psychoanalysis was no more than "a small-minded 'Victorian' patriarch confronted by incredible numbers of sex-starved hysterical women" (Mitchell, *Psychoanalysis* xx). The science he founded has had its detractors. Typical is the off-hand manner of Hans Eysenck, who defined psychoanalysis in a recent book as "a theory about mental activity and mental disease which tried to explain human behavior. It failed completely to live up to its major claim, namely, to be able to cure mental patients, and has now no scientific pretensions of any kind" (4). Mitchell poured scorn on Eysenck's statements made in the 1950s to the effect that psychoanalysis did not cure patients' symptoms (340 note 2).

17. Valenzuela's Argentinian punctuation is retained. For further discussion of her work see Magnarelli, *Reflections/Refractions*.

18. Valenzuela alludes extensively to Lacanian theory in "Mis brujas favoritas." She refers to the "célebre deslizamiento del significado por debajo del significante," which she describes as "hoy tan vital como lo fue en su momento el encuentro fortuito del paraguas con la máquina de coser" (89) and to Lacan's theory of the phallus as the site of Lack, arguing that it is as a result of this Lack that "la humanidad en pleno gira en torno a una carencia, con cada sexo instalado en ubicación opuesta en lo que al falo como hito se refiere" (90).

19. In this poem Castellanos describes herself rejected by her mother, Malinche: "Arrojada, expulsada / del reino, del palacio y de la entraña tibia / de la que me dio a luz en tálamo legítimo / y que me aborreció porque yo era su igual / en figura y en rango / y se contempló en mí y odió su imagen / y destrozó el espejo contra el suelo" (see Crow 100).

20. Most of the stories in *Ciudad real* focus on the slave-master relationship. As Alfonso González has pointed out: "El único lenguaje operante es el que gira alrededor de la relación amo-siervo y que aísla al individuo o al grupo débil del más fuerte, creando una familia o una sociedad estratificada e incomunicada" (107). For further discussion of this topic in Castellanos's short stories, see Paley Francescato and Miller.

IV
POETRY, CULTURE, NEUROSIS

César Vallejo (1893-1938) and Pablo Neruda (1904-1973) are undoubtedly the two most famous poets of Latin America. In this chapter my aim is to analyze their respective views of culture (taken in the broadest sense of the word) and compare them with that of the Spanish poet Vicente Aleixandre (1898-1984). The twentieth-century Latin-American writer, unlike his European counterpart, typically has demonstrated a schizoid attitude to the Western concept of culture, compounded by the Latin American republics' unsettling experience of the expansion of North American capitalism, especially during the 1920s and 1930s. I will firstly delineate the different ways in which Vallejo and Neruda reacted to the discourse of Western culture as well as its counter-discourse of Marxism. Both Vallejo and Neruda embraced Marxism, Vallejo as a result of his reading of Marxist-Leninist theory in the late 1920s and Neruda as a result of his experience of the Spanish Civil War. In the case of both poets it will be necessary to review some background biographical material which illuminates this issue (in Vallejo's case his relationship with his mother, and in Neruda's case his timidity and paranoia as a young man). Vicente Aleixandre, as we shall see, used the discourse of surrealism and its perception of the Other Scene of the Unconscious to unravel the secrets of his obsessions.

Vallejo: Incest and the Matriarchal Utopia

The role of the "mother figure" is a crucial one in the work of César Vallejo, and, as we shall see, the Oedipal path traced in Vallejo's early poetry was superseded in his later work by a vision of the mother as "mothering" a new socialist utopia. It is a critical commonplace that Vallejo had an ambiguous relationship with his mother. Juan Espejo Asturrizaga recalls that, when he heard news of his mother's death in August 1918 (he was in Lima at the time), Vallejo was emotionally and intellectually paralyzed for days: "Por estos días Vallejo atravesó una etapa de total paralización intelectual a la vez que desesperación y angustia" (70). Armando Bazán suggests an interesting ramification. Vallejo apparently found it difficult to have a sexual relationship with another woman because of the vivid image of his mother, who seemed to disapprove of his sexual desires. When attempting to kiss a girl, whom Bazán discreetly calls Hirondelle, in the Bois de Boulogne, the following Oedipal scene took place:

> Mientras tanto, sin delaciones de ningún género, Hirondelle le enlaza el cuello con un brazo de sedas fragantes. Le atrae el rostro y lo aproxima al suyo hasta hacer de los dos un monolito, con apariencia de terracita

angustiada y de mármol radiante, mitad a mitad. "César ... César querido ..." Ya él se ha hundido en la noche tenebrosa del pasado, en la cual impera majestuosa una voz inmortal. ¿En qué forma se combinan, se enredan o se enfrentan y entran en tan terrible conflicto la ternura materna que embarga a su alma y el amor apasionado de la muchacha aquella que ha logrado penetrar hasta lo más noble de su sangre y de su espíritu? Lo único cierto es que tal conflicto repercute como una campanada de terror absurdo en la conciencia del desventurado, que ante la inminencia de besar virilmente en trance de posesión, no sabe si es amante o es hijo y sólo acierta a sollozar, poniéndose de pie, con el rostro crispado y rogando a Hirondelle que haga lo mismo y que camine hasta la barca. (84-85)

This event, which took place soon after Vallejo's arrival in Europe and within five years of his mother's death, shows how the confusion between his sexual feelings and his love of his mother made him distraught, in this case reducing him to tears. Faced with a sexual adventure, Vallejo was unable to differentiate between seeing himself as lover or son. Likewise, Hirondelle oscillated between lover and mother, and this oscillation caused him to break down. Even if we take into account the rather literary style in which Bazán's account is couched, these biographical details serve to demonstrate that, according to his biographers, Vallejo had ambiguous feelings towards his mother. This emotional ambivalence is reflected in the images of the mother which occur in his poetry.

In *Los heraldos negros* (1919), Vallejo's first collection of poems, his mother is, though alive at the time (most of the poems were written between 1915 and 1917, that is, before her death in August 1918), strangely absent. Even in "Canciones de hogar," she is metaphorized rather blandly as "como una Dolorosa" (*Obra poética* 111) or appears in a banal context: "Otras veces le hablaba a mi madre / de impresiones urbanas, de política" (113). Compared to the overbearing presence of the poet's father and the poet's brother, Miguel, the mother seems trivial, unimportant, non-central.

It was, however, as a result of her death that Vallejo's mother came to occupy a central role in Vallejo's poetic expression. Some critics have claimed that the mother's death was a crucial biographical factor influencing the form that *Trilce* (1922) was to take.[1] In this work, Vallejo deconstructs linguistic hierarchies, allowing neologisms, archaisms, and typographical experimentation to rub shoulders with literary language, scientific terminology and legal jargon. The phallogocentric discourse of *Los heraldos negros* gives way to a shattered text in which all certainties—whether religious, political or epistemological—are radically subverted. As we shall see, in *Trilce* Vallejo gives voice to what I have called, following Lacan's lead, the "Name-of-the-Mother" and, before the analysis of the poems, some general points about this term seem appropiate.

The "Name-of-the-Mother" is an allusion to Lacan's term *le nom-du-père*, which has already been discussed in this work. Lacan uses this term on a specifically Freudian level to indicate the authority attaching to the *paterfamilias*. The term thus indicates the transference of the family name from father to sibling (given the play on the homophonous *le non-du-père*) as well as the authority invested in the father to prohibit the sibling's antisocial behavior. To paraphrase Lacan still further, language, as a gift from the father, confers identity at the same time that it introduces an awareness of lack. To pass from the Imaginary Order, which is related to a prelinguistic phase, to the Symbolic Order, which is embodied in the world of language, is to pass through what Lacan called the mirror stage, which is when "one is no longer the same as one's mother." This split in consciousness is dependent, in Lacan's view, on the recognition of the Name-of-the-Father. In Vallejo's poetry, as I hope to show, the Lacanian paradigm is disrupted. It is the figure of the mother who takes the place of the father and who initiates the split in identity normally attached to the figure of the father. Vallejo thus deconstructs the configuration of the classical "Family Romance." As we shall see, the death of the mother transforms her into an empty signified, forever absent and thereby giving birth to an endless chain of self-effacing signifiers. Her death gives birth to what might be termed an "Oedipalization" of poetic language in which the Name-of-the-Mother stumbles into speech. In order to discuss this idea I intend to look first of all at two poems from *Trilce*, which are Tr. XXIII and Tr. LXV.

Both of these poems strive to immortalize the mother, the first by the poet's regressing to a mother-infant relationship and the second by his attempt through the medium of language to de-sexualize her presence/absence, thereby closing her potentiality for sexual repetition. The first of these poems runs as follows:

Tahona estuosa de aquellos mis bizcochos
pura yema infantil innumerable, madre.

Oh tus cuatro gorgas, asombrosamente
mal plañidas, madre: tus mendigos.
Las dos hermanas últimas, Miguel que ha muerto
y yo arrastrando todavía
una trenza por cada letra del abecedario.

En la sala de arriba nos repartías
de mañana, de tarde, de dual estiba,
aquellas ricas hostias de tiempo, para
que ahora nos sobrasen
cáscaras de relojes en flexión de las 24
en punto parados.
Madre, y ahora! Ahora, en cuál alvéolo
quedaría, en qué retoño capilar,
cierta migaja que hoy se me ata al cuello
y no quiere pasar. Hoy que hasta
tus puros huesos estarán harina
que no habrá en qué amasar
¡tierna dulcera de amor!,
hasta en la cruda sombra, hasta en el gran molar
cuya encía late en aquel lácteo hoyuelo

> que inadvertido lábrase y pulula ¡tú lo viste tanto!
> en las cerradas manos recién nacidas.
>
> Tal la tierra oirá en tu silenciar,
> cómo nos van cobrando todos
> el alquiler del mundo donde nos dejas
> y el valor de aquel pan inacabable.
> Y nos lo cobran, cuando, siendo nosotros
> pequeños entonces, como tú verías,
> no se lo podíamos hacer arrebatado
> a nadie; cuando tú nos lo diste,
> ¿di, mamá? (134-35)

    This poem, as Eduardo Neale-Silva has pointed out, centers on "el contraste entre el encantamiento de la infancia y la aspereza de la realidad presente" (343). It (re-)presents a failed attempt by the poetic persona to return from the Symbolic Order to the Imaginary Order, which is here epitomized by the unspeaking and unspoken relationship between mother and sibling. The main image of the poem is the food which is given freely in the symbiotic and narcissistic mother-child relationship. This image also appears in Tr. XXVIII, where food which is not given by the mother tastes of death or of the earth, for it articulates "amor ajeno" rather than the desired "amor propio" (139). The animality of this relationship is stressed by the ornithological references ("tus cuatro gorgas"). The children's pre-verbal state is suggested by the poet's reference to himself as "yo arrastrando todavía / una trenza por cada letra del abecedario." The sacramental nature of the feeding is underlined by the references in the third verse to the biscuits as "hostias" and the room where they were shared out as "la sala de arriba" (recalling the Last Supper which took place in the Upper Room; see Mark 14: 14-16).[2] The fall into the Symbolic Order experienced by the poet has made itself felt in the transition from eternity to the world of time ("Cáscaras de relojes en flexión de las 24 / en punto parados"). In the fourth stanza the reference to the crumb getting stuck in the poet's throat has a dual function. On the one hand, it expresses the poet's desire to regress to the pre-solid food stage of development characteristic of the Imaginary Order (the image of a child drinking its mother's milk appears at the end of the fourth stanza). Secondly, the image of the undigested crumb reveals how this desire is unattainable; the subject, in attempting to regress from the Symbolic to the Imaginary Order, will get stuck, left in a limbo region which is neither one nor the other.

    Stanza 5 attempts to resurrect the dead mother from the tomb, as its anguished last question makes clear ("¿di, mamá?"). The juxtaposition of the two worlds centers once more on food. In the last stanza, which idealizes a pre-capitalist world in which values are not exchanged between members of a society, but freely received from the mother ("no se lo podíamos haber arrebatado / a nadie, cuando tú nos lo diste"), the poet bases his right to possession on the Name-of-the-Mother who, though absent, lays down the law from the grave. Yet her voice from beyond the grave, as the last stanza makes clear, is silent: "Tu silenciar" (line 1); "¿di, mamá?" (line 9). The voice of the mother remains un(der)heard in a phallocentric society.

Tr. XLV likewise attempts to validate the Name-of-the-Mother; but whereas Tr. XXIII had voiced a desire to cross the space separating the Imaginary order from the Symbolic Order, Tr. LXV accepts that space and makes of its necessity a virtue. Tr. LXV, which was composed very shortly after Vallejo heard of his mother's death, runs as follows (Espejo Asturrizaga 70):

> Madre, me voy mañana a Santiago,
> a mojarme en tu bendición y en tu llanto.
> Acomodado estoy mis desengaños y el rosado
> de llaga de mis falsos trajines.
>
> Me esperará tu arco de asombro,
> las tonsuradas columnas de tus ansias
> que se acaban la vida, me esperará el patio,
> el corredor de abajo con sus tondos y repulgos
> de fiesta. Me esperará mi sillón ayo,
> aquel buen quijarudo trasto de dinástico
> cuero, que pára (*sic*) no más rezongando a las nalgas
> tataranietas, de correa a correhuela.
>
> Estoy cribando mis cariños más puros.
> Estoy ejeando ¿no oyes jadear la sonda?
>   ¿no oyes tascar dianas?
> estoy plasmando tu fórmula de amor
> para todos los huecos de este suelo.
> Oh si se dispusieran los tácitos volantes
> para todas las cintas más distantes,
> para todas las citas más distantes.
>
> Así, muerta inmortal. Así.
> Bajo los dobles arcos de tu sangre, por donde
> hay que pasar tan de puntillas, que hasta mi padre
> para ir por allí,
> humildóse hasta menos de la mitad del hombre,
> hasta ser el primer pequeño que tuviste.
>
> Así, muerta inmortal.
> Entre la columnata de tus huesos
> que no puede caer ni a lloros,
> y a cuyo lado ni el destino pudo entrometer
> ni un solo dedo suyo.
> Así, muerta inmortal.
> Así. (166-67)

In this poem, as James Higgins has pointed out, the poet's mother, through death, is transfigured into "a kind of saint or personal divinity" (Vallejo, *Anthology* 20). The focal image of the poem is the arch which suggests, on the one hand, a commemoratory monument which can withstand the flow of time and, on the other, the arch of female legs as a structure under which all men must pass. The reference in the first stanza to "tu arco de asombro" is a mid-way image beween the arch of the entrance to the family house and the arch of the mother's legs, which is the entrance to the womb. It is here that life not only begins but also ends ("las tonsuradas columnas de tus ansias / que se acaban la vida"). In the final stanza stanza of the poem, reference is made to the father's entry into the mother's womb, described as "el primer pequeño que tuviste." The father, as a result of the sexual act, becomes like a child before his mother; he is symbolically castrated and reduced to half the man he was ("hasta menos de la mitad del hombre"). The use of the archaic neologism ("humildóse"), rather than the more normal "se humilló," is an apt way of describing the movement back in time. Just as the father regresses to his childhood, so language regresses to a prelapsarian archaic state.[3]

The following stanza voices the desire to fetishize the mother's body, turning it into a "columnata de tus huesos" which cannot fall down, despite (the poet's) grief. In this act of fetishization, the poetic voice enacts a closure of the mother's womb; no longer an object of sexual desire, therefore no finger of Destiny can pierce open its magic space. The womb has been closed for eternity, becoming a timeless monument to death: "Así, muerta inmortal. / Así."

Some of these basically Oedipal preoccupations extend into the collection which immediately follows *Trilce* chronologically, namely, *Poemas en prosa*. In one of the poems from this collection, "Lánguidamente su licor," the separate realms of the authority of the father and the (non-)authority of the mother are contrasted in the very first two sentences of the poem: "Tendríamos ya una edad misericordiosa, cuando mi padre ordenó nuestro ingreso a la escuela. Cura de amor, una tarde lluviosa de febrero, mamá servía en la cocina el yantar de oración" (181). In contrast to the father, whose being is incarnated in authority and the social world of school which stands outside the family home, the mother is associated with innerness, service, food and love. The irruption of the world of school into the children's cozy world, the child's first experience of the irruption of society into its private world, is represented later on in the poem as a knock at the door:

—Tocan a la puerta—mi madre.
—Tocan a la puerta—mi propia madre.
—Tocan a la puerta—dijo toda mi madre, tocándose las entrañas a trastes infinitos, sobre toda la altura de quien viene. (182)

The image of the mother touching her womb suggests how the children are about to be expelled from the second "womb" of the family home into the social world outside.[4] As the father's subsequent command makes clear, the outside world is associated with the Law-of-the-Father:

¡Qué diestra de subprefecto, la diestra del padrE, revelando, el hombre, las falanjas filiales del niño! Podía así otorgarle la ventura que el hombre deseara más tarde. Sin embargo:

> —Y mañana, a la escuela,—disertó magistralmente el padre, ante el público semanal de sus hijos.
>
> —Y tal, la ley, la causa de la ley. Y tal también la vida. (182)

The poem ends with a displaced image of the significance of the child's entry into the outside world, its departure from the Imaginary Order to the Symbolic Order:

> Más, luego, de improviso, salió de un albañal de aguas llovedizas y de aquel mismo patio de la visita mala, una gallina, no ajena ni ponedora, sino brutal y negra. Cloqueaba en mi garganta. Fue una gallina vieja, maternalmente viuda de unos pollos que no llegaron a incubarse. origen olvidado de ese instante, la gallina era viuda de sus hijos. Fueron hallados todos los huevos. la clueca después tuvo el verbo.
>
> Nadie la espantó. Y de espantarla, nadie dejó arrullarse por su gran calofrío maternal.
>
> —¿Dónde están los hijos de la gallina vieja?
>
> —¿Dónde están los pollos de la gallina vieja?
>
> ¡Pobrecitos! ¡Dónde estarían!

Through an animal allegory, this stanza describes the child's entry into the Symbolic Order and the experience of Lack ("Fueron hallados vacíos todos los huevos"), as well as the realm of language ("La clueca después tuvo el verbo"), here echoing the first lines of the Gospel according to John (John 1: 1-4). In Vallejo's poem, the act of leaving the infantile nest is experienced by the mother as Lack. The hen is "maternalmente viuda de unos pollos que no llegaron a incubarse" (183). The experience of Lack, which is intrinsic to the subject's passage into the Symbolic Order, is a radical one for the subject and conditions his experience indefinitely. Many of the poems Vallejo wrote at this period about, and sometimes actually addressed to the mother, constantly relive the experience of Lack. The mother not only experiences Lack, she embodies Lack and transfers her experience on to her children. When the children leave home and go to school, their experience of Lack is centered on the physical absence of the mother. When the mother eventually dies, this experience of Lack is reconfirmed, as Vallejo's poem reveals. The mother's death is thus seen as confirming an intrinsic feature of her relationship with her siblings, as seen through Vallejo's eyes. The mother will always be Other. Mother will never be there.

"El buen sentido," written when Vallejo had already travelled to Paris (where he arrived in 1923), voices the desire for an Oedipal fusion with the mother. This desire for union is mitigated in intensity, and thereby displaced, by the physical distance between Lima and Paris. It is indicative that the Oedipal wish only surfaces in Vallejo's text as a result of two stages of displacement: firstly, the mother's death, and secondly, Vallejo's own journey to Paris. Mother and son are thereby separated by time and space. The Oedipal wish surfaces most unambiguously in the third stanza of "El buen sentido":

> La mujer de mi padre está enamorada de mí, viniendo y avanzando de espaldas a mi nacimiento y de pecho a mi muerte. Que estoy dos veces suyo: por el adiós y por el regreso. La cierro, al retornar. Por eso me dieran tánto sus ojos, justa de mí, in fragranti de mí, aconteciéndose por obras terminadas, por pactos consumados. (179)

In a paradoxical image, the mother is described as advancing backwards to the poet's birth while advancing forwards towards his death.[5] The poet's final return to the mother, as he suggests here, is going to take place when he dies. This *regressus ad uterum* will be a final return to pre-lapsarian bliss. There will be no more goodbyes inevitably followed by a return; in a contemporary poem, Vallejo remarks how: "¡Alejarse! ¡Quedarse! ¡Volver! ¡Partir! Toda la mecánica social cabe en estas palabras" ("Algo te identifica . . ." 194). But the social mechanics of leaving and returning will finally be subsumed by the *regressus ad uterum* which will, in effect, close the womb up, barring it to any unwanted future intruders. The fifth stanza explores the ways in which this return will echo the blissful peace of the baby in the womb before birth: "Ante mi vida de regreso, recordando que viajé durante dos corazones por su vientre, se ruboriza y se queda mortalmente lívida, cuando digo, en el tratado del alma: Aquella noche fui dichoso" (179). The reference to the mother's embarrassment and to the poet's blissful experience "aquella noche" suggests an Oedipal relationship is being delineated. The Oedipal resonance of the return is made clearer later on in the poem when described as something which transforms the son into a man:

> Mi adiós partió de un punto de su ser, más externo que el punto de su ser al que retorno. Soy, a causa del excesivo plazo de mi vuelta, más el hombre ante mi madre que el hijo ante mi madre. Allí reside el candor que hoy nos llama con tres llamas. (188)

The verbal communication originated in an organ (the mouth), which is more external than the "inner" organ of the womb to which the poet now feels he is returning. The reference to how the poet feels he becomes a man rather than a son before his mother suggests how he has adopted the paternal role, fulfilling an Oedipal destiny. This (sublimated) desire for incest does not, however, bring blindess, as in the classical version of Oedipus' plight. Rather it brings "candor" and transcendence (suggested by the trinitarian image "three flames," the number three here being, as so often in Vallejo's work, an image of transcendence). The mother seems to connive in the expression of prohibited desire veiled by the reference to Paris:

> —Hay, madre, en el mundo un sitio que se llama París. Un sitio muy grande y muy lejano y otra vez grande.

> La mujer de mi padre, al oírme, almuerza y sus ojos mortales descienden
> suavemente por mis brazos. (180)

In the transition from "madre" to "la mujer de mi padre" lies a blurring of the distinction between the separate roles of mother and wife. The ambiguous image of the mother's eyes "running down" the poet's arms could be innocent, but it could also suggest connivance in the prohibited wish. Reinforcing the symbiotic overtones of the mother-son relationship is the reference to food (the mother is having lunch), which is invariably related to the Imaginary Order, as we have already seen.

Throughout these early pre-political poems, it is the mother's death and her inescapable absence which leads to an Oedipalization of language. As Vallejo suggests in "La violencia de las horas," "Murió en mi revólver mi madre" (181). The phallic allusiveness of the revolver is associated with the mother's death. It is through death, and its concomitant experience of existential Lack, Vallejo suggests, that the Oedipal complex is articulated. The "revolver" is also, however, a displaced image of the pen. It is through Vallejo's writing, through his text, that the mother's absence is not only articulated but also produced. His text registers but also produces the Lack of the Name-of-the-Mother.

In *Poemas humanos*, the figure of the mother hardly appears; but she does re-appear in *España, aparta de mí este cáliz*, now totally sublimated and associated with the body of Spain ravaged by the Civil War (1936-1939). Poem XV in particular represents a call to the children of the world to save "mother Spain." The mother, who was originally associated with the Imaginary Order, has now been fully integrated into the Symbolic Order:

> ¡Niños del mundo, está
> la madre España con su vientre a cuestas;
> está nuestra maestra con sus férulas,
> está madre y maestra,
> cruz y madera, porque os dio la altura,
> vértigo y división y suma, niños;
> está con ella, padres procesales! (303)

Once associated with the forbidden and extra-societal, the mother figure has been sublimated to form a whole with a nation-state, itself a semantic cluster originally associated with the Law-of-the-Father, society and school, as evident in "Lánguidamente su licor." The mother has now become a teacher who knows the secret of division and addition, this knowledge being at once associated with culture (arithmetic in school) and with nature (the mother's procreative qualities). As we read later on in the poem:

> Niños,
> hijos de los guerreros, entretanto,
> bajad la voz, que España está ahora mismo repartiendo

> la energía entre el reino animal,
> las florecillas, los cometas y los hombres. (303)

The archetypal mother figure is shown sustaining the animal kingdom, the vegetable kingdom, and even the stars (that is "los cometas," which are often associated with "destiny" in Vallejo's poetry), as well as mankind. There is a suggestion, therefore, that the world the Republican army is attempting to bring into being through war is based on a projection of the symbiotic mother-sibling relationship, that is, a union between the natural and the female. The poem concludes by evoking the possibility of the mother-state's demise, but voices that absence as ultimately re-traceable, and not irredeemably absent:

> ¡Bajado el aliento, y si
> el antebrazo baja,
> si las férulas suenan, si es de noche,
> si el cielo cabe en dos limbos terrestres,
> si hay ruido en el sonido de las puertas,
> si tardo,
> si no veis a nadie, si os asustan
> los lápices sin punta, si la madre
> España cae—digo, es un decir -
> salid, niños del mundo; id a buscarla! . . . (304)

Most of the possibilities delineated by the "if" clauses suggest the idea of death or extinction of the body ("si / el antebrazo baja") or a progression between the two realms of life and death ("si el cielo cabe en dos limbos terrestres") or the "blunting" of culture ("los lápices sin punta," pencils, like pens, words and letters in *España, aparta de mí este cáliz*, having the meaning of the new script of Republican culture).[6] In this poem, then, the mother figure has finally achieved sublimation as a projection into the Symbolic Order of the State. She has thereby achieved some of the knowledge normally retained within the Name-of-the-Father. The Oedipalization of language characteristic of *Trilce* and *Poemas en prosa* has passed into the sublimation of the mother figure in which death is seen not as a loss but as a prelude to a greater unity.

Pablo Neruda: Revolution, Culture and Paranoia

It is now almost a commonplace to assert that the work of the Chilean poet Neftalí Ricardo Reyes, alias Pablo Neruda, reveals a writer with many faces. Apart from the more obvious case of his adopted *nom de plume*, a hybrid creation combining his early identification with the French poet Paul Verlaine and the Czeck novelist Jan Neruda and adopted largely as anonymous protection against his father's hostility, Neruda also masked himself in many *personae* during his long poetic career. In his study *Neruda: el viajero inmóvil* (1977), Emir Rodríguez Monegal drew attention specifically to Neruda's projection of various poetic *personae*:

> En el curso de su larga carrera, Neruda ha proyectado poéticamente varias personas visibles: el muchacho perdido entre los ponientes de la gran ciudad hostil de su primer libro, *Crepusculario*; el hondero entusiasta, embriagado por la contemplación del espacio infinito y (sobre todo) por el espacio poético que crea con sus versos de Sabat Ercasty; el nuevo Bécquer, americano, que enseñará a varias generaciones el arte melancólico y desesperado del amor adolescente; el poeta desatado e inconexo de *Tentativa del hombre infinito*, tan inadvertido que hasta Amado Alonso omitió considerarlo; el sonambúlico espectador despavorido de un mundo en permanente proceso de desintegración que documenta *Residencia en la tierra*; el testigo que ha visto la sangre por las calles y crea una poesía deliberadamente impura para transmitir el estupor y la esperanza de *España en el corazón*; el narrador que se levanta desde la arena nutricia y el océano para cantar la gloria y la miseria de la América hispánica en el *Canto general*; el satisfecho y enamorado viajero del mundo que ordena sus deberes poéticos en *Las uvas y el viento*; el amante secreto que inventa, o segrega, otro poeta anónimo para cantar *Los versos del capitán*; el poeta popular que pulsa la guitarra de los pobres para entonar sucesivas y alfabéticas *Odas elementales*; el hombre que llegado al otoño conversa coloquialmente sobre las reglas y los deberes, los ritos de la vida y de la muerte, sobre sí mismo y sobre la mujer amada, en ese libro de estupenda libertad que se llama *Estravagario*. (*Neruda* 22)

Rodríguez Monegal has argued that it was as a direct result of his timidity that Neruda created various masks: "Como todos los tímidos, el niño para sobrevivir se inventa un personaje" (38). Neruda certainly gives this impression in his memoirs, describing himself, for example, as "demasiado tímido y ensimismado" to form more than a superficial relationship with Gabriela Mistral, whom he met in Temuco as a young man (*Confieso* 33).[7] One section of his autobiography is entitled "La timidez," and in it Neruda makes the following statement:

> La timidez es una condición extraña del alma, una categoría, una dimensión que se abre hacia la soledad. También es un sufrimiento inseparable, como si se tienen dos epidermis, y la segunda piel interior se irrita y se contrae ante la vida. Entre las estructuraciones del hombre, esta calidad o este daño son parte de la aleación que va fundamentando, en una larga circunstancia, la perpetuidad del ser. (53)

What is interesting here is that Neruda sees timidity as a permanent quality of character, rather than a state of mind associated with youth. Neruda's timidity may help to explain why he used to dress outlandishly while a student in Santiago, wearing a "larga capa española," although the primary reason he gives for this is poverty (53). In a superficial way, Neruda's attitudinizing can be compared to that of the archetypal Spanish Romantic poet, José Espronceda, who, according to one school of thought, "deliberately acted and wrote in such a way as to make the public think that he was a dangerous rebel, merely to cast an aura of romanticism about his person" (Pattison 1126). Neruda's antics as a young aspiring poet, as described in his memoirs, show him very much playing the part of the Romantic poet. Yet Neruda was not simply "maintaining a pose," as Espronceda was. The different identities which he projected sprang from his anguished sense of the elusive multivalency of the self, rather than simply from a desire to pull the wool over the eyes of his contemporaries. The "large Spanish cape" which surfaces in his memoirs is intriguing not only because of its clear Romantic links, but also because, by being an article of clothing, it suggests an archetypal means of hiding from the world, like a mollusc within its shell, a metaphor which Neruda uses to describe himself at one stage (*Confieso* 47). As we shall see, the image of clothes was destined to play an important role in Neruda's later poetry.

In this discussion of the work of Pablo Neruda, I shall be following the direction of Monegal's insight but concentrating specifically on the Janus-like qualities of the poet's face, one side of which makes him appear to be an iconclastic post-romantic seer and the other side a revolutionary political pragmatist. What is striking about these two at first glance different façades is that both stances can be interpreted as unconsciously driven by an underlying complex which psychoanalysis would define as paranoia. The use of a term such as paranoia in the context of a "sane" poet such as Neruda needs some further elucidation. The dictionary defines paranoia as a "mental derangement; spec. chronic mental unsoundness characterized by delusions or hallucinations, esp. of grandeur, persecution, etc." (*Oxford English Dictionary* 460). Freud further defines paranoia as an example of thoughts and feelings from the unconscious forcing their way through to consciousness. He also suggests that it is a feature of those who suffer from paranoia that they feel threatened by others and "attach the greatest significance to the minor details of other people's behaviour which we ordinarily neglect, interpret them and make them the basis of far-reaching conclusions" (*Psychopathology* 255).[8]

Much of Neruda's poetry, from his non-political verse, such as *Residencia en la tierra*, to his political verse, such as *Canto general*, delineates a poetic *persona* who is obsessed with *naming* his enemies. For when Neruda is rejecting undefined enemies who recur incessantly in *Residencia en la tierra*, he is exploring in psychological terms a projection outwards of a hostility complex which, in his later political poetry, would be directed at specific people. Whether political or non-political, Neruda's poetry derives its impetus from the drive to *name* the enemy, to exorcise his power, and render him impotent. In this section, I intend to explore the implications of Neruda's cathartic gesture and thereby suggest an implicit link between the *prima facie* discontinuous cells of his pre-political and post-conversion poetry.

Residencia en la tierra, published in 1933 and 1935, was the last work in which Neruda's poetry was iconoclastic rather than revolutionary; the Spanish Civil War marks a watershed in his work, since it was the main historical event which persuaded him to embrace communism. Neruda wrote *Residencia en la tierra* while he was in the Far East. In his memoirs, Neruda speaks of the East as dislocated, strange, Other: "el Oriente me impresionó como una grande y desventurada familia humana, sin destinar sitio en mi conciencia para sus ritos ni para sus dioses. No creo, pues, que mi poesía de entonces haya reflejado otra cosa que la soledad de un forastero trasplantado a un mundo violento y extraño" (*Confieso* 120-21). It is for this reason that *Residencia en la tierra* demonstrates one of the fundamental reactions common to neurotic obsession as identified by Freud, namely, *Wiederholungswang* (the compulsion to repeat), that is, a compulsion derived from the daemonic power of the repressed striving for expression.[9] Neruda in fact described the poems which would one day come together in the form of *Residencia en la tierra* as "una sola cosa comenzada, como eternamente ensayada sin éxito" (Rodríguez Monegal, *Neruda* 80).[10] As we shall see, this repetition of the same idea throughout the poem, which Neruda in another letter calls "monotonous" and "ritualistic," is intrinsic to the expression of the poem. Each stanza repeats the same basic seme, exploring it in greater depth, perhaps, but always simply revealing its existence, leaving it unresolved, uncathected. Just as each of the stanzas often seems to rework the central theme, so each poem seems to "rehearse" ("without success," as Neruda would say) the same obsessive thought; each poem within the (dis)unity of the collection, as well as each stanzaic unit within the poem, is a painful revelation of a psychological dilemma. Paranoiac feelings are expressed constantly in *Residencia en la tierra*. In "Caballero solo," the poet feels persecuted by "enemigos establecidos contra mi alma," who are variously described as "young homosexuals," "girls in love," "long widows," "pregnant wives," and even "hoarse cats" (55).

Paranoia implies awareness of an enemy, and the enemy in *Residencia en la tierra* is human Culture understood in its widest sense. As Neruda said in the same letter to Eandi quoted above: "Tengo hasta cierto desprecio por la cultura, como interpretación de las cosas me parece mejor un conocimiento sin antecedentes, una absorción física del mundo, a pesar y en contra de nosotros" (79-80). One is reminded of Luis Buñuel's statement that in his work he was attempting to destroy "Culture."[11] Neruda's iconoclastic intent is most evident in "Ritual de mis piernas," in which he uses the clothes which cover our bodies as an image of the grotesque repression which underwrites human culture. Opening with a mock-ironic description of his legs, seen alternatively as the "legs of a divine women" or "brutal, thick arms," Neruda leads on to a vituperative tirade against the moral code which governs our everyday lives:

> Las gentes cruzan el mundo en la actualidad
> sin apenas recordar que poseen un cuerpo y en él la vida,
> y hay miedo, hay miedo en el mundo de las palabras que designan el cuerpo,
> y se habla favorablemente de la ropa,
> de pantalones es posible hablar, de trajes,
> y de ropa interior de mujer (de medias y ligas de "señora"),

> como si por las calles fuera las prendas y los trajes vacíos por completo
> y un oscuro y obsceno guardarropas ocupara el mundo.

The body is veiled in a repressive shroud; clothes take the place of the body. The presence of the body, through the mechanism of the superego which polices our thoughts and our language, is suppressed and turned into absence. In a mechanism typical of the displacement of the superego, it is then the clothes which take on the attributes of presence. The poem subsequently reveals that the point at which human culture is articulated is the point where the enemy of the poet's consciousness lies; it is to be found neither in the poet's legs nor in the earth beneath his feet, but somewhere in between, in his shoes, that is, within the cultural veil splitting body from world, those clothes and shoes which, as Chris Perriam has pointed out, are "classic images of nerudian weariness" (169):

> En mis pies cosquillosos,
> y duros como el sol, y abiertos como flores,
> y perpetuos, magníficos soldados
> en la guerra gris del silencio,
> todo termina, la vida termina definitivamente en mis pies,
> lo extranjero y lo hostil allí comienza:
> los nombres del mundo, lo fronterizo y lo remoto,
> lo sustantivo y lo adjetivo que no caben en mi corazón
> con densa y fría constancia allí se originan.

It is interesting that Neruda should include not only clothes, but also language, as his references to "the nouns of the world" implies. Here Neruda iconoclastically rejects a whole system of alliances/parallelisms underlying the Western tradition in which eloquence is associated with human clothing. As Cicero argued: "For just as clothes were first invented to protect us against cold and afterwards began to be used for the sake of adornment and dignity as well, so the metaphorical employment of words was begun because of poverty, but was brought into common use for the sake of entertainment" (Coleman 77).[12] Neruda deconstructs this ontological system, unriveting the bases on which it has been built. As the last stanza of the poem suggests, the enemy is human culture which, like the poet's shoes, stands between him and the world:

> Siempre,
> productos manufacturados, medias, zapatos,
> o simplemente aire infinito.
> Habrá entre mis pies y la tierra
> extremando lo aislado y lo solitario de mi ser,
> algo tenazmente supuesto entre mi vida y la tierra,
> algo abiertamente invencible y enemigo. (57-59)

In his attack upon human culture, its "manufactured products," its "stockings," "shoes" and even its abstractions such as "infinity," Neruda sought to unleash the repressed energies of the unconscious mind. In tearing off the clothes of culturality, Neruda unveiled the Adamic splendor of the human body. In a sense reduplicating Freudian knowledge, Neruda reveals how the urges of the body revolve around sexual desire and the death drive, *eros* and *thanatos*. Neruda's obsession with death as the deepest level of our being surfaces clearly in a poem such as "Sólo la muerte" which outlines, in macabre fashion, the death which is gnawing away at all of us from within:

> Pero la muerte va también por el mundo vestida de escoba,
> lame el suelo buscando difuntos,
> la muerte está en la escoba,
> es la lengua de la muerte buscando muertos,
> es la aguja de la muerte buscando hilo.
> La muerte está en los catres:
> en los colchones lentos, en las frazadas negras
> vive tendida, y de repente sopla:
> sopla un sonido oscuro que hincha sábanas,
> y hay camas navegando a un puerto
> en donde está esperando, vestido de almirante. (77)

Death takes one of its numerous chameleon disguises, as a broom, a tongue, a needle; in the last stanza, it is death which is carrying us on its bed to what seemed to be a safe haven, but in the port of call death is waiting for us, dressed as an admiral, in a way reminiscent of Quevedo's death poetry.[13] In other poems, death is not necessarily mentioned but is the force animating the things which surround the poet's consciousness. "Unidad," for example, opens with the description of a nameless force: "Hay algo denso, unido, sentado en el fondo, / repitiendo su número, su señal idéntica." Neruda explores this idea in the remainder of the first and the second stanzas. It is only in the third stanza that we learn implicitly that it is death which is creating life around us: "Trabajo sordamente, girando sobre mí mismo, como el cuervo sobre la muerte, el cuervo de luto" (17).

Sex plays a similar role to that of death in *Residencia en la tierra*. While suppressed by the superego it incessantly surfaces, its force seeking to destroy the edifice of culture. "Agua sexual" articulates the dynamics of this to and fro movement between cathexis and repression. The poem opens with a description of water moving, as yet untied to any specific person or chain of events:

> Rodando a goterones solos,
> a gotas como dientes,
> a espesos goterones de mermelada y sangre,
> rodando a goterones,
> cae el agua,
> como una espada en gotas,
> como un desgarrador río de vidrio,
> cae mordiendo,
> golpeando el eje de la simetría, pegando en las costuras del alma
> rompiendo cosas abandonadas, empapando lo oscuro.

The repetition of certain key words (such as "goterones" and "gotas") reveals the obsessive nature of the poet's thoughts. The use of the conjunctive "como," which in normal usage serves to elucidate a framework of comparison, here only adds to the indeterminacy of the referent.[14] The use of present participles, such as "rodando," "mordiendo," and "golpeando," itself a typical feature of *Residencia en la tierra*, serves to emphasize the flux-like qualities of sexual desire. Relevant too are its associations with violence (the sexual drive is like water with "teeth," it has the shape of a "sword" and is like a "river of glass"). In the second verse, when this rather abstract type of water is related to a concrete human situation, again the violence underlying the sexual drive is stressed:

> veo sangre, puñales y medias de mujer,
> y pelos de hombre,
> veo camas, veo corredores donde grita una virgen,
> veo frazadas y órganos y hoteles.

Neruda is fusing together the events of the unseen and unspoken scene, a virgin being deflowered in a hotel, but the reader's vision is only partial, based on glimpses. Even during expression, repression distorts, displaces, avoids. The final stanza of the poem alludes to the orgasm and the poet's half-grasped awareness of the creation of new life:

> Y aunque cierre los ojos y me cubra el corazón enteramente,
> veo caer un agua sorda,
> a goterones sordos.
> Es como un huracán de gelatina,
> como una catarata de espermas y medusas.
> Veo correr un arco iris turbio.
> Veo pasar sus aguas a través de los huesos. (105-07)

Neruda's revolution not only involved the questioning of moral codes and the defiance of social taboo, the desire to mention the unmentionable. It also included a radical deconstruction of the premises underlying our notions about language. The epistemological revolution Neruda is advocating in *Residencia en la tierra*, on a purely literary level, involved the deconstruction of Juan Ramón Jiménez's concept of "pure poetry," itself inherited from the French Symbolist poets, Stéphane Mallarmé and Paul Valéry.[15] Thus Neruda, in 1935, was promoting "poesía impura," that is, a type of poetry which is "gastada como por un ácido por los deberes de la mano, penetrada por el sudor y el humo, oliente a orina y azucena, salpicada por las diversas profesiones que se ejercen dentro y fuera de la ley" ("Sobre una poesía sin pureza").

Neruda's revolution was not only part of the divergence from his literary forebears which any strong poet must inititate; it also embodied a deconstruction of logocentrism. In "Establecimientos nocturnos," for example, Neruda pours scorn on two professions, opera singers and astronomers, as examples of a logocentric order placed over an existence which cannot be understood in logical terms:

> Oh Dios, cuántas ranas habituadas a la noche, silbando y roncando con gargantas de seres humanos a los cuarenta años, y qué angosta y sideral es la curva que hasta lo más lejos me rodea! Llorarían en mi caso los cantores italianos, los doctores de astronomía ceñidos por esta alba negra, definidos hasta el corazón por esta aguda espada. Y luego esa condensación, esa unidad de elementos de la noche, esa suposición, puesta detrás de cada cosa, y ese frío tan claramente sostenido por estrellas. (*Residencia* 53)

Neruda, in a bitterly sarcastic aside, remarks on how the logocentric gesture, by seeing unity where there is none, and placing suppositions behind things, will arrive at absurd hypotheses, such as the theory that the "cold" is "clearly sustained" by the stars. Metaphysics has been turned upside-down. Rather than seeing, or supposing there to be, a cause behind an effect, Neruda sees only absence and in effect reverses the metalepsia installed by the hermeneutic categories of logocentrism. Absence is indeed a word which turns up again and again in *Residencia en la tierra* and serves to illuminate the repetitive gesture of the obsessed mind:

> el tejido del día, su lienzo débil,
> sirve para una venda de enfermos, sirve para hacer señas
> en una despedida, detrás de la ausencia (16)

Other examples include the conclusion of "El joven monarca," in which Neruda dreams about getting married and remarks ironically: "acercada ya la noche, desencadenado su molino, escucho a mi tigre y lloro a mi ausente" (52). In dismantling the logocentric desire to see a cause preceding each effect, Neruda is simply left not with structure but chaos, not cause and effect, but rather an endless chain of self-effacing signifiers. Cause and effect become co-substantial rather than chronologically dependent. The effect becomes its own cause. In "Sistema sombrío," for example, the poet's days follow each other and substitute each other endlessly:

> mis rostros diferentes se arriman y encadenan
> como grandes flores pálidas y pesadas
> tenazmente substituidas y difuntas (43)

Self-substitution becomes almost a physical property of the universe; thus Neruda speaks of "el dios de la substitución" (47). By using the rather archaic form "substitución" rather than "sustituición" Neruda is reconstructing the etymological root of the word, throwing into focus how the substituted element is under ("sub") its physical appearance.

Turning from *Residencia en la tierra* to *Canto general* (1950) is at first to experience discontinuity between two opposing systems of thought. *Residencia*, as we have seen, expresses paranoid knowledge, refusing to see culture in its myriad manifestations as a second nature (put in Freudian terms, the ego refuses to accommodate to the reality principle). But *Canto general* seems to have changed into a new gear. Now there are no false starts; the engine of the world purrs contentedly. Like the "new art" espoused by Trotsky, *Canto general* is "realistic, active, vitally collectivist, and filled with a limitless creative faith in the future" (*Literature* 15).[16] It sings the genesis of the South American peoples. Like the Old Testament, it exudes a fascination with the genealogical along with the joy of new creation. The poet becomes the scribe of the limitless, unnamed reservoir of experience of the past: "Yo vengo a hablar por vuestra boca muerta / Acudid a mis venas y a mi boca. / Hablad por mis palabras y mi sangre" (*Canto* I, xii, 38-39). Neruda writes, or rather re-writes, the historical epic of the South American peoples not from the point of view of Columbus and his descendants who "discovered" South America. Instead Neruda writes his epic from a worm's-eye view, from the vantage point of the down-trodden Indians, the negro slaves, the working masses, the communists.

The structure of Neruda's epic lies not in its form, for it is consciously formless, thereby epitomizing what Lukács has called the epic mentality's "total indifference to any form of architectural construction" (67). Its structure devolves from the poet's fixed narratological focus. *Canto general* was not intended to be a false history as written by bourgeois scribes, but the discourse of the opposition. Some Spanish-American writers have felt the absence of a clear-cut literary tradition in Spanish America to be a consciously experienced lack. Others, such as Vargas Llosa, have felt it as a cause for jubilation, a pretext for a proliferation of discourses:

> La falta de una tradición cultural significa un vacío que es también suprema libertad. No sólo porque el "bárbaro," ese huérfano, puede saquear con igual comodidad todas las reservas culturas de la tierra (lo que el "civilizado" no puede hacer, limitado como está frente a las otras culturas por la visión que de ellas le impone la suya propia), sino, sobre todo, porque su condición adánica, de pionero, constituye un aliciente para su ambición: autoriza a ésta todos los excesos, el ímpetu y la audacia de la inocencia. (208)[17]

Yet Neruda veers away from discursive promiscuity, choosing to combine the Adamic discourse of the Old Testament with the progressivist historicism of Marxism. The fusion of these two discourses seems, *prima facie*, to have been achieved successfully, in order to bring about in *Canto general* a semantic sureness of step and a discourse which is the garantor of its own truth.

Despite its initial appearance of epistemological coherence, however, the garantor of its fixed ideology is based on a contradiction, that is, a truth which perpetually moves its own hermeneutical standards. In short, we are faced with one of those "flagrant discontinuities" to which Paul Julian Smith has pointed in Neruda's work. Smith has focused on the strategies employed in Neruda's *Odas elementales*, which tend to naturalize man "as universal subject of language and vision" (156) and thereby represent the female as a "passive object of this vital male force" (144). A similar contradiction occurs in other types of hermenetical oppositions that Neruda fabricates in his poetry, such as between conqueror/conquered, oppressor/oppressed, and Culture/Nature. With the possible exception of the first book of *Canto general*, the poetic discourse owes its origin to the foregrounding of the political struggle. In Book II, Neruda speaks against the Macchu Pichu monument in favor of the slaves who lost their lives during its construction, addressing the monument with the words: "devuélveme el esclavo que enterraste" (I, ii, 36), those nameless human beings entombed in the bowels of history whom Neruda later epistemologizes as Juan Cortepiedras, Juan Comefrío and Juan Piesdescalzos (I, ii, 37). A similar kind of opposition is set up in Book III, where Neruda becomes the unspoken brother of the Indians who perished at the hands of the Conquistadors:

> Entraron matando a caballo,
> cortaron la mano que daba
> el homenaje de oro y flores,
> cerraron la plaza, cansaron
> los brazos hasta agarrotarse,
> matando la flor del recuerdo,
> hundiendo hasta el codo en la sangre
> de mis hermanos sorprendidos. (I, ii, 49)

Book IV likewise sets up a clear juxtaposition between two powers, two knowledges, two discourses. On the one hand, we have the oppressors, and on the other, the liberators. The latter include Fray Bartolomé de las Casas, a priest who argued for a more humane treatment of the Indian slaves, the Indians who executed Pedro de Valdivia (a particularly hated Conquistador), Tupac Amaru (an Indian liberator), San Martín and Bolívar, who, inspired by the French Revolution, spearheaded the movement for Independence from the Spanish Crown in the colonies at the beginning of the nineteenth century, as well as Recabarren, who founded the Chilean Communist Party in the 1920s.[18] In setting up and then dramatizing a political conflict which, though with different *dramatis personae*, always enacts the same plot of oppressed destroying oppressor, Neruda often groups together people of very different political aims. It is not transparent, for example, that the Indians who executed Pedro de Valvivia in a particularly gruesome way would have been politically aligned with Fray Bartolomé de las Casas. Even less transparent is the link posited between San Martín and Bolívar, progressive nineteenth-century liberals, and Recabarren, a twentieth-century communist. This spoken historical scene (re)veils an unseen inner scene. In seeing the same drama enacted in the external space of history over and over again, Neruda is repeating a structure from his psychological life. If we return to the Freudian paradigm enunciated in the first half of this essay, it is feasible that this periodic rebellion against authority, what Lacan in another context called *le-nom-du-père*, can be assimilated with the violent impulses of the id.[19] By identifying his poetic *persona* with the successive eruptions of political violence in the history of Latin America, Neruda the poet seeks to cathect his own schizoid emotions. History becomes the palimpsestic manuscript in which he (re)reads the dynamics of repression within his own mind.

But the id is not, in this case, simply a voiceless, nameless reservoir of psychical energy. For, like the power called the Name-of-the-Father, this repressed discourse is able to speak out and name its oppressors. Just as he names Franco in his Spanish Civil War poetry as the enemy of the people, so Neruda names González Videla in his *Canto general*:

> Gabriel González Videla. Aquí dejo su nombre,
> para que cuando el tiempo haya borrado
> la ignominia, cuando mi patria limpie
> su rostro iluminado por el trigo y la nieve,
> más tarde, los que aquí busquen la herencia
> que en estas líneas dejo como una brasa verde
> hallen también el nombre del traidor que trajera
> la copa de agonía que rechazó mi pueblo.
> (I, iv, 202; see a similar idea in "Serán nombrados," II, xii, 138)

It is now that his ego has achieved fixity, through promoting communism as a guarantor of meaning, that the poet is able to name the enemy with confidence. In *Residencia en la tierra*, Neruda had expressed a poetic *persona* repressed and oppressed by Culture, a space which could not be harmonized with the desires of the id; his text therefore had no option but to express paranoid knowledge. By substituting his former vision of Culture as id-repressive with a notion of Culture as id-expressive, the poetic *persona* now is able to achieve harmonization between apparently antagonistic elements.

It is symptomatic of the idiosyncracy of Neruda's communism that its laws should be based on those of Nature. The land is identified so intimately with the proletariat that it bears the latter's name. Land and proletariat become characterized not by Otherness but Ipseity:

> Detrás de los libertadores estaba Juan
> trabajando, pescando y combatiendo,
> en su trabajo de carpintería o en su mina mojada.
> Sus manos han arado la tierra y han medido
> los caminos.
>   Sus huesos están en todas partes.
> Pero vive. Regresó de la tierra. Ha nacido.
> Ha nacido como una planta eterna.
> ("La tierra se llama Juan," II, viii, 60)

By re-inscribing Culture within Nature, Neruda is employing an organicist frame of reference which orthodox Marxist thinkers would reject as revisionist.[20] In identifying Marxist Culture with Nature, endowing it with the air of a "second nature" which is "eternal," Neruda, though (or perhaps because) he diverged from orthodox Marxist teleology, was able to harmonize contradictory discourses in a way which the early *persona* of *Residencia en la tierra* would scarcely have thought possible. And yet there are links between the apparently discontinuous cells of Neruda's pre- and post-political poetry. Whereas in *Residencia en la tierra* the enemy was human culture, in *Canto general* that enemy shifts political ground slightly in order to take up position as specifically "bourgeois" culture. Yet the desire to name the enemy through the written word, and thereby exorcise his power, remains constant.

Vicente Aleixandre and the "Other Scene"

An analysis of the interaction of psychoanalysis and literature in the Hispanic field would be incomplete without reference to Surrealism, the one twentieth-century movement which was indisputably inspired by the investigations of Sigmund Freud. André Breton, the founder of Surrealism, used Freud's psychoanalytic techniques to "cure" the medical patients he came into contact with as an Army Doctor during World War I (33-34).[21] He subsequently used psychoanalytical techniques such as free association and automatic writing as a scientific prop for the new literary movement he founded in 1924 with the publication of his *Premier manifeste du Surréalisme*.[22] The Surrealists' fascination with Freud's work was not reciprocated. Freud appears to have had no professional interest in the Surrealists. He met Breton in 1932 but nothing came of their meeting; he also later met Salvador Dalí but simply dismissed him as an eccentric.[23] Quite the opposite was the case with regard to the relationship between Lacan and the Surrealists. As a result of his thesis, entitled *Psychose paranoïaque dans ses rapports avec la personnalité* (1932), Lacan became something of a *cause célèbre* with the Parisian Surrealists. In 1933 he published two pieces in the Surrealist magazine *Le Minotaure*, one of which was on paranoia and accompanied a contribution by Salvador Dalí on the same subject (Turkle 68).[24] David Macey has argued that much of Lacan's innovative thinking runs parallel to the Surrealists' verbal experiments; in particular he cites Lacan's view of word-play as thought-constitutive rather than simply thought-reflective as having much in common with the Surrealists' word-games (44-74).[25] In one of his rare pronouncements on Surrealism, Lacan described the movement as "a tornado on the edge of atmospheric depression where the norms of humanist individualism founder," which suggests that he saw Surrealism as an epistemologically radical movement comparable to psychoanalysis (Macey 46).

A name which suggests itself automatically in a discussion of the interaction of psychoanalysis and literature in the Hispanic field is that of the Spanish poet Vicente Aleixandre. Aleixandre was one of the few poets of the 1927 Generation to read not only the French Surrealists but also Freud's work in Spanish translation. He read Freud's *The Interpretation of Dreams* in 1928, which left a lasting impression on him. As Lucie Personneaux suggests: "L'influence de Freud sur le poète s'est surtout exercée dans son acceptation du désir comme loi de toute vie" (193).[26] Along with Juan Larrea, Aleixandre has been seen by Vittorio Bodini as "il solo professionista del surrealismo, nel senso che mentre per gli altri poeti della Generazione del Ventisette il surrealismo fu un'esperienza limitata al giro di pochi anni o a un solo libro, per loro fu sostanza e condizione de loro mesaggio poetico" (lxxx-lxxxi). The impact of Surrealism is most pronounced in three of Aleixandre's poetic collections: *Pasión de la tierra* (1928-29), *Espadas como labios* (1930-31) and *La destrucción o el amor* (1932-33). Pedro Salinas hailed this latter work as a perfect embodiment of the Surrealist mode in Spanish literature (214-21).

It needs to be stressed at a preliminary stage that Aleixandre's poetry is radically different from the work of both César Vallejo and Pablo Neruda because of the apparent absence of any overt political ideology.[27] This can be explained geographically as reflecting the difference between the European mentality and the Spanish-American experience at that particular historical juncture. However, a distinction drawn on these lines works only up to a point. For there is no lack of "politicized" Spanish poets, as of non-politicized Spanish-American poets of the same period. What is intriguing about the case of Aleixandre is that his conversion to Freud's world-vision was so complete as to foreclose any other possible later conversions. Thus Aleixandre did not experience a political conversion as a result of the Spanish Civil War, as Neruda did, for example. In one of the few poems in which Aleixandre referred specifically to the Civil War, he did so in such a way that the personal dimension occludes the political level of the poem. In Aleixandre's poetry the political dimension is subsumed within the knot of antagonistic forces operating within the id. The Civil War becomes simply another link in the chain of endless destruction perpetrated by the death drive.[28]

In the following analysis I shall be arguing that psychoanalytical concepts inform in a fundamental sense the poetic expression of Aleixandre's Surrealist verse. The main focus of this section is provided by Lacan's notion of the "Other Scene," a realm whose contours Aleixandre's poetry is concerned to delineate. Aleixandre's work reveals a poetic subject in the act of unveiling a kingdom whose meaning he is ultimately blind to and over which he has little control. Despite the poet's lack of mastery over the "language of his dreams," or perhaps because of it, we are "seduced" by his text.

In his study *The Seductions of Psychoanalysis* (1990), John Forrester has argued that the psychoanalytic reading "must involve some crucial reference to the causal efficacy of sexuality" (263). As we shall see, this observation fits perfectly with Aleixandre's Surrealist poetry, in which the sexual drive is the over-riding motive behind poetic expression. Forrester further clarifies that reference to the "causal efficacy of sexuality" should not be restricted to the investigation by the critic of the "sexuality of characters met with in fiction." As he continues:

> it is not so much much that the text is the sexual object of the reader, though there is always a dimension of the pleasuring reader. Rather, it is the reader who is the sexual object of the text: quite simply, reading is being seduced by the text. (264)

We do not simply "overhear" the poet's thoughts, as one critic would have it, as if we were innocent bystanders.[29] Rather, the thoughts are directed to us; we are seduced by the poet's words. But how, we might ask, does this process come about? Through transference. As Forrester suggests, reading is akin to the process of transference in the psychoanalytic situation:

> when the subject in analysis addresses the analyst directly with a demand or a desire, that demand or desire not only specifies the fantasy as it coalesces around the figure of the analyst, but also specifies a position of the subject in that fantasy. Transference constitutes the scene of desire in which the patient has already been seduced. (265)

Here "transference" is to be understood in the Freudian technical sense of the phenomenon which occurs in analysis whereby thoughts and feelings which are associated with a forgotten event in the past are transferred to the present and crystallize around the person of the analyst ("Observations" 159-71). As readers we are implicated in a similar way in Aleixandre's fantasies, allowing ourselves to become the space in which these desires are staged.

The process of transference whereby the reader is transformed into a space around which the textual fantasies coalesce must be seen as a secondary process, since it is dependent on a primary transference whereby the poetic subject projects his libido into a universe of words which masquerades as the world of nature. The reader/text transferential relationship is thus predicated on the poetic self/world interface. But before discussing how the reader is "drawn" into the text, let us analyze the mechanism whereby the poetic subject transfers a demand or a desire to the phenomenal world. The most typical example of this technique in Aleixandre's verse is the image of the sea, which invariably operates as a projection of the unconscious mind. As Kessel Schwartz, for example, has pointed out, "an examination of the sea symbolism in Aleixandre's poetry reveals the neurotic motivation behind and preoccupation with the equation that love equals death" (*Vicente Aleixandre* 46).[30] It is not always the case in Aleixandre's poetry, however, that the Freudian parallel *eros-thanatos* appears in the context of sea symbolism. In the poem "Muerte," for example, love and death appear interlocked, but sea imagery is absent:

> He acudido. Dos clavos están solos
> punta a punta. Caricia, yo te amo.
> Bajo tierra los besos no esperados,
> ese silencio que es carbón, no llama. (*Espadas* 223)

Typically, however, the twin expressions of the id *are* accompanied by images of fluidity in Aleixandre's poetry. One of the most transparent examples of this tendency is to be found in "Unidad en ella":

> Quiero amor o la muerte, quiero morir del todo,
> quiero ser tú, tu sangre, esa lava sangriente

>   que regando encerrada bellos miembros extremos
>   siente así los hermosos límites de la vida. (*La destrucción* 308)

What is intriguing about Aleixandre's poem is how it presents the id as accepting, and even rejoicing in, the limits of life, described as "hermosos." Aleixandre's poem thus seems to fly in the face of traditional Freudian knowledge, which emphasizes how the id seeks cathexis at any cost. In Aleixandre's poem the containment of the lover's blood within her body is a cause for rejoicing. Notice how Aleixandre's imagery echoes that of Lorca, in whose plays, as we have seen in Chapter I, blood acts as a metaphor of the id. Unlike in Lorca's work, however, where blood is depicted as an unstoppable force, Aleixandre revels in the beauty of containment. As the final verse of this poem suggests:

>   Este beso en tus labios como una lenta espina,
>   como un mar que voló hecho un espejo,
>   como el brillo de un ala,
>   es todavía unas manos, un repasar de tu crujiente pelo,
>   un crepitar de la luz vengadora,
>   luz o espada mortal que sobre mi cuello amenaza,
>   pero que nunca podrá destruir la unidad de este mundo. (308)

In what seems at first to be a highly essentialist gesture, Aleixandre concludes his poem on a note of unity ("la unidad de este mundo"). This unity, however, masks an ambivalent, dynamic reality; as Hernán Galilea has pointed out, Aleixandre's poetic universe is "simultáneamente atraído y rechazado entre el ser y el no-ser" (72). It is significant that the poem suggests how the unity underlying the sea is achieved via its transformation into a mirror ("como un mar que voló hecho un espejo"). The mirror functions here, as in Lacan's work, as a sign of the unity of identity. The image of the mirror often appears, for example, in Aleixandre's work when the unity of self and world, or of self and love, is actualized verbally within the poem. In Lacan's work, however, the mirror, and in particular the mirror stage, functions as a pointer towards the spurious creation of identity through language (the "ego" rather than the "subject").[31] Also relevant to this discussion is the Freudian substratum of Lacan's insight. As Forrester has pointed out, Lacan's theory of the mirror stage is "linked closely to Freud's concept of narcissism and to the notion that both the ego and love are fundamentally narcissistic in character" (110). Aleixandre's poem "Unidad en ella" reveals that the moment of transcendence desired by the poetic subject is that point of union at which the sea turns into a mirror, and at which, we might gloss, the poetic subject is caught at the mirror stage. Rather than describing the evolution of the self passing through the mirror stage into the Symbolic Order, Aleixandre catches the ego before the transformation of identity takes place. This limbo realm in which the poetic subject is transfixed lies between the fluidity of the id (the sea) and the solidity of the ego (the mirror). Its main characteristics are silence (since it is quintessentially pre-Oedipal) and narcissism.

We meet with a similar exploitation of this motif in "El aire ligero":

El mar bate sólo como un espejo,
como una ilusión de aire,
ese cristal vertical donde la sequedad del desierto
finge un agua o un rumor de espadas persiguiéndose.

El mar, encerrado en un dado,
desencadena su furia o gota prisionera,
corazón cuyos bordes inundarían al mundo
y sólo pueden contraerse con su sonrisa o límite. (*La destrucción* 309)

The first of these two stanzas employs the opposite terms of sea and mirror to actualize the dialectical forces striving to shape the identity of the ego. The notion that the sea is like a mirror is referred to as "una ilusión de aire," which is an ambiguous grammatical phrase since the object of the genitive possessive "de" is not specified. One way to interpret this phrase is to view it as referring to the desire experienced by the sea to break out of its liquid identity and enter another dimension of matter, which is, in this case, air. The third and fourth lines of the same stanza are an apt illustration of how objects metamorphose with alarming rapidity in Aleixandre's poetic universe. The air is now likened to "vertical crystal" (or "glass"), which is then transformed into a dry desert, which in turn gives way to an image of water or the "sound of swords chasing one other." Both of these latter images are references to the id. Water is universally acknowledged by Aleixandre's critics to be a projection of the id (and, in particular, see Schwartz's reference above, p. 109); the second image is tantalizing. On a literalist level the "espadas" can be read as phallic symbols; but more intriguing is the force of the reflexive verb "persiguiéndose," which underlines the narcissism which structures the id's desires.

The second of the quoted stanzas returns to the same dialectical metamorphosis. It extends the basic premise of the first stanza, while further exploring the id's status as alternating between cathexis ("desencadena," "gota," "inundarían," "sonrisa") and containment ("encerrado," "prisionera," "bordes," "límite"). By juxtaposing the two stanzas we recognize an intrinsic feature of Aleixandre's poetic manner, namely, his use of accumulation, redefinition and the repetition of binary oppositions, all of which give a sense of the flow of the poetic discourse. A key image in this particular stanza is "el mar, encerrado en un dado," which suggests once more how the poetic subject is determined to create a poetic universe which lies in limbo between the sea of the Unconscious and the land of the Conscious mind, and perhaps best defined as the line of the tide which is neither one nor the other.

We find an illuminating reference to this limbo region poised delicately between the two realms in two poems from *La destrucción o el amor*, "Orillas del mar" and "Quiero saber." The first of these poems opens with a scene which we readily recognize as central to the setting of many of Aleixandre's poems, the sea-scape:

> Después de todo lo mismo da el color que el frío,
> una dulce hormiguita color naranja,
> una guitarra muda en la noche,
> una mujer tendida como las conchas,
> un mar como dos labios por la arena.

The first line of the stanza begins with the premise that all is one and that contraries have merged, a technique of suggestion which is common in many of Aleixandre's poems. It is in the last two lines of the stanza that we realize the motive behind the poet's desire to fuse opposites; it springs from the wish to actualize the Other Scene of the Unconscious within the visible world, to see the "woman" lying within the shells on the beach (one is inevitably reminded of Botticelli's *Birth of Venus*) and "two lips" contained within the sea. The poetic device Aleixandre uses here is similar to Dalí's formula of paranoia-criticism which involves employing the image of an object which "without the least figurative or anatomical modification can at the same time represent another, absolutely different object" (Wilson 18).[32] The two lips can be interpreted as the "two lips" of one person or the "lips" of two people. Given the explanatory reference to "por la arena," it is likely that Aleixandre intends the reader to read this image as alluding to the (elusive) "kiss" of the sea and the sand. This "kiss" within the world of nature is one which Aleixandre returns to obsessively in his poetry of this period, almost as if he saw it as an embodiment of the unseen "primary scene" (of which, more later). An important feature of this "kiss" is its transient, ungraspable nature. For if we picture in our minds the tide moving up and down the beach, we find it difficult to conceptualize the "kiss" as occurring within the movement of the waves. The most striking visual image associated is that of the dividing line between the water's edge and the sand. Rather than a sense of the unproblematic union between two elements, implying an experience of "misticismo panteísta," as one critic has it (Bousoño 38), we are left with an image of the dividing line between the two elements, a line which is elusive to the point of non-existence. A similar notion of the dividing line between elements occurs in a later image of the poem which alludes to "Tu corazón redondo como naipe / visto de perfil es un espejo" (*La destrucción* 333), in which it is the profile of the object which governs its identity.

This hermeneutical dilemma reoccurs with some urgency in "Quiero saber." The poem opens with an investigation into identity which then leads to a reflection about the laws governing the separation of elements in the phenomenal world:

> Dime pronto el secreto de tu existencia;
> quiero saber por qué la piedra no es pluma,
> ni el corazón un árbol delicado,
> ni por qué esa niña que muere entre dos venas ríos
> no se va hacia la mar como todos los buques.
>
> Quiero saber si el corazón es una lluvia o margen,
> lo que se queda a un lado cuando dos se sonríen,

> o es sólo la frontera entre dos manos nuevas
> que estrechan una piel caliente que no separa. (335)

The crux of the dilemma for the poetic self is epitomized in the question as to whether the heart "es una lluvia o margen". This could be re-expressed as whether the seat of human emotion is able to achieve expression ("rain" being an image of liquidity denoting cathexis in Aleixandre's poetry), or whether it is intrinsically incapable of achieving satisfaction and therefore doomed to being caught at the frontiers of expression. In the following stanza the image of the "frontier" is linked specifically to poetic expression:

> Flor, risco o duda, o sed o sol o látigo:
> el mundo todo es uno, la ribera y el párpado,
> ese amarillo pájaro que duerme entre dos labios
> cuando el alba penetra con esfuerzo en el día. (336)

The imagery of the stanza suggests that a parallel is being drawn between the riverbank (which separates the river from the land and therefore operates as a symbol of the dividing line between the Unconscious mind and Consciousness), the eyelid (which separates the eye from its vision of the world), and lips (which stand between the poet's song, the "yellow bird," and the phenomenal world). The river bank, the eyelid and the lips all operate as symbols of liminality and point once more to an underlying theme of Aleixandre's verse, namely, the (paranoiac) desire to capture within words the elusive limbo realm which lies between the fluidity of the id (the sea) and the solidity of the ego (the mirror).

It will be clear from the reference in the above stanza to the poet's verse as "ese amarillo pájaro" that language plays a crucial role in Aleixandre's poetry. Thus in the process whereby the self is caught at the mirror stage, language unavoidably has a constitutive rather than merely a descriptive function for, as Lacan has suggested, an essential function of entry into the Symbolic Order is played by language acquisition. In Aleixandre's poetry, it is language which becomes the mirror before which, like Medusa, the poetic subject is entranced.

In a number of Aleixandre's poems language appears to play a conventional role. In the opening poem of *Espadas como labios*, for example, entitled "Mi voz," Aleixandre expresses the desire (that few poets have not at one time shared) of speaking the same language as the phenomenal world. As the poem concludes:

> Entonces son posibles ya las luces, las caricias, la piel, el horizonte,
> ese decir palabras sin sentido
> que ruedan como oídos, caracoles,
> como un lóbulo abierto que amanece
> (escucha, escucha) entre la luz pisada. (219)

But appearances can be deceptive. In the same poem Aleixandre refers to the writing of poetry in terms of birth (which is conventional enough), but then specifies, interestingly enough, that the birth occurred between "two pauses": "He nacido una noche de verano / entre dos pausas." Poetic identity is thereby defined by its liminality, a feature which, as we have seen, is constant in Aleixandre's verse and gives it a conceptual depth. Occasionally Aleixandre comes close to echoing Lacan's vision of the Unconscious as "structured like a language." Particularly striking is the opening stanza of "El más bello amor":

> Anteayer distante.
> Un día muy remoto
> me encontré con el vidrio nunca visto,
> con una mariposa de lengua,
> con esa vibración escapada de donde estaba bien sujeta. (243)

All of the images in this stanza suggest how the sensation of love, which the poem goes on to describe, is remote from the conscious mind. It is temporally distant ("un día muy remoto"), invisible ("nunca visto") and inexpressible (it makes the tongue vibrate as if it were a butterfly). The final line of the stanza explores the ramifications of this latter idea and seeks to conjure up the Other Scene of the unconscious mind from which this vibration emanates ("esa vibración escapada de donde estaba bien sujeta"). Though once trapped within the Unconscious, the knowledge of the id has now emerged in the poet's voice, albeit fleetingly (the butterfly being an archetypal image of transience).[33] Language is thus a route to the Unconscious. As one poem has it, "la palabra, esa arena machacada" (260), namely, the realm of the conscious through which the Other Scene can speak. In the opening poem of *El amor o la destrucción*, "La selva y el mar," Aleixandre reveals the antagonistic relationship between the poet, here imaged as the bird, and the Unconscious, which appears in its usual guise as the sea:

> Pájaro de la dicha,
> azul pájaro o pluma,
> sobre un sordo rumor de fieras solitarias,
> del amor o castigo contra los troncos estériles,
> frente al mar remotísimo que como la luz se retira. (300)

Again the Unconscious is presented as a remote region; here it is fading from view. The Other Scene is never fully visible. We know of its existence through its traces. "Cuerpo de piedra" concludes on a similar image, this time associated with the traces of love left on the body: "no, ya no quema el fuego que en las ingles / aquel remoto mar dejó al marcharse" (394). At times language gives way to silence, as in the poem "Silencio" which describes "El paisaje es la risa. Dos cinturas amándose. / Los árboles en sombra segregan voz. Silencio" (*Espadas* 227). The authentic language of the Unconscious, Aleixandre's poem suggests, is silence.

As we can see, a primordial characteristic of the Other Scene is its remoteness. One other important feature is its spatial elusiveness, for it simultaneously inhabits a number of different spaces, such as a space beyond the horizon, as we have already seen, as well as a limbo realm after death and, most importantly of all, the inner scene of the body. In a number of poems, Aleixandre Freudianizes the Christian concept of an afterlife. His poem "Después de la muerte," for example, presents a world after death which, in its fusion of love and death, is clearly modelled on Freud's vision of the Unconscious:

> La realidad que vive
> en el fondo de un beso dormido,
> donde las mariposas no se atreven a volar
> por no mover el aire tan quieto como el amor. (*La destrucción* 303)

But the best example of this theme is the masterful poem from *Pasión de la tierra*, "La muerte o antesala de consulta," which manages to bring together the naturalistic scene of a doctor's waiting room with entry into the afterlife, as well as entry into the Other Scene of the Unconscious. As this poem concludes:

> La puerta, presta a abrirse, se teñía de amarillo lóbrego lamentándose de su torpeza. Dónde encontrarte, oh sentido de la vida, si ya no hay tiempo. Todos los seres esperaban la voz de Jehová refulgente de metal blanco. Los amantes se besaban sobre los nombres. Los pañuelos eran narcóticos y restañaban la carne exangüe. Las siete y diez. La puerta volaba sin plumas y el ángel del Señor anunció a María. Puede pasar el primero. (154)

The beauty of this poem is that it leads the reader to the point at which she is about to go through the door, but then stops at the threshold. The Other Scene remains undescribed because undescribable.

An intrinsic feature of the Other Scene is the confusion of inner and outer worlds, which in turn echoes the fusion of the conscious and unconscious realms (itself often imaged, as we have noted, as the union of the land and sea). A good example of this occurs in "Poema de amor," in which the poet delineates a utopian universe contained within the space of the body:

> yo me muevo y, si giro, me busco, oh centro, oh centro,
> camino, viajadores del mundo, del futuro existente
> más allá de los mares, en mis pulsos que laten. (*Espadas* 246)

This sense of a utopian world within "mis pulsos que laten" is explored in other poems, mainly by means of a comparison between the fluidity of the sea and that of human blood. This leads to some typically Surrealist images, such as the description of how small red fish are circulating, like corpuscles, in the bloodstream:

> Quizás por la garganta del cuerpo juvenil
> los rojos pececillos circulan,

> se extinguen,
> los besos son burbujas,
> son ese gris que falla en el fondo de la copa
> cuando alguien intenta acercarle los labios;
> son ese ojo profundo sin párpado que en el fondo
> demuestra con su fijeza que nunca ha de acabarse. (*La destrucción* 327)

Like Freud, Aleixandre evidently sees the force of the id as indestructible ("nunca ha de acabarse"). We find a similar telescopic vision of the inner world of the body in "Quiero pisar," which alludes at one stage to "ese pecho de ámbar por cuya agua íntima pececillos transcurren" (383).

It will be clear from the preceding discussion that Aleixandre's poetry is concerned with unveiling the Other Scene of the unconscious mind. The favorite trope employed to express this Other Scene is the sexual act, which is depicted as played out within the body of Nature. Nearly every poem of Aleixandre's Surrealist phase refers at some point to sexual penetration, which is normally presented in a displaced manner as occurring in the natural world, such as when tree roots penetrate the earth ("La selva y el mar," *La destrucción* 299), or the moon opens up like a body ("Verbena," 378) or, most common of all, the sea and the beach unite in foam, with which male issue has a visual similarity ("Resaca," *Espadas* 242). As readers, we are thus privy to the spectacle of love which, though expressed in displaced images, remains tied to its personal, private origins. The reader is thereby cast in the position of voyeur. And a question will inevitably be posed: put crudely, why is the poet telling us these things, why is he revealing these thoughts to us? One way of answering this question is to refer perhaps to the poetic conventions which provide a sheen of acceptability to the poet's sexual revelations. But this would not be enough to explain why the poetic subject needs to repeat the "unveiling" process. To say the secret once is enough; to reiterate it in various guises in successive poems shows an obsession with the act of revelation rather than with the secret itself. Judging by the poet's obsessiveness, it is likely that each of the poems, thus, can be seen as a stage on which the primal scene is being acted out, in a way reminiscent of the mind of the neurotic.[34] The reference here to a primal scene is not meant to be understood in a literalist sense as specifically implying mysterious goings on in the parental bed. The primal scene as represented in Aleixandre's verse is concerned as much with textuality as sexuality; it can be seen as relating simultaneously to the birth of meaning within the poem, to which the poet returns obsessively.[35] Aleixandre's Surrealist poetry, thus, repeats this hermeneutical gesture and thereby recreates the pleasure of sexual union in words. The ultimate aim of the word for Aleixandre is to "know" the body of language, to be understood as much in a biblical as a Lacanian sense.

Aleixandre's conversion to the Freudian world vision led him to marginalize the validity of Marxism, unlike Vallejo and Neruda who, as we have already noted in this chapter, embraced the value of political revolution in the 1920s and 1930s respectively. Aleixandre shares, however, with both Latin-American poets an obsessiveness which borders on neurosis. But while the neurosis expressed by Vallejo and Neruda was fixated on culture, Aleixandre's neurosis sprang from a desire to capture the poetic self in a liminal zone on the threshold of the Unconscious.

NOTES

1. In a sensible article, "En los orígenes de *Trilce*: Vallejo entre modernismo y vanguardia," Paoli argues against giving too much importance to biographical material.
2. For further discussion of the role of religion in Vallejo's work, see Hart, *Religión política y ciencia en la obra de César Vallejo*.
3. For further discussion of the role of archaisms in Vallejo's poetry, see Hart, "El arcaísmo y la motivación etimológica en *Trilce* de César Vallejo."
4. The emptiness of the house as an image of existential Lack is common in Vallejo's poetry; see, for example, Tr. LXI and "No vive ya nadie . . ." For a dicussion of images of emptiness in Vallejo's poetry, see Ferrari 35-38.
5. For other examples of upside-down images in Vallejo's work, see Hart, "The World Upside-Down in the Work of César Vallejo," and Paoli, "El lenguaje conceptista de César Vallejo."
6. In "Himno a los voluntarios de la República," the Nationalist forces are accused of destroying books, language and even auxiliary verbs: "Matan al libro, tiran a sus verbos auxiliares, / a su indefensa página primera!" (285). As Franco comments on this passage: "By throwing out the 'auxiliary' verbs, the Fascists destroy a part of the sentence which has no function in isolation but without which no sense is possible. Perhaps we might read this as a reference to the individual, to the 'defenceless first page' who can neither exist alone nor be dispensed with" (*César Vallejo* 237).
7. In a penetrating study of Neruda's memoirs, Labanyi shows how Neruda projects a public self which is a "mask designed to hide one's inner contradictions." She also argues that Neruda "shows no awareness of the fact that he has cast himself in the role of a performer: a mask ('persona') incapable of contradiction or change" (212).
8. As Freud goes on to point out, "a person who has harboured frequent evil wishes against others, but has been brought up to be good and has therefore repressed such wishes into the unconscious, will be especially ready to expect punishment for his unconscious wickedness in the form of trouble threatening him from without" (*Psychopathology* 260). The poetic *persona* delineated in *Residencia en la tierra* seems to operate on a similar basis of "conscious ignorance" and "unconscious knowledge."
9. As Freud argues, a dangerous instinctual impulse once repressed becomes an "outlaw," expelled from the ego. If the danger situation changes, the "new impulse will run its course under an automatic influence or, as I should prefer to say, under the compulsion to repeat." As Freud further suggests, the "fixating factor in repression" is "the unconscious id's compulsion to repeat" ("Inhibitions" 153).
10. Letter written from Rangoon to Héctor Eandi, 24 April 1929.
11. As Buñuel pointed out to Francisco Aranda, "our Surrealism was fighting against 'Culture' " (Aranda 46).
12. Coleman cites other examples of the association in the classical mind between rhetoric, ornament and clothes.
13. For further discussion of this theme, see Loyola 101-23; see also Hart, "Quevedo, Góngora y su vigencia en la poesía contemporánea."

14. For further discussion of the use of conjunctives in this way, see Hart, " 'Galope muerto' Revisited"; see also Lozada 213-22.

15. On this topic see Gullón.

16. For discussion of Neruda's political conversion, see Rodríguez Fernández.

17. As Borges also suggested, "nuestra tradición es toda la cultura occidental," in "El escritor argentino y la tradición" (160).

18. For a succint description of the historical backdrop see Pendle.

19. *Le nom-du-père*, as Lacan understood the term, not only covered the province of what Freud understood by the term "superego" and its associations with religious, societal and parental authority (the *No* of the father), but also the power of language transmitted from generation to generation in the form of the family name (the *Name* of the father) (*Écrits. A Selection* 199 and chapter II, note 14).

20. See Eagleton's critique of George Eliot's "nostalgic organicism" (110-25). For further discussion of the use of images of nature in *Canto general*, see Reiss and Villegas.

21. For interesting feedback about Surrealism from the medical field, see Breton 71-75.

22. Breton's definition of Surrealism as "la croyance à la réalité supérieure de certaines formes d'association négligées jusqu'à lui [i.e., Surrealism], à la toute-puissance du rêve, au jeu désintéressé de la pensée" (37-38), for example, was clearly adopted from Freud's own observations about the Unconscious.

23. Dalí and Freud met in 1938, and Freud is said to have remarked of the Catalan painter, "What a fanatic!" (Parinaud 120-21). Dalí made a quick sketch of Freud on a piece of blotting paper (Wilson xxv, 183 and 184).

24. Schneiderman lists Dalí as one of Lacan's closest friends (vi).

25. As Macey concludes, Lacan "is not influenced by Surrealism, as though it were some external factor impinging upon his subjectivity; his writing is part of the same web" (74).

26. Freud's works were published in Spanish translation by the Biblioteca Nueva between 1923 and 1934, following the suggestion of José Ortega y Gasset. Aleixandre began reading Freud from 1928 onwards. In an interview given in 1960 Aleixandre stated that without the impression of Freud, *Pasión de la tierra* "would not have taken the form which it took, although I was not then aware of it" (Schwartz, *Vicente Aleixandre* 48). For a general discussion of the impact of Surrealism in Spain, see Morris and Bodini. As the Catalan poet J.V. Foix suggested in *Sol, i de dol* (1936), "Del son, grosser, ja en parla Sigmund Freud; / Tots som el pacient número u / I un llavi destenyit no és tabú" (Morris 36).

27. Molho, however, notes some stylistic similarities between Aleixandre's work and Neruda's pre-political verse, especially his *Residencia en la tierra* (143).

28. See Hart, "War Within a War: Poetry and the Spanish Civil War," esp. 112-14. For a lucid discussion of poetry and politics in Latin America, and in particular Nicaragua, see Beverley 123-51.

29. Frye argues, for example, that "the lyric is preeminently the utterance that is overheard. The lyric poet normally pretends to be talking to himself or to someone else" (249).

30. Schwartz has also related Aleixandre's early poetry to the psychoanalytic theory of Otto Isakower ("The Isakower Phenomenon").

31. In his essay "The mirror stage as formative of the function of the I as revealed in psychoanalytical experience" (1949), Lacan described mirror stage identification as a stage in the psychical development of the child between six and eighteen months of age which permanently situates the human subject in a line of alienation. Whereas infants of the pre-mirror stage experience their body and their surroundings in terms

of fragmentation, the infant during the mirror stage (6-18 months) is able to recognize his own image in the mirror, thereby establishing a feeling of unity and fixity. As Ellie Ragland-Sullivan points out, such unity is, however, "imposed from without and consequently is asymmetrical, fictional, and artificial. Lacan explodes the supposed 'unity' of the neo-Freudian ego as a tenuous illusion. His mirror stage must, therefore, be understood as a metaphor for the vision of harmony of a subject essentially in discord" (26-27).

32. For a good discussion of the image in Aleixandre's work, see Personneaux 137-47.

33. Juan Ramón Jiménez, in his poem "Mariposa de luz," uses the butterfly like Aleixandre to symbolize the elusiveness of poetic expression (163). See also a similar use of this image in Lorca's "Vuelta de paseo," discussed above, p. 29.

34. del Amo discusses the parallels between the neurotic and the artist in his study *Literatura y neurosis*; see esp. 11-31.

35. Ilie has pointed, in a similar vein, to the ways in which love and the writing of poetry are associated in Aleixandre's work.

CONCLUSION

In this study an attempt has been made to analyze the inter-penetration between psychoanalytical knowledge and a selection of hispanic texts. Though the texts have been drawn from different genres—the time-honored trinity of drama, novel and poetry—it has been possible to identify the continuing presence of specific concepts, such as the Unconscious, the castration-complex, and the "Family Romance," which inform the form-giving intention in works which, if analyzed from a structural point of view, seem opposed rather than related. Certain themes have naturally enough predominated in certain chapters. Chapter I, which focused on drama, attempted to trace the coincidence between specific dramatic masterpieces (plays written by the Spanish Romantics, García Lorca and Carlos Fuentes) and Freudian notions such as the "Family Romance," primary and secondary repression, and others borrowed from Lacan's writings, such as the Other. Chapters II and III, which concentrated on the novel in its masculine and feminine forms, strove to analyze the interface between psychoanalytic notions such as castration, the Oedipal Complex and the Unconscious and a selection of twentieth-century novels ranging from Martín-Santos's *Tiempo de silencio* to Castellanos's *Oficio de tinieblas*. Chapter IV employed the concept of neurosis to offer a psychoanalytic reading of the work of three major twentieth-century poets: César Vallejo, Pablo Neruda and Vicente Aleixandre. While Vallejo and Neruda transformed their neuroses and produced a vision of a utopian culture, Aleixandre, especially in his Surrealist writings, sought to regress to a pre-cultural space on the borders of the unconscious mind.

In quite unexpected ways, these psychoanalytic readings have drawn attention to coincidences of world-vision and of technique in the work of writers who are not normally seen as related. Martín-Santos's *Tiempo de silencio* seems at the furthest remove from Lorca's *La casa de Bernarda Alba*, and yet both works, though opposed as far as genre is concerned, probe the paradoxical complementarity existing between castration and creativity. Rulfo's *Pedro Páramo* investigates the mysterious power attaching to the father figure in a way which is curiously similar to the father-fixation evident in Spanish Romantic drama. It can, of course, always be argued that to privilege the role of concepts such as castration, the Name-of-the-Father, and their like in the work of these authors is to do so at the expense of other possible readings. This I would of course accept; yet, as Harold Bloom has pointed out, anyone who has not misread a text has not read it either. As Stuart Schneiderman confirms: "Anyone who has not entered into a dialogue with a text, who has not asked it questions and listened to its answers, not attempted to find within it even better answers, not selected some parts for special emphasis while omitting consideration of others, anyone who has not done this has not read the text" (31-32).

And yet the task of criticism—asking the text questions and listening to its answers, as Schneider puts it—is a morbid preoccupation, for texts are dead creatures and authors rarely alive (in the sense that the text is always something already written, already past, already dead). Like the dead, texts are silent. Criticism is thus a type of halfway house between the dead and the living. It is indeed not fortuitous that death fulfills a creative function in the work of many of the authors analyzed in this study. The death of the Romantic hero, Adela's suicide in Lorca's play, Pedro Páramo's ever-recurring death, the death of the Colonel in Valenzuela's short story—all are needed before the text can be staged or represented before our eyes. César Vallejo's mother needed to pass away before her voice could pass into her son's text. The presence of death in these works is not simply a well-rehearsed theme; it articulates the text, gives it birth. It is through the rites of passage provided by criticism that the death of literature is able to speak to the subject. Death can finally (re)veil its secret.

What is the text's secret, we may well ask? In one sense, to know the secret of the text spells death for the subject, since it is a knowledge based on a theft. Lacan has argued that Freud's discovery of the other scene of the unconscious was like Prometheus's act of stealing from the Gods. As Schneiderman suggests:

> Relations between the living and the dead never take place in an atmosphere of communication leading to interpersonal and mutual understanding. In place of this humanistic model for therapy, Lacan proposed one based on the elements of theft and sacrifice. Prometheus is the most striking example of this for his stealing of fire from the gods or the immortals. And he does this through the exercise of cunning, of his wits. The gods, however, must have some recompense, for man has through an act placed himself in debt to them. Thus man offers sacrifice that the dead may either accept or reject. (60-61)

Literary criticism, to misread Scheiderman's argument, is simultaneously a theft from and an offering to the text. It steals the knowledge of the text in order to pay back its debt in kind, namely, with different coinage, with other words. It is a debt, however, which, like Prometheus's, can never be repaid in full.

WORKS CONSULTED

Abrams, Fred. "The Death of Zorrilla's Don Juan and the Problem of Catholic Orthodoxy." *Romance Notes* 6 (1964): 42-46.

Aguirre, J.M. "Apostillas a 'El sonambulismo de Federico García Lorca.'" *Bulletin of Hispanic Studies* 53 (1976): 127-32.

Ahern, Maureen and Mary Seale Vásquez, eds. *Homenaje a Rosario Castellanos*. Valencia: Albatros, 1980.

Aleixandre, Vicente. *La destrucción o el amor. Poesías completas de Vicente Aleixandre*. Madrid: Aguilar, 1960.

———. *Espadas como labios. Poesías completas de Vicente Aleixandre*. Madrid: Aguilar, 1960.

———. *Pasión de la tierra. Poesías completas de Vicente Aleixandre*. Madrid: Aguilar, 1960.

d'Ambrosio Servodidio, Mirella. "A Case of Pre-Oedipal and Narrative Fixation: *El mismo mar de todos los veranos*." *Anales de la Literatura Española Contemporánea* 12 (1987): 157-74.

———. "Perverse Pairings and Corrupted Codes: *El amor es un juego solitario*." *Anales de la Literatura Española Contemporánea* 11 (1986): 237-54.

Andermatt Conley, Verena. *Hélène Cixous: Writing the Feminine*. Nebraska: University of Nebraska, 1984.

Anderson, C.L. "Mueca's Consort: The Great Mother Archetype in *Tiempo de silencio*." *Revista Canadiense de Estudios Hispánicos* 12 (1988): 287-95.

Andioc, René. "Sobre el estreno del *Don Álvaro*." *Homenaje a Juan López-Morrillas*. Ed. José Amor y Vázquez and A. David Kossoff. Madrid: Castalia, 1982. 63-86.

Aranda, Francisco. *Luis Buñuel: A Critical Biography*. Trans. David Robinson. London: Secker and Warburg, 1975.

Aristotle. *Classical Literary Criticism*. Trans. T.S. Dorsch. Harmondsworth: Penguin, 1965.

Auerbach, Nina. *Communities of Women: An Idea in Fiction*. Cambridge, Massachusetts: Harvard University Press, 1978.

Babcock, Barbara A. *The Reversible World: Symbolic Inversion in Art and Society*. Ithaca, New York: Cornell University Press, 1978.

Barthes, Roland. *S/Z*. Paris: Seuil, 1970.

Bazán, Armando. *César Vallejo: dolor y poesía*. Buenos Aires: Ediciones de la Biblioteca Universitaria, 1958.

Bellver, Catherine. "The Language of Eroticism in the Novels of Esther Tusquets." *Anales de la Literatura Española Contemporánea* 9 (1984): 13-27.

Benvenuto, Bice and Roger Kennedy. *Jacques Lacan: an Introduction*. London: Free Association Books, 1986.

Benjamin, Jessica. "A Desire of One's Own: Psychoanalytical Feminism and Intersubjective Space." *Feminist Studies/Critical Studies*. Ed. Teresa de Lauretis. London: Macmillan, 1988. 78-101.

Bergmann, Emilie. "Reshaping the Canon: Intertextuality in Spanish Novels of Female Development." *Anales de la Literatura Española Contemporánea* 12 (1987): 141-56.

Bersani, Leo. *The Freudian Body: Psychoanalysis and Art*. New York: Columbia University Press, 1986.

Beverley, John. *Del "Lazarillo" al sandinismo: Estudios sobre la función ideológica de la literatura española e hispanoamericana*. Minneapolis: The Prisma Institute and Ideologies and Literatures, 1987.

Binding, Paul. *Lorca: The Gay Imagination*. London: GMP, 1985.

Bodini, Vittorio. *I poeti surrealist spagnoli*. Torino: Giulio Einaudi, 1963.

Borges, Jorge Luis. "El escritor argentino y la tradición." *Obras completas de Jorge Luis Borges*. Vol. I. Buenos Aires: Emecé, 1964. 151-62.

Bousoño, Carlos. "La poesía de Vicente Aleixandre." *Vicente Aleixandre. El escritor y la crítica*. Ed. José Luis Cano. Madrid: Taurus, 1977. 31-65.

Bower, Gary. "Fuentes de Fuentes: Paz y las raíces de *Todos los gatos son pardos*." *Latin American Theater Review* 5 (1971): 59-68.

Bowie, Malcolm. *Freud, Proust and Lacan: Theory as Fiction*. Cambridge: Cambridge University Press, 1987.

Bowlby, Rachel. "Still Crazy After All These Years." *Between Feminism and Psychoanalysis*. Ed. Teresa Brennan. London: Routledge, 1989. 40-59.

Boyle, Catherine. *Thematic Development in Chilean Theatre since 1973: In Search of the Dramatic Conflict*. Rutherford: Fairleigh Dickinson University Press, 1990.

Bradford, E. *Christopher Columbus*. New York: The Viking Press, 1973.

Brennan, Teresa, ed. *Between Feminism and Psychoanalysis*. London: Routledge, 1989.

Breton, André. *Manifestes du surréalisme*. Paris: Gallimard, 1972.

Brotherston, Gordon. *The Emergence of the Latin American Novel.* Cambridge: Cambridge University Press, 1977.

Bull, Judith M. " 'Santa Barbara' and *La casa de Bernarda Alba.*" *Bulletin of Hispanic Studies* 47 (1970): 117-23.

Burgess, R.D. *The New Dramatists of Mexico, 1967-1985.* Lexington: Kentucky University Press, 1990.

Busette, Cedric. *Obra dramática de García Lorca.* New York: Las Américas, 1971.

Cano, José Luis. *García Lorca: biografía ilustrada.* Barcelona: Destino, 1962.

Carr, Raymond. *Spain 1808-1936.* Oxford: Clarendon, 1966.

Cassell's German-English English-German Dictionary (London: Cassell, 1978).

Castellanos, Rosario. *Album de familia.* Mexico: Joaquín Mortiz, 1971.

———. *Ciudad real.* Mexico: Novaro, 1974.

———. *Meditation on the Threshold.* New York: Bilingual Press, 1988.

———. *Oficio de tinieblas.* 2nd ed. Mexico: Joaquín Mortiz, 1966.

———. *A Rosario Castellanos Reader.* Ed. Maureen Ahern. Austin: University of Texas Press, 1988. 236-44.

Castillo del Pino, Carlos. "La psiquiatría española (1939-1975)." *La cultura bajo el franquismo.* Barcelona: Ediciones del Bolsillo, 1977. 79-102.

Cavilgia, John. "A Simple Question of Symmetry: Psyche as Structure in *Tiempo de silencio.*" *Hispania* 60 (1977): 452-60.

Chodorow, N.J. *Feminism and Psychoanalytic Theory.* New Haven: Yale University Press, 1989.

Chrzanowski, Joseph A. "Consideraciones temáticas-estéticas en torno a *Todos los gatos son pardos.*" *Latin American Theater Review* 9 (1975): 11-17.

Cleary Nichols, Geraldine. "The Prison House (and Beyond): *El mismo mar de todos los veranos.*" *The Romanic Review* 75 (1984): 366-85.

Clément, Cathérine. *The Lives and Legends of Jacques Lacan.* Trans. Arthur Goldhammer. New York: Columbia University Press, 1983.

Coleman, D. *The Gallo-Roman Muse.* Cambridge: Cambridge University Press, 1979.

Cortés, Hernán. *Cartas de relación de la conquista de México.* 4th ed. México: Espasa-Calpe Mexicana, 1961.

Crow, Mary, ed. *Woman Who Has Sprouted Wings: Poems by Contemporary Latin American Women Poets*. Pittsburgh: Latin American Review Press, 1984.

Dalí, Salvador. *The Secret Life of Salvador Dali*. New York: Dial Press, 1942.

de Jongh, Nicholas. "The House of Bernarda Alba." *The Guardian* (19 January 1987).

de Man, Paul. "Form and Intent in the American New Criticism." *Blindness and Insight. Essays in the Rhetoric of Contemporary Criticism*. Minneapolis: University of Minnesota Press, 1983. 20-35.

de Vega, Lope. *Peribáñez y el comendador de Ocaña*. Ed. J.M. Ruano and J.E. Varey. London: Tamesis, 1980.

del Amo, Javier. *Literatura y neurosis*. Madrid: Editora Nacional, 1974.

del Río, Ángel. *Vida y obra de Federico García Lorca*. Zaragoza: Heraldo de Aragón, 1952.

Díaz, Janet W. "Luis Martín-Santos and the Contemporary Novel." *Hispania* 51 (1968): 232-38.

Dolan, Kathleen. "Time, Irony and Negation in Lorca's Three Last Plays." *Hispania* 63 (1980): 514-22.

Eagleton, Terry. *Criticism and Ideology: a Study in Marxist Literary Theory*. London: NLB, 1976.

Ehrenzweig, Anton. *The Hidden Order of Art*. London: Weidenfeld, 1967.

Elliott, J.H. *Imperial Spain 1469-1716*. Harmondsworth: Penguin, 1978.

Empson, William. *Seven Types of Ambiguity*. Harmondsworth: Penguin, 1977.

Espejo Asturrizaga, Juan. *César Vallejo: itinerario del hombre*. Lima: Mejía Baca, 1965.

Eysenck, Hans. *Rebel with a Cause: The Autobiography of Hans Eysenck*. London: WH Allen, 1990. Reviewed by Mary Warnock. *The Sunday Times: Books* (1 April 1990): 4.

Feal Deibe, Carlos. "García Lorca y el psicoanálisis. Apostillas a unas apostillas." *Bulletin of Hispanic Studies* 54 (1977): 311-14.

Felman, Shoshana. *Jacques Lacan and the Adventure of Insight: Psychoanalysis in Contemporary Culture*. Cambridge, Massachusetts: Harvard University Press, 1987.

——. "To Open the Question." *Yale French Studies* 55-56 (1977): 5-10.

Fernández Cifuentes, Luis. "García Lorca y el éxito de *Bodas de sangre*." *Lecciones sobre Federico García Lorca*. Ed. A.S. Olmedo. Granada: Comisión Nacional del Cincuentenario, 1986.

Ferrari, Américo. *El universo poético de César Vallejo*. Caracas: Monte Avila, 1972.

Fiddian, Robin W. and Peter W. Evans. "*Tiempo de silencio*: 'Los españoles pintados por sí mismos.' " *Challenges to Authority: Fiction and Film in Contemporary Spain*. London: Tamesis, 1988. 30-46.

Fisher, Claudine. "Hélène Cixous's Window of Daring through Clarice Lispector's Voice." *Continental, Latin-American and Francophone Women Writers*. Ed. Eunice Myers and Ginette Adamson. Lanham, MD: University Press of America, 1987. 21-27.

Fitz, Earl E. *Clarice Lispector*. Boston: Twayne, 1985.

———. "Hélène Cixous's Debt to Clarice Lispector: The Case of *Vivre L'Orange* and 'l'écriture féminine.' " *Revue de Littérature Comparée* 1 (1990): 235-49.

Flanagan, Mary. Review of Uta Ranke-Heineman, *Eunuchs for Heaven: The Catholic Church and Sexuality*. London: Deutsch, 1990. *The Sunday Times: Books* (8 April 1990): 10.

Forrester, John. *The Seductions of Psychoanalysis: Freud, Lacan and Derrida*. Cambridge: Cambridge University Press, 1990.

Forster, Merlin H. "Carlos Fuentes as Dramatist." *Carlos Fuentes*. Ed. Robert Brody and Charles Rossman. Austin: University of Texas Press, 1984. 184-92.

Foster, David William. *Estudios sobre teatro mexicano contemporáneo: Semiología de la competencia teatral*. New York: Peter Lang, 1984.

Foucault, Michel. *Histoire de la sexualité I: La volonté de savoir*. Paris: Gallimard, 1976.

Franco, Jean. *César Vallejo: The Dialectics of Poetry and Silence*. Cambridge: Cambridge University Press, 1976

———. *Plotting Women: Gender and Representation in Mexico*. London: Verso, 1989.

Freud, Sigmund. *The Basic Writings of Sigmund Freud*. Trans. A.A. Brill. New York: Random House, 1938.

———. "Formulations regarding the two principles in mental functioning." *The Standard Edition of the Complete Psychological Works of Sigmund Freud*. Vol. IV. Trans. James Strachey. London: Hogarth, 1973. 13-21.

———. "Femininity." *New Introductory Lectures on Psycho-Analysis and Other Works*. Vol. XXII. London: Hogarth, 1973. 112-35.

——. "The Great Reservoir of Libido." *The Ego and the Id, and Other Works. The Standard Edition of the Complete Psychological Works of Sigmund Freud.* Vol. XIX. London: Hogarth, 1973. 63-66, Appendix B.

——. "Inhibitions, Symptoms and Anxieties." *An Autobiographical Study; Inhibitions, Symptoms and Anxieties; The Question of Lay Analysis; and Other Works.* Vol. XX. Trans. James Strachey. London: Hogarth, 1973. 77-175.

——. *The Interpretation of Dreams.* Trans. James Strachey. Harmondsworth: Penguin, 1978.

——. *Moses and Monotheism. The Standard Edition of the Complete Psychological Works of Sigmund Freud.* Vol. XXIII. Trans. James Strachey. London: Hogarth, 1973.

——. "Observations on Transference-Love." *The Standard Edition of the Complete Psychological Works of Sigmund Freud.* Vol. XII. Trans. James Strachey. London: Hogarth, 1973. 159-71.

——. *The Psychopathology of Everyday Life.* Vol. VI. Trans. James Strachey. London: Hogarth, 1973.

Frye, Northrop. *Anatomy of Criticism.* Princeton, NJ: University of Princeton, 1957.

Fuentes, Carlos. *La nueva novela hispanoamericana.* México: Joaquín Mortiz, 1972.

——. *Carlos Fuentes: Obras completas.* 3 vols. Mexico City: Aguilar, 1986.

Galilea, Hernán. *La poesía superrealista de Vicente Aleixandre.* Santiago, Chile: Editorial Universitaria, 1971.

Gallop, Jane. *Reading Lacan.* Ithaca: Cornell University Press, 1986.

García Gutiérrez, Antonio. *El Trovador.* Ed. José Hesse. Madrid: Aguilar, 1966.

García Lorca, Federico. *Bodas de sangre. Yerma.* 12th ed. Madrid: Espasa-Calpe, 1984.

——. *La casa de Bernarda Alba.* Ed. and with an introduction by Herbert Ramsden. Manchester: Manchester University Press, 1983.

——. *García Lorca. Obras completas.* Madrid: Aguilar, 1974.

——. *Poet in New York.* Ed. and with an introduction by Christopher Maurer. Trans. Greg Simon and Steven F. White. 1989.

Gascón Vera, Elena. "Rosa Montero ante la escritura femenina." *Anales de la Literatura Española Contemporánea* 12 (1987): 59-77.

Gaunt, William. *The Surrealists.* London: Thames and Hudson, 1972.

Gibson, Ian. *The Death of Lorca*. London: W.H. Allen, 1973.

———. *La represión nacionalista de Granada en 1936 y la muerte de Federico García Lorca*. Paris: Ruedo Ibérico, 1971.

Gilbert, Sandra and Susan Gubar. *The Madwoman in the Attic*. New Haven: Yale University Press, 1979.

Girard, René. *Violence and the Sacred*. Trans. Patrick Gregory. Baltimore: John Hopkins Press, 1979.

Gold, Janet N. "Reading the Love Myth: Tusquets with the Help of Barthes." *Hispanic Review* 55 (1987): 337-46.

Gombrich, Ernst. *Art and Illusion: A Study in the Psychology of Pictorial Representation*. London: Pantheon, 1960.

González, Alfonso. "La soledad y los patrones del dominio en la cuentística de Rosario Castellanos." *Homenaje a Rosario Castellanos*. Ed. Maureen Ahern and Mary Seale Vásquez. Valencia: Albatros, 1980. 107-13.

González Boixo, J.C. *Claves narrativas de Juan Rulfo*. León: Universidad de León, 1983.

Griffin Crowder, Dianne. "Amazons and Mothers? Monique Wittig, Hélène Cixous and Theories of Women's Writing." *Contemporary Writing* 24 (1983): 117-44.

Gullón, Ricardo. "Relaciones Pablo Neruda-Juan Ramón Jiménez." *Hispanic Review* 39 (1971): 141-46.

Gyurko, Lanin A. "Vindication of La Malinche in Fuentes' *Todos los gatos son pardos*." *Iberoamerikanisches Archiv* 3 (1977): 233-66.

Harris, Derek. "Green Death: An Analysis of the Symbolism of the Colour Green in Lorca's Poetry." *Readings on Spanish and Portuguese Poetry for Geoffrey Connel*. Ed. N. Round. Glasgow: University of Glasgow Department of Hispanic Studies, 1985. 80-97.

Harss, Luis and Barbara Dohmann. *Into the Mainstream. Conversations with Latin American Writers*. New York: Harper and Row, 1967.

Hart, Stephen M. "El arcaísmo y la motivación etimológica en *Trilce* de César Vallejo." *Quaderni Iberoamericani* 57-58 (1985): 20-35.

———. "El compromiso en el teatro de César Vallejo." *En torno a César Vallejo*. Ed. Antonio Merino. Madrid: Júcar, 1988. 209-219.

———. " 'Galope muerto' Revisited." *Hispanic Journal* 9 (1987): 107-114.

———. "Quevedo, Góngora y su vigencia en la poesía contemporánea." *Iberoromania* 32 (1990): 55-81.

———. *Religión, política y ciencia en la obra de César Vallejo*. London: Tamesis, 1987.

———. "Vargas Llosa. 1936." *Research Guide to Biography and Criticism: Drama*. Ed. Walton Beacham. Washington, D.C.: Research Publishing, 1986. 668-73.

———. "War Within a War: Poetry and the Spanish Civil War." *¡No pasarán! Art, Literature and the Spanish Civil War*. Ed. Stephen M. Hart. London: Tamesis, 1988. 106-22.

———. "The World Upside-Down in the Work of César Vallejo." *Bulletin of Hispanic Studies* 62 (1985): 163-77.

Hartzenbusch, Eugenio. *Los amantes de Teruel. La jura en Santa Gadea*. Ed. A.G. Albacete. Madrid: Espasa-Calpe, 1974.

Havard, Robert. "The Hidden Parts of *La casa de Bernarda Alba*." *Romance Notes* 26 (1985): 102-08.

———. "The Symbolic Ambivalence of 'Green' in García Lorca and Dylan Thomas." *Modern Language Review* 67 (1972): 810-19.

Hoffman, Frederick J. *Freudianism and the Literary Mind*. Ann Arbor, Michigan: Michigan State University Press, 1967.

Holdsworth, C.A. "The Scholar and the Earth Mother in *Tiempo de silencio*." *Hispanófila* 92 (1988): 41-48.

Inés de la Cruz, Sor Juana. *Obras completas de Sor Juana Inés de la Cruz*. México: Fondo de Cultura Económica, 1957.

Ilie, Paul. *The Surrealist Mode in Spanish Literature*. Ann Arbor, Michigan: Michigan State University Press, 1968.

Irigaray, Luce. *Ce Sexe qui n'en est pas un*. Paris: Minuit, 1977.

———. *This Sex Which Is Not One*. Trans. Catherine Porter. Ithaca: Cornell University Press, 1985.

———. "Women, the sacred and money." *Paragraph* 8 (1986): 6-18.

Jakobson, Roman. *Selected Writings*. The Hague: Mouton, 1971.

James, Henry. "Gustave Flaubert, 1902." *Henry James: Literary Criticism*. Ed. Morris Shapira. Harmondsworth: Penguin, 1968. 252-81.

Jameson, Fredric. *Marxism and Form: Twentieth-Century Dialectical Theories of Literature*. Princeton, NJ: Princeton University Press, 1971.

Jerez-Farrán, C. " 'Ansiedad de influencia' versus intertextualidad autoconsciente en *Tiempo de silencio* de Martín-Santos." *Symposium* 42 (1988): 119-32.

Jiménez, Juan Ramón. *Juan Ramón Jiménez. Antología poética*. Ed. Eugenio Florit. Madrid: Biblioteca Nueva, 1981.

Jones, Ann Rosalind. "Writing the Body: Towards an Understanding of *l'écriture féminine*." *Feminist Studies* 7.2 (1981): 247-306.

Jones, Ernest. *Sigmund Freud. Life and Work*. London: Hogarth, 1972.

Josipovici, Gabriel. *The World and the Book*. Stanford: Stanford University Press, 1971.

Joyce, James. *Selected Letters of James Joyce*. Ed. Richard Ellmann. London: Faber and Faber, 1975.

Kristeva, Julia. *La Révolution du language poétique: L'Avant-garde à la fin du XIXe siècle: Lautréamont et Mallarmé*. Paris: Seuil, 1974.

———. "Within the Microcosm of the Talking Cure." Ed. Joseph H. Smith and William Kerrigan. *Interpreting Lacan*. New Haven: Yale University Press, 1983.

Labanyi, Jo. "The Construction/Deconstruction of the Self in the Autobiographies of Pablo Neruda and Juan Goytisolo." *Forum for Modern Language Studies* 36 (1990): 212-21.

———. *Ironía e historia en "Tiempo de silencio."* Madrid: Taurus, 1985.

Lacan, Jacques. *Écrits*. Paris: Seuil, 1966.

———. *Écrits. A Selection*. Trans. Alan Sheridan. London: Tavistock, 1977.

———. "God and the *Jouissance* of The Woman." *Feminine Sexuality: Jacques Lacan and the "école freudienne."* Ed. Juliet Mitchell and Jacqueline Rose. London: Macmillan, 1982. 137-48.

———. "L'inconscient freudien et le notre." *Les quatre concepts fondamentaux de la psychanalyse*. Paris: Seuil, 1973. 21-30.

———. *The Language of the Self: The Function of Language in Psychoanalysis*. Trans. with notes and commentary by Anthony Wilden. New York: Delta, 1975).

———. *Speech and Language in Psychoanalysis*. Trans. with notes and commentary by Anthony Wilden. Fourth printing. Baltimore: The Johns Hopkins University Press, 1976.

Langer, Marie, Enrique Guinsberg and Jaime del Palacio. *From Vienna to Managua: Journey of a Psychoanalyst*. Trans. Margaret Hooks. London: Free Association Books, 1989.

Laraque, Frank. *La Révolte dans le théâtre de Sartre*. Paris: Encyclopédie, 1976.

Larra, Mariano José de. *"El trovador." Artículos de costumbres.* Ed. Azorín. Madrid: Austral, 1980. 123-27.

Lastinger, Valerie C. "Humor in a New Reading of Clarice Lispector." *Hispania* 72 (1989): 130-37.

Lévi-Strauss, Claude. *The Elementary Structures of Kinship.* London: Social Science Paperbacks, 1969.

Lispector, Clarice. *Near to the Wild Heart.* Trans. and with an afterword by Giovanni Pontiero. Manchester: Carcanet, 1990.

——. *Perto do coração selvagem.* São Paolo: Edition Nova Fronteira, 1944.

Lovett, Gabriel H. *Napoleon and the Birth of Modern Spain.* New York: New York University Press, 1965.

Loyola, Hernán. *Ser y morir en Pablo Neruda.* Santiago: Horizonte, 1967.

Lozada, Alfredo. *El monismo agónico de Pablo Neruda.* México: B. Costa-Amic, 1971.

Lukács, Georg. *The Theory of the Novel.* Trans. Anna Bostock. London: Merlin, 1971.

Lyon, J.E. "Don Pedro's Complicity: An Existential Dimension of *Tiempo de silencio.*" *Modern Language Review* 74 (1979): 69-78.

——. "Love, Imagination and Society in *Amor de don Perlimplín* and *La zapatera prodigiosa.*" *Bulletin of Hispanic Studies* 63 (1986): 235-45.

MacAdam, Alfred J. *Modern Latin American Narratives.* Chicago: The University of Chicago Press, 1977.

MacCabe, Colin, ed. *The Talking Cure.* London: Macmillan, 1981.

Macey, David. *Lacan in Contexts.* London: Verso, 1988.

Magnarelli, Sharon. *The Lost Rib. Female Characters in the Spanish-American Novel.* Cranbury, NJ: Associated University Presses, 1983.

——. *Reflections/Refractions: Reading Luisa Valenzuela.* New York: Peter Lang, 1988.

Mandrell, James. "*Don Juan Tenorio* as *Refundición*: the Question of Repetition and Doubling." *Hispania* 70 (1987): 22-30.

Mansour, George P. "Parallelism in *Don Juan Tenorio.*" *Hispania* 61 (1978): 245-53.

Manteiga, Robert C. "El triunfo del Minotauro: ambigüedad y razón en *El mismo mar de todos los veranos* de Esther Tusquets." *Letras Femeninas* 14 (1988): 22-31.

Marcuse, Herbert. *Eros and Civilization: A Philosophical Inquiry into Freud.* London: Sphere Books, 1969.

Martín-Santos, Luis. *Libertad, temporalidad y transferencia en el psicoanálisis existencial: para una fenomenología de la cura psicoanalítica*. Barcelona: Seix Barral, 1975.

———. *Tiempo de silencio*. 12th ed. Barcelona: Seix Barral, 1978.

———. *Tiempo de destrucción*. Barcelona: Seix Barral, 1975.

Maurer, Christopher, ed. *Federico García Lorca: Poet in New York*. Harmondsworth: Penguin, 1989.

Mazzeo, Guido E. "*Don Juan Tenorio*: Salvation or Damnation?" *Romance Notes* 5 (1964): 151-55.

Meyers, Jeffrey. *Disease and the Novel, 1880-1960*. London: Macmillan, 1985.

Miller, Beth. *Uma consciência feminista: Rosário Castellanos*. São Paulo: Editora Perspectiva, 1987.

Millett, Kate. *Sexual Politics*. London: Virago, 1970.

Mitchell, Juliet. *Psychoanalysis and Feminism*. Harmondsworth: Penguin, 1982 (first published 1974).

———. *Women: The Longest Revolution*. New York: Pantheon, 1984.

Molho, Mauricio. "La aurora insumisa de Vicente Aleixandre." *Vicente Aleixandre. El escritor y la crítica*. Ed. José Luis Cano. Madrid: Taurus, 1977. 139-45.

Montrelay, Michèle. "Inquiry into Femininity." *French Feminist Thought: A Reader*. Ed. Toril Moi. Oxford: Basil Blackwell, 1987. 227-49.

———. *L'Ombre et le Nom: Sur la fémininité*. Paris: Minuit, 1977.

Mora, Gabriela and Karen S. Van Hooft, eds. *Theory and Practice of Feminist Literary Criticism*. Ypsilanti, Michigan: Bilingual Press, 1982.

Morris, C.B. *Surrealism in Spain. 1920-1936*. Cambridge: Cambridge University Press, 1972.

National Geographic (supplement) 169.4 (April 1986): 466A.

Navajas, Gonzalo. "Repetition and the Rhetoric of Love in Esther Tusquets' *El mismo mar de todos los veranos*." *Nuevos y novísimos: Algunas perspectivas críticas sobre la narrativa española desde la década de los 60*. Ed. Ricardo Landeira and Luis T. González-del-Valle. Boulder, Colorado: Society for Spanish and Spanish-American Studies, 1987. 113-29.

Neale-Silva, Eduardo. *César Vallejo en su fase trílcica*. Madison, Wisconsin: The University of Wisconsin, 1975.

Neruda, Pablo. *Canto general*. 7th ed. Buenos Aires: Losada, 1978.

———. *Confieso que he vivido: Memorias*. Barcelona: Seix Barral, 1976.

———. *Literature and Revolution*. Trans. Rose Strunsky. London: Faber, 1925.

———. *Residencia en la tierra*. Buenos Aires: Lozada, 1973.

New Schöffler-Weis Compact German and English Dictionary. London: Harrap, 1969.

Newbury, Wilma. "Patterns of Negation in *La casa de Bernarda Alba*." *Hispania* 59 (1976): 802-09.

Nichols, Geraldine Cleary. "The Prison House (and Beyond): *El mismo mar de todos los veranos*." *The Romanic Review* 75 (1984): 366-85.

Nomland, John B. *Teatro mexicano contemporáneo (1900-1950)*. México: Instituto Nacional de Bellas Artes, 1967.

Olmedo, A.S., ed. *Lecciones sobre Federico García Lorca*. Granada: Comisión Nacional del Cincuentenario, 1986.

Ordóñez, Elizabeth J. "Inscribing Difference: 'L'écriture féminine' and New Narrative by Women." *Anales de la Literatura Española Contemporánea* 12 (1987): 45-58.

Oxford English Dictionary. Oxford: Clarendon, 1933.

Paley Francescato, Marta. "Transgresión y aperturas en los cuentos de Rosario Castellanos." *Homenaje a Rosario Castellanos*. Ed. Maureen Ahern and Mary Seale Vásquez. Valencia: Albatros, 1980. 115-20.

Palley, Julian. "The Periplus of Don Pedro." *Bulletin of Hispanic Studies* 48 (1971): 239-54.

Paoli, Roberto. "El lenguaje conceptista de César Vallejo." *Cuadernos Hispanoamericanos* 456-57 (1988): 945-59.

———. "En los orígenes de *Trilce*: Vallejo entre modernismo y vanguardia." *Mapas anatómicos de César Vallejo*. Florence: Casa Editrice d'Anna, 1981. 31-50.

Parinaud, André. *The Unspeakable Confessions of Salvador Dali*. Trans. Harold J. Salemson. London: W.H. Allen, 1976.

Patai, Daphne. "Clarice Lispector and the Clamor of the Ineffable." *Kentucky Romance Quarterly* 27 (1980): 133-49.

Pattison, Walter T. "On Espronceda's Personality." *Publications of the Modern Language Association of America* 41 (1946): 1126-1145.

Paz, Octavio. *El laberinto de la soledad*. México: Fondo de Cultura Económica, 1964.

———. *The Labyrinth of Solitude*. Trans. Lysander Kemp. New York: Grove Press, 1961.

———. Discussion of *Pedro Páramo*. *Corriente alterna*. Mexico: Siglo XXI, 1967. 17-18.

Peers, Alison. *A Short History of the Romantic Drama Movement*. Liverpool: Liverpool University Press, 1949.

Pendle, George. *A History of Latin America*. Harmondsworth: Penguin, 1980.

Peñuela Cañizal, Eduardo. "Myth and Language in a Play by Carlos Fuentes." *Latin American Theater Review* 13:1 (1979): 15-27.

Perriam, Chris. *The Late Poetry of Pablo Neruda*. Oxford: The Dolphin Book Co., 1989.

Perrota, L.A. "Aplicaciones clínicas del psicoanálisis." *Sobre Psiquitaría y Psicoanálisis: Memorias Martes del Paraninfo*. Ed. Luz Elena Ochoa Vélez. Medellín, Colombia: Universidad de Antioquía, 1982. 133-53.

Personneaux, Lucie. *Vicente Aleixandre ou une poésie du suspens*. Montpellier: Université Paul Valéry, 1980.

Piñol, Rosa María. "Nueve autoras de distintas culturas coinciden en asociar escritura y libertad." *La Vanguardia* (23 June 1990).

Pontiero, G. "Clarice Lispector: An Intuitive Approach to Fiction." *Knives and Angels: Women Writers in Latin America*. Ed. Susan Bassnett. London and New Jersey: Zed Books Ltd., 1990). 74-85.

———. "Testament of Experience: Some Reflections on Clarice Lispector's *A Hora da Estrela*." *Iberoamerikanisches Archiv* 10 (1984): 13-22.

Pound, Ezra. *ABC of Reading*. London: Faber, 1973.

Ragland-Sullivan, Ellie. *Jacques Lacan and the Philosophy of Psychoanalysis*. London: Croom Helm, 1986.

Ramsden, Herbert. *Lorca's "Romancero Gitano": Eighteen Commentaries*. Manchester: Manchester University Press, 1988.

Ranke-Heineman, Uta. *Eunuchs for Heaven: The Catholic Church and Sexuality*. London: Deutsch, 1990.

Read, Herbert. *A Concise History of Modern Painting*. London: Thames and Hudson, 1980.

Reiss, Frank. *The Word and the Stone: Language and Imagery in Neruda's "Canto general."* Oxford: Oxford University Press, 1972.

Rey, Alfonso. *Construcción y sentido de "Tiempo de silencio."* Madrid: José Porrúa Turanzas, 1977.

Rivas, Duque de. *Don Álvaro o la fuerza del sino*. Ed. María Socorro Perales. Madrid: Editorial Burdeos, 1988.

Rodríguez Fernández, Mario. " 'Reunión bajo las nuevas banderas' o de la conversión política de Pablo Neruda." *Aproximaciones a Pablo Neruda*. Ed. Angel Flores. Barcelona: Llibres de Sinera, 1974. 151-64.

Rodríguez Monegal, Emir. "Carlos Fuentes." *Homenaje a Carlos Fuentes*. Ed. Helmy F. Giacoman. New York: Las Américas, 1971. 23-65.

———. *Neruda: el viajero inmóvil*. Caracas: Monte Avila, 1977.

Rose, Jacqueline. *Feminine Sexuality: Jacques Lacan and the "école freudienne."* Ed. Juliet Mitchell and Jacqueline Rose. London: Macmillan, 1982.

Rowland, Beryl. *Animals with Human Faces: A Guide to Animal Symbolism*. London: George Allen and Unwin, 1974.

Rubia Barcia, J. "El realismo mágico de *La casa de Bernarda Alba*." *Federico García Lorca. El escritor y la crítica*. Ed. Ildefonso-Manuel Gil. Madrid: Taurus, 1973. 301-21.

Rulfo, Juan. *Pedro Páramo*. Mexico: Fondo de Cultura Económica, 1977.

Sahuquillo, A. *Federico García Lorca y la cultura de la homosexualidad: Lorca, Dalí, Cernuda, Gil-Albert, Prados y la voz silenciada del amor homosexual*. Stockholm: author's edition, 1986.

Said, Edward. *Orientalism*. New York: Vintage, 1979.

Salinas, Pedro. "Vicente Aleixandre entre la destrucción y el amor." *Vicente Aleixandre. El escritor y la crítica*. Ed. José Luis Cano. Madrid: Taurus, 1977. 214-21.

Sánchez Vidal, Agustín. *Buñuel, Lorca, Dalí: el enigma sin fin*. Barcelona: Planeta, 1988.

Sartre, Jean-Paul. *L'Être et le Néant*. Paris: Gallimard, 1943.

Saussure, Ferdinand de. *Cours de linguistique générale*. Paris: Gallimard, 1967.

Schneiderman, Stuart. *Jacques Lacan: the Death of an Intellectual Hero*. Cambridge, Massachusetts: Harvard University Press, 1983.

Schoenberg, Jean-Louis. *Federico García Lorca: L'homme - l'oeuvre*. Paris: Plon, 1956.

Schopenhauer, Arthur. *Schopenhauer. Essays and Aphorisms*. Harmondsworth: Penguin, 1976.

Schwartz, Kessel. "The Isakower Phenomenon and the Dream Screen." *Critical Views on Vicente Aleixandre's Poetry*. Ed. Vicente Cabrera and

Harriet Boyer. Boulder, Colorado: Society of Spanish and Spanish-American Studies, 1979. 39-46.

———. *Vicente Aleixandre*. Boston: Twayne, 1970.

Searle, Mary L. "Hangman and Victim: An Analysis of Martin-Santos's *Tiempo de silencio*." *Hispanófila* 44 (1972): 45-52.

Shaw, Donald. *Nueva narrativa hispanoamericana*. Madrid: Cátedra, 1983.

———. "Spain/Romántico-Romanticismo-Romancesco-Romanesco-Romancista-Románico." *"Romantic" and Its Cognates. The European History of a Word*. Ed. Hans Eichner. Manchester: Manchester University Press, 1972. 341-71.

Showalter. Elaine, ed. *The New Feminist Criticism: Essays on Women, Literature, and Theory*. London: Virago, 1989.

Smith, Joseph H. and William Kerrigan. eds. *Interpreting Lacan*. New Haven: Yale University Press, 1983.

Smith, Paul Julian. *The Body Hispanic: Gender and Sexuality in Spanish and Spanish American Literature*. Oxford: Oxford University Press, 1989.

Solís, Ramón. *El Cádiz de las Cortes*. Madrid: Alianza, 1969.

Stais, James. "*Todos los gatos son pardos*: un acto de rebelión en nueve escenas." *Homenaje a Carlos Fuentes*. Ed. Helmy F. Giacoman. New York: Las Américas, 1971. 465-71.

Summers, Joseph. *After the Storm. Landmarks of the Modern Mexican Novel*. Albuquerque: University of New Mexico Press, 1968.

Tanner, Tony. *Adultery in the Novel: Contract and Transgression*. Baltimore: The John Hopkins Press, 1979.

Taylor, D. *Theatre in Crisis: Drama and Politics in Latin America*. Lexington, Kentucky University Press, 1990.

Ter Horst, Robert. "Ritual Time Regained in Zorrilla's *Don Juan Tenorio*." *The Romanic Review* 170 (1979): 80-93.

Thibaudet, A. *Gustave Flaubert*. Paris: Gallimard, 1935.

Thom, Martin. "The Unconscious Structured like a Language." *The Talking Cure*. Ed. C. MacCabe. London: Macmillan, 1981. 1-44.

Traba, Marta. "Hipótesis sobre una escritura diferente." *Quimera* 13.11 (1981).

Trend, J.B. *Lorca and the Poetic Tradition*. Oxford: Basil Blackwell, 1956.

Trotsky, Leon. *Literature and Revolution*. Trans. Rose Strunsky. London: Faber, 1925.

Trudgill, Peter. *Sociolinguistics: An Introduction to Language and Society*. Harmondsworth: Penguin, 1974.

Turkle, Sherry. *Psychoanalytical Politics: Jacques Lacan and Freud's French Revolution*. London: Burnett Books, 1979.

Tusquets, Esther. *El mismo mar de todos los veranos*. 3rd ed. Barcelona: Lumen, 1979.

Ugarte, Michael. "*Tiempo de silencio* and the Language of Displacement." *Modern Language Notes* 96 (1981): 240-57.

Valenzuela, Luisa. *Cambio de armas*. Hanover: Ediciones de Norte, 1982.

———. "Mis brujas favoritas." *Theory and Practice of Feminist Literary Criticism*. Ed. Gabriela Mora and Karten S. Van Hooft. Ypsilanti, MI: Bilingual Press, 1982. 88-95.

Vallejo, César. *César Vallejo. An Anthology of his Poetry*. Ed. James Higgins. Oxford: Pergamon Press, 1970.

———. *César Vallejo. Obra poética completa*. Madrid: Alianza Tres, 1983.

Valls, Fernando. "La literatura femenina en España: 1975-1989." *Insula* 512-513 (1989): 13.

Vargas Llosa, Mario. *García Márquez: historia de un deicidio*. Barcelona: Barral, 1971.

Vásquez, Mary S. "Image and Linear Progression Toward Defeat in Esther Tusquets's *El mismo mar de todos los veranos*." *La Chispa '83: Selected Proceedings*. Ed. Gilbert Paolini. Baton Rouge: Louisiana State University, 1983. 307-13.

———. "Tusquets, Fitzgerald and the Redemptive Power of Love." *Letras Femeninas* 15 (1988): 10-21.

Vezzetti, Hugo. *Freud en Buenos Aires, 1910-1939*. Buenos Aires: Puntosur, 1989.

Villegas, Juan. *Estructuras míticas y arquetipos en el "Canto general" de Pablo Neruda*. Barcelona: Planeta, 1976.

Wattman Frank, Francine. "Women's Language in America." *Women's Language and Style*. Ed. Douglas Butturff and Edmund L. Epstein. Akron, Ohio: University of Akron, 1978. 47-61.

Williams, Raymond. *Drama from Ibsen to Brecht*. Harmondsworth: Penguin, 1978.

Wilson, Stanley. Introduction. *Salvador Dalí. The Tate Gallery*. London: The Tate Gallery, 1980. 9-20.

Wittig, Monique. *Le Corps lesbien*. Paris: Minuit, 1973.

Woolf, Virginia. *A Room of One's Own*. London: Hogarth, 1929.

Wright, Elizabeth. *Psychoanalytical Criticism*. London: Methuen, 1984.

Year's Work in Modern Language Studies 1988 50 (1989): "Literature, 1898-1936," 362-82.

Zorrilla, José de. *Don Juan Tenorio*. Ed. Aniano Peña. Madrid: Cátedra, 1984.

INDEX

Abrams, Fred 38, 123
Aguirre, J.M. 4-5, 123
Agustín, José 30
Aladrén, Emilio 19
Aleixandre, Vicente 3, 4, 87, 107-21, 123, 124, 128, 133, 135-36
Allende, Isabel 3, 68
d'Ambrosio Servidodio, Mirella 84, 123
Amor Vázquez, José 123
Andermatt Conley, Verena 84, 123
Anderson, C.L. 62, 123
Andioc, René 38, 123
Aquinas, Thomas 64
Aranda, Francisco 117, 123
Aristotle 64-65, 73, 78, 123
Auerbach, Nina 64, 123
Babcock, Barbara A. 123
Barthes, Roland 45, 57, 60, 124, 129
Bazán, Armando 87-88, 124
Benjamin, Jessica 62, 124
Benvenuto, Bice 124
Bergmann, Emilie 84, 124
Bersani, Leo 74-75, 79, 124
Beverley, John 118, 124
Binding, Paul 19, 38-39, 124
Bodini, Vittorio 107, 119, 124
Borges, Jorge Luis 118, 124
Bousoño, Carlos 112, 124
Bower, Gary 40, 124
Bowie, Malcolm 6, 73, 124
Boyle, Catherine 40, 124
Bradford, E. 40, 124
Brennan, Teresa 124
Breton, André 107, 118, 124
Brotherston, Gordon 62, 125
Bull, Judith M. 39, 125
Busette, Cedric 39, 125
Camus, Albert 37
Carballido, Emilio 30
Carr, Raymond 37-38, 125
Castellanos, Rosario 3, 29, 39-40, 63, 65, 72, 74, 78-83, 85, 121, 123, 125, 129, 133, 134; and political unconscious 78-83
Castillo del Pino, Carlos 6, 125

castration 3, 25, 41, 43-46, 50-52, 92, 121; and representation 3, 43-51
Cavilgia, John 62, 125
Chesterton, G.K. 72
Chrzanowski, Joseph A. 40, 125
Clément, Cathérine 1, 34, 125
Coleman, Dorothy 100, 117, 125
Cortés, Hernán 3, 30-36, 40, 51, 78, 125
Crow, Mary 40, 126
Dalí, Salvador 39, 107, 112, 118, 126, 136, 139
de Beauvoir, Simone 80, 84
de Jongh, Nicholas 24, 126
de Man, Paul 126
del Amo, Javier 119, 126
del Río, Ángel 18-19, 126
Díaz, Janet W. 62, 126
Dohmann, Barbara 51, 57, 62, 130
Dolan, Kathleen 39, 126
Eagleton, Terry 118, 126
Eandi, Héctor 99, 117
écriture féminine 3, 65-69, 71-72, 83-84, 127, 131, 134
Ehrenzweig, Anton 126
Electra 44, 51
Empson, William 126
Espejo Asturrizaga, Juan 87, 91, 126
Espronceda, José 97-98, 135
Eurydice 61
Evans, Peter W. 62, 127
Eysenck, Hans 85, 126
"Family Romance" 3, 7-9, 11, 14, 18
Feal, Carlos Deibe 4, 5, 126
Fechner, G.T. 1, 2
Felman, Shoshana 5, 8-9, 126
Ferrari, Américo 117, 127
Fiddian, Robin W. 62, 127
Fitz, Earl E. 69, 70, 84, 127
Flaubert, Gustave 25, 39, 62, 63, 130, 137
Foix, J.V. 118
Forrester, John 108-10, 127
Forster, Merlin H. 30, 127
Foster, David William 30, 127
Foucault, Michel 13-16, 127

Franco, Francisco 4, 6, 18, 38, 43-46, 71, 106
Franco, Jean 80, 117, 127
Freud, Sigmund 1-3, 6, 7-12, 18, 20, 23, 26, 31, 37, 39, 43, 51-56, 65, 72-75, 84, 98-99, 107-08, 110, 115, 116-17, 118, 122, 124, 127-28, 131, 133, 138; and Unconscious 1-3, 30-33, 72-78, 111-18, 121; and *eros/thanatos* 21, 101, 109
Frye, Northrop 118, 128
Fuentes, Carlos 3, 7, 40, 51, 121, 124, 127-37; and drama 29-37
Galilea, Hernán 110, 128
Gallop, Jane 128
García Gutiérrez, Antonio 9, 128
García Lorca, Federico 3, 4, 7, 18-19, 29, 121, 123, 125-30, 133-34, 136-37; and *Bodas de sangre* 3, 19-21, 24-25, 38, 127, 128; and *La casa de Bernarda Alba* 3, 19, 23-26, 39, 121, 125, 128, 130, 134, 136; and gayness 18-19, 39
García Morales, Adelaida 68
Gascón Vera, Elena 84, 128
Gaunt, William 128
Gibson, Ian 19, 38, 129
Gilbert, Sandra 22, 26, 28-29, 129
Girard, René 62, 129
Gombrich, Ernst 129
González Boixo, J.C. 54, 129
González-del-Valle, Luis T. 133
Gorostiza, Celestino 30
Griffin Crowder, Dianne 85, 129
Gubar, Susan 22, 26, 28-29, 129
Gullón, Ricardo 118, 129
Gyurko, Lanin A. 33, 35, 129
Harris, Derek 39, 129
Harss, Luis 51, 57, 62, 129
Hart, Stephen M. 117-18, 129-30
Hartzenbusch, Eugenio 9, 130
Havard, Robert 39, 130
Hawthorne, Nathaniel 63
Hernández, Luisa Josefina 30
Higgins, James 91, 138
Hoffman, Frederick J. 73, 130
Holdsworth, C.A. 62, 130
Ibargüengoitia, Jorge 30
Ilie, Paul 119, 130
Inés de la Cruz, Sor Juana 62-63, 80-82, 130
Irigaray, Luce 20, 26, 39, 66, 130

Isakower, Otto 118, 136
Jakobson, Roman 60, 130
Jameson, Fredric 37, 73-74, 130
Jerez-Farrán, C. 62, 130
Jones, Ernest 72, 84, 131
Josipovici, Gabriel 12, 131
Jung, Karl 4
Kennedy, Roger 124
Kerrigan, William 131, 137
Klein, Melanie 6
Kossoff, David A. 123
Kristeva, Julia 24, 51, 131
Labanyi, Jo 62, 117, 131
Lacan, Jacques 1-4, 6-7, 12, 30, 32, 34, 43, 46, 54-57, 60, 62, 65-66, 76, 77, 85, 88-89, 105, 107-08, 110, 113, 114, 118-19, 121-22, 124-28, 131-32, 135-38; and the "Other Scene" 74, 76, 87, 107-08, 112, 114-16, 122; and mirror stage 77, 89, 110, 113, 118-19; and *nom-du-père* 11, 66, 88, 105, 118
Laing, R.D. 84
Landeira, Ricardo 133
Langer, Marie 6, 131
Laraque, Frank 37, 131
Larra, Mariano José de 38, 132
Lauretis, Teresa de 124
Lawrence, D.H. 41
Leñero, Vicente 30
Lévi-Strauss, Claude 28, 33, 34, 48, 132; and libido, as phallic 10, 20-22, 29, 32, 39, 42, 67, 73, 109; and fluidity 20, 36, 69, 109, 110, 113, 115
Lispector, Clarice 3, 71-72, 83-84, 127, 132, 134-35; and *écriture féminine* 69
Lovett, Gabriel H. 37, 132
Loyola, Hernán 117, 132
Lukács, Georg 104, 132
Lyon, J.E. 39, 44, 132
MacAdam, Alfred J. 61, 132
MacCabe, Colin 132, 137
Macey, David 107, 118, 132
Magnarelli, Sharon 61, 85, 132
Malinche 34-35, 40, 51, 78, 85, 129
Mallarmé, Stéphane 102, 131
Mandrell, James 38, 132
Mansour, George P. 38, 132
Marcuse, Herbert 27, 132

Martín-Santos, Luis 3, 41-43, 45-50, 62, 69, 121, 126, 130, 133; and *Tiempo de silencio* 3, 41-51, 69, 121, 123, 125, 127, 130, 131-33, 135, 137-38
Martínez de la Rosa, Francisco 9
Marxism 73, 74, 87, 104, 106, 116, 126, 130; and Neruda 105-07; and Vallejo 95-96
Mayoral, Marina 68
Mazzeo, Guido E. 38, 133
Meyers, Jeffrey 41, 133
Miller, Arthur 30
Miller, Beth 85, 133
Millett, Kate 26, 84, 133
"miscourse," definition of 46-50, 62
Mitchell, Juliet 23, 64-66, 84-85, 131, 133, 136
Moctezuma, in Fuentes's drama 3, 30-36
Molho, Mauricio 118, 133
Montero, Rosa 68
Montrelay, Michèle 43, 45, 133
Mora, Gabriela 15, 38, 133, 138
Morris, C.B. 118, 130, 133
myth, use in fiction 30-31, 34, 36, 49, 51, 61
narcissism 110, 111
Navajas, Gonzalo 85, 133
Neale-Silva, Eduardo 90, 133
Neruda, Pablo 3, 87, 96-108, 116-18, 121, 129, 131-33, 135-36, 138
neurosis, role in Aleixandre 112; in Martín-Santos 50; in Neruda 98
Newbury, Wilma 39, 134
Nichols, Geraldine Cleary 85, 125, 134
Nomland, John B. 40, 134
obstacle-love, definition of 3, 10
Oedipal Complex 95, 121
Oedipus 7, 33, 34, 41, 44, 61, 73, 94
Olmedo, A.S. 127, 134
Ominous Decade 9
Ordóñez, Elizabeth J. 68, 84, 134
Orpheus 44, 61
Ortiz, Lourdes 68
"Other Scene" 2-3, 6, 74, 76, 87, 107-08, 112, 114-16, 122
Palley, Julian 62, 134
Paoli, Roberto 117, 134
Pattison, Walter T. 98, 134
Peers, Alison 9, 135
Pendle, George 118, 135

Peñuela Cañizal, Eduardo 40, 135
Peri Rossi, Cristina 68
Perriam, Chris 100, 135
Personneaux, Lucie 107, 119, 135
Pontiero, Giovanni 69, 84, 132, 135
primal scene 35, 116
psychoanalysis 4-6, 8-9, 41, 43, 50, 65, 66, 72-73, 84-85, 98, 107-08, 124-27, 131, 133, 135; and literature; and Surrealism 87, 107-08, 117, 118; in the Spanish-speaking world 4, 6
Quevedo, Francisco de 101, 117, 129
Ragland-Sullivan, Ellie 119, 135
Ramsden, Herbert 6, 38, 128, 135
Rank, Otto 8
Ranke-Heineman, Uta 127, 135
Read, Herbert 135
Recabarren 105
regressus ad uterum 28, 44, 94
Reich, Wilheim 84
Reiss, Frank 118, 135
Rey, Alfonso 62, 135
Reyes Palacio, Felipe 30
Riera, Carme 68
Rivas, Duque de 9, 13, 136
Rodríguez Fernández, Mario 118, 136
Rodríguez Monegal, Emir 30, 35, 97, 99, 117, 136
Romantic drama 3, 7-14, 16-18, 35, 121, 135
Rubia Barcia, J. 23, 136
Said, Edward 40, 136
Salemson, Harold J. 134
Salinas, Pedro 108, 136
Sánchez Vidal, Agustín 40, 136
Sartre, Jean-Paul 37, 47, 62, 131, 136
Saussure, Ferdinand de 136
Schneiderman, Stuart 121-22, 136
Schoenberg, Jean-Louis 19, 38, 136
Schopenhauer, Arthur 10, 136
Schwartz, Kessel 109, 111, 118, 136-37
Searle, Mary L. 62, 137
Sebastian, Saint 29, 39
Shakespeare, Freudian interpretation of 7
Shaw, Donald 37, 58, 137
Showalter, Elaine 64, 137
Smith, Joseph H. 131, 137
Smith, Paul Julian 38-39, 104, 137
Solís, Ramón 37, 137
Solórzano, Carlos 30

Stais, James 30, 137
Summers, Joseph 54, 137
Tanner, Tony 12-13, 137
Ter Horst, Robert 38, 137
Thibaudet, Albert 39, 137
Thom, Martin 6, 137
Todorov, Tzvetan 31
Traba, Marta 68, 137
transference, in literature 6, 42, 53, 88, 109, 128
Trend, J.B. 6, 19, 137
Trotsky, Leon 104, 137
Tupac Amaru 105
Turkle, Sherry 107, 138
Tusquets, Esther 3, 71-75, 124, 129, 132-33, 138
Ugarte, Michael 50, 138
Ulysses 44, 61, 69
Umbral, Francisco 68
Usigli, Rodolfo 29-30
Valdivia, Pedro de 105
Valenzuela, Luisa 3, 66, 72-76, 83, 85, 122, 132, 138; and political unconscious 72-78
Valéry, Paul 102
Vallejo, César 3, 29, 40, 87-89, 91, 93-96, 108, 116-17, 121-22, 124, 126, 127, 129-30, 133-34, 138
Valls, Fernando 68, 138
Van Hooft, Karen S. 133, 138
Vargas Llosa, Mario 29, 40, 104, 129, 138
Vásquez, Mary S. 84, 138
Vezzetti, Hugo 6, 138
Villegas, Juan 118, 138
Wattman Frank, Francine 84, 138
Wilden, Anthony 1-2, 131
Williams, Raymond 40, 138
Wilson, Stanley 112, 118, 139
Wolff, Charlotte 64
Woolf, Virginia 64-65, 83, 139
Wright, Elizabeth 9, 139
Zorrilla, José de 9, 12, 38, 123, 137, 139